ALL THE LOVELY LIES

A Novel

MARY KAY LEATHERMAN

Also by Mary Kay Leatherman

Cowboys to Camelot
Vanity Insanity

Surviving Your Friend's Divorce: 10 Simple Rule to Help You Both
Sharing the Fatih with Your Child: From Birth to Age Four

Library of Congress Control Number: 2013910110
Copyright 2025 Mary Kay Leatherman
All rights reserved.

ISBN: 978-1-968000-52-3 Paperback
ISBN: 978-1-968000-53-0 Hardcover

To my Mother, as constant as the moon

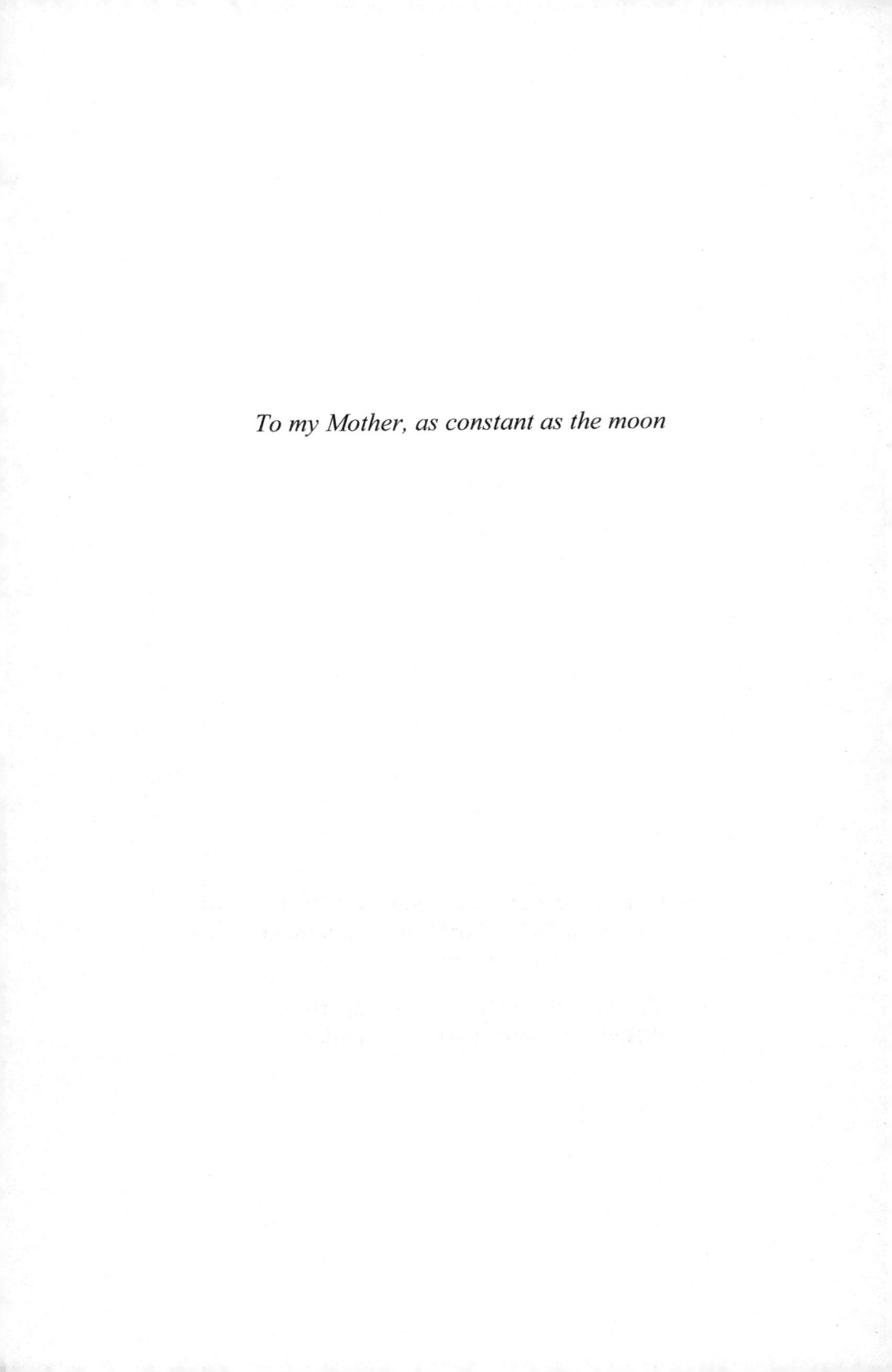

7 Days of Lies

The Before	1
The Releasing	2
The Revealing	115
The Rapture	250
The After	354
Acknowledgements	361

THE BEFORE

Man is not what he thinks he is, he is what he hides.
Andre Malraux

We are all broken—that's how the light gets in.
Ernest Hemingway

THE RELEASING

Pay no attention to the man behind the curtain!

The Wizard of Oz

1

Esther

DAY ONE 1976

The first time my mother died, we had spaghetti for dinner.

The sauce dribbled down my brother's chin as he prodded my dad. "When's Momma coming home?" Frankie had asked at least fifteen times before asking again.

"She went for milk." Still in his blue General Electric uniform after a long day at work, my dad answered as he looked down at the untouched food on his plate.

"She went for milk lots of days ago."

Four years younger than I, Frankie was relentless. I tried to get him to look at me as I picked up his plate. He ignored my glare and challenged my dad. "Is she dead?"

Olivia dropped her fork.

Twin to Frankie, five-year-old Olivia could not be more different from the chatty, energetic brother who usually played with me. Daddy didn't look at Frankie as he slammed his fists on the card table we used in our kitchen. "Yes, she's dead." The twins looked at me, and I shook my head no as my dad stormed out of the kitchen and swung open the front door, slamming it as he left.

"Dead," Olivia whispered as she played with her pasta, a blonde wisp of hair veiled one big brown eye.

It took me twenty minutes to scrape the plates, my hands shaking as I stood by the sink. I'd told Olivia and Frankie to go out and play after dinner. Through the kitchen window, I watched them—Frankie throwing something at the back of the fence and Olivia pulling weeds from the unkempt flowerbed and laying them side by side on the grass. Daddy had come back into the house and was sitting in the living room, his head in his hands. Something bad had happened, but I had no idea what. The kitchen calendar showed the dark X's made by me: the days that my mom had been gone, one week to the day, seven days, as the end of a perfect summer melted away. During those X'd out days, Daddy told me not to answer the telephone when he was at work except for a call he'd make to home at 12:05 each day.

The phone rang all day, every day, way more than before Momma left. I sat by the phone, watching our new digital clock each day, waiting for the 12:05 call. The clock was a reminder of one of the few times I witnessed my parents disagreeing. The two had argued briefly about getting the latest fad. Money was always tight, and—as my mom had argued—I was just learning to tell time, and she didn't want me to depend on the digital clock. Daddy won for once, and the digital anomaly was one of the few highlights of 1976.

Our mom had disappeared from our world, quietly and suddenly. She had disintegrated like an ice cube in a glass of lemonade on a really hot day; she had been here, but we looked away and looked back to see all the ice had melted. Daddy told Frankie that Momma was dead, but I knew that he meant she was dead to him. The sadness that lingered in his blue eyes in the days after she disappeared told me that maybe she had gone for milk and decided that a better life was out there. My dad stood at the front window, looking for her. He checked the mail every day after he came home from work, something she did when she was here. Maybe our mother was tired of taking care of Olivia, Frankie, and me. Maybe she had fallen out of love with our life, a life that I believed was so perfect.

The summer, before our mother vanished, had been a scorcher but a perfect three months. Momma was with us every day while Daddy worked. My dad had given my mom the greatest hits album of *ABBA* for her birthday months before, and Frankie and I knew every word to every song, as Momma played the album repeatedly as she worked around our little house. Dad would come home, and we would be complete. After dinner, I played in the backyard with the Junior Mints, a nickname my dad had for Frankie and Olivia. "And you, Esther, you are my big Milky Way. Your love is as big as the universe." We were the little candies in Tara and Clark Duvall's world. No one had a better life.

Fireflies sparkled around us as the silhouette of my parents danced in the kitchen, the white curtains sheering the tenderness of the moment. The song playing on an old record player in the house was *I do, I do, I do, I do, I do*. Only a hint of light from the day reminded us that we were on borrowed time before heading into bed. The sliding glass door opened, and my mother's silky voice called out to us, "Alright, my little angels, time to come in. Time to shut off the day." That's what Momma said every night. It's almost like we could just flip a switch and turn off the day and rest before a new one. And we did. Until we didn't.

Maybe Momma just wanted to shut off this life and turn on a new one.

Most people can't say that their mother had disappeared.

Not that this is anything to be proud of. Throughout my life, I've tried to make sense of and even find humor in that unique experience in the summer of 1976. I would imagine social situations with icebreakers to help people get to know each other. The icebreaker leader would throw out the question: What was your greatest life tragedy? Most people would be grouped into lesser tragedies: a broken engagement, a failed class, an unplanned pregnancy, the death of a special pet—all truly distressing at the time. But for these people, after their initial panic, time usually brought relief, as they recognized greater blessings and came to see their tragedy as a windfall. And if they could, they would write a little note to God in all caps: THANK YOU.

At this hypothetical icebreaker activity, where tragedies were grouped, I'd be left standing with a guy whose dad was sucked into a tornado, and the host would group us together since there really weren't many tragedies like disappearing mothers and sucked-up fathers. We didn't fit in with the rest of the room. And then, in this imaginary scenario, we would do some other ice breaker activity, and we'd all get to know each other even more, but the others would always look at us—the two strangest tragedies in the room—with pity and distance, as if our unique tragedy just might rub off on them.

Our mother had disappeared.

True. But I knew a few other things to be true that I hoped meant that she would be coming back. I knew that my tenth birthday was a week away, and my mom would never be gone on my birthday. I knew that she had a meeting with a teacher at my school to talk about special programs for Olivia when the time came for her to start school after Labor Day. I knew that she'd told me the day before she left that we'd go shopping for school supplies before the first day. And I knew that our mother loved us all more than life. She told us that every night as she tucked us in.

As I wiped down the counter, my dad walked back into the kitchen. He stood in the doorway holding a piece of paper and cleared his throat. "How'd you and the Junior Mints like to go to Peony Park?" We had been to the amusement park only once, on my seventh birthday. I didn't have a party with the kids from school, but a day with my family had been just fine by me. "Esther, I'm sorry I put an awful lot on you this past week... I keep forgetting you're only ten."

Technically still nine.

Daddy's eyes filled up with tears. "I think a night out would be good. Don't you?"

My dad's dark hair, striking blue eyes, and tall, lean frame were noticeable. I never really thought about adults being attractive at that time, but I knew that my father, along with my beautiful mother, stood out in any room. Momma's long, smooth, dark hair showered down her back, and her big green eyes were the first thing you saw when she entered that room. The green was almost golden, like my favorite marble in my cigar box filled with all different ordinary-colored marbles.

"Sounds good. I'll get Frankie and Olivia to come in and clean up. Are you sure we can afford ...?"

"Grab the Junior Mints and let's head to the car."

I opened the sliding glass door to the backyard. "Hey, you two want to go on an adventure?"

"To find Momma?" Frankie asked, no smile on his face.

"To Peony Park. Remember, with the airplane ride?"

Olivia and Frankie moved toward the door. "I want her home."

"I do too, Frankie, but I think it'd be better if you don't mention Momma tonight. Daddy's sad."

Frankie said nothing and took Olivia's hand as they walked into the house.

We drove to Peony Park in our old brown station wagon while the sun sat like an orange ball on the horizon, too beautiful for the sorrow in my heart. Frankie and Olivia said nothing as I sat up front with Daddy, where Momma should have been. The lights from the rides popped against the dark sky as we drove closer. Music from the park that could be heard even in the parking lot was enough to lift the mood from the tense dinner exchange and, if only for a brief time, remind us that happy times still might happen when mothers disappear.

"I want to be up there," Frankie yelled, pointing to the top of the Ferris wheel. Olivia hummed and laughed beside him.

"Then let's go there first." Daddy took Frankie's hand, and I took Olivia's, and the four of us moved toward the front entrance. We rode the Ferris wheel together and laughed as we moved toward the top. The laughter felt really good. "I wish we could go live on the moon, Esther," Frankie yelled, his head of dark curls holding the shine from the moonlight as he looked up in the sky.

From the tip top of our ride, I looked out across the city lights twinkling and wondered if Momma was out there somewhere. Living a new life, not even thinking of us. She was not dead. I could not go there in my head. I would not go there. While I looked out over the city for our mother, Daddy was looking down. I followed his taut stare to a woman near a tree at the bottom of the Ferris wheel. A tall woman with shoulder-length blonde hair wearing a black sundress and sunglasses stood near a big tree.

"When will this ride move?" Daddy said. "We can't sit up here forever."

Frankie held his hands up high. "Why not? I want to stay up here forever." Olivia moved her hands up to the sky with Frankie.

I looked back down to see that the woman near the tree was no longer there. The Ferris wheel moved on, and we got off. After bumper cars and big vanilla ice cream cones, Frankie and Olivia rode in the little kiddie planes that flew so slowly around that I wasn't sure you could still call it a ride, but the Junior Mints seemed to enjoy them as they flew past us again and again. I stood with my dad outside the ride, and the two of us waved each time they flew by.

"Well, look who's enjoying the end of their summer." The voice came from Mrs. Krisco, a woman whose red lipstick screamed when she spoke. The short, large woman was also the mother to one of the most annoying girls in my class: Kathy Krisco. Kathy stood next to her mother, with her hands on her hips, wearing a pair of bright pink shorts, a striped pink and yellow shirt, and a pair of pink sandals. Pink personified.

"We had our kick-off Daisy meeting tonight. All the girls picnicked over in the area near the pool." Mrs. Krisco spoke to my dad as if he cared.

"Oh," Daddy said as the Junior Mints squealed from their plane. We waved.

"We tried all week to get a hold of your wife," Mrs. Krisco said. She held a yellow purse against her large yellow pantsuit. There is such a thing as too much yellow. "But no one answered. We assumed you were out of town. Were you all on vacation?"

The closest thing to a vacation for the Duvall family had been the summer before when we drove up I-29 toward Sioux City, Iowa, to hear some odd lady talk about campers. Momma had read in the paper that families who ventured to the campground to hear a presentation about the latest fads on campers would receive a free gift—which is actually redundant—and the ad showed three boxes with words on each box: a thousand dollars, a barbecue grill, and a bottle of French perfume. If you could sit still for a full hour as a lady showed you pictures of the new 1976 pop-up campers with the latest bells and whistles, you would win one of the three prizes. Momma wore a dress and put the Junior Mints and me in our best clothes. Daddy grinned as Momma packed snacks and drinks for the afternoon adventure. She laughed and said, "We won't be poor and simple folk forever, Clark." I'm pretty sure Momma probably dreamed about all the bills we could pay off or a new kitchen table on that ride north. I remember thinking that we were really going to buy a camper. We drove our old car up I-29 for about a half hour along the Nebraska/Iowa border with all our windows open to fan us off in the heat of the day.

We arrived early and sat in the front row. When no one else showed up, a tall lady with frizzy hair and a lisp began her camper song-and-dance routine. Frankie ran around, and Olivia fussed as the woman droned on about the new camper that turned camper set-up time into family fun-time. When she finally stopped talking, Momma went up to the coffee can the woman was holding and pulled out a piece of paper with our prize: French Perfume.

Daddy laughed out loud. "Big surprise."

Momma looked shocked that we didn't win the thousand dollars. The perfume smelled nasty, and we drove home without money or a new camper. Momma cried a little on the long ride home. Daddy held her hand as Frankie, Olivia, and I fell asleep in the backseat, and we all went back home to be poor and simple folk.

"A vacation is always a fun way to end a summer." Mrs. Krisco prodded my dad.

"She's just been busy. I'll let her know." Daddy didn't look at Mrs. Krisco as he spoke; I wasn't sure if he avoided eye contact because he'd just lied or because he didn't like Kathy's mom. Whenever her name had come up in past conversations, Daddy always called her Queen Krisco, Queen of the Busy Bodies. The queen and her posse had said something once that had made Momma cry. My mom was clearly younger than the other mothers and never fit in. I overheard my parents talking in the kitchen after the Junior Mints and I had been put to bed.

"I'll kill 'em," Daddy's voice got louder as he spoke.

"No... I just..." My mother took a deep breath between sobs.

"Who said it? I'll kill her," my dad repeated.

"Babe, I'm sorry I said anything. I'm overreacting. I'm tired."

Daddy was no fan of Queen Krisco.

"Well, we'd sure like to see her get more involved with the PTA, Clark. We could always use more help."

"Are you sure you even want to be a Daisy?" Pink Kathy twirled her blonde hair as she challenged me. I could not be more different from the little princess. She was petite, blonde, and perfect. I was taller, with dark hair and an unusual name.

I shrugged. That was my answer.

"Well, maybe I'll just stop by this week to talk to Tara about the Daisy troop, the PTA, and whatnot." Queen Krisco would not let it go.

"I said I'll have her call you. Last round," he yelled to the Junior Mints. He said nothing more to Mrs. Krisco. I'm not sure if Mrs. Krisco or Kathy had ever been brushed off, but the two stood in shock as my dad moved toward the area where the mini flyers exited. Frankie and Olivia ran toward us from the ride while the queen and her pink princess walked away from the ride. The night was over.

The Junior Mints were asleep in the backseat before we were out of the Peony Park parking lot. Daddy was mad.

"Mrs. Krisco can be like that." I wanted him to know that I didn't like her either. Daddy said nothing as he started the car and turned on the radio.

"I don't even want to be a dumb Daisy."

Not a word after that. As we drove into our neighborhood, James Taylor crooned to his friend that he'd always be there. My dad, who had always worked for the electric company in Omaha, had told my mother that one day, he would make enough money to take her to a James Taylor concert. We sat in the driveway after he turned off the car.

"Does Momma not love us anymore?" The words in my head tumbled out of my mouth.

"Esther, why would you ever say something like that? Of course, she loves you more than life."

Loves.

Present tense.

I knew better than to ask where she was, like Frankie did. "Do you think she'll ever come home?"

Dad stared at our front door for a long time before he spoke. "Sometimes, it's hard to explain why people do what they do."

"You lied to Mrs. Krisco." I knew I was risking setting him off again, but I said it anyway.

Daddy took the keys out of the ignition.

The last time I'd lied to my parents, I'd had to sweep out the garage and weed the small garden in the backyard. I'd told Momma my homework was done so that I could watch *Welcome Back, Kotter*. She checked my folder as I relaxed on the couch, and you would have thought I had stabbed her through the heart as she scolded me, waving the blank addition/subtraction worksheet at me. Daddy's lie to Mrs. Krisco and Momma's lie to us that she loved us forever surely outweighed the unfinished math sheet. The double standard of parenting was both confusing and infuriating, but I knew that the topic of my dad lying was over for good.

We put the Junior Mints to bed; neither argued. I said goodnight to Daddy as he stood in the kitchen looking out the window.

"See you tomorrow," I said and paused.

"No answering the phone, remember."

"Right." Daddy wasn't a hugger or one to say he loved us. I missed Momma more than ever as I walked to my room.

"Esther," Daddy called out.

"Yep," I called from the hall.

"Sometimes a lie is the only answer."

I didn't know how to respond.

Daddy looked down but spoke. "Love you, Esther."

"You too, Daddy."

"Oh... and one more thing. Let's try and stay inside as much as possible tomorrow."

The only way I could get to sleep that night was to think of good things. I thought about Daddy taking the first day of school off last year to walk me to school with Momma and the Junior Mints. I thought of the snowman we had built the year before that looked kind of like the grumpy man across the street. I thought of the beautiful music box that Momma had given me for my sixth birthday. The music was from her favorite movie, *The Wizard of Oz*.

My thoughts then went where I could not stop them.

The secrets.

I knew of three secrets that my mother kept.

I knew that my mother kept a stash of M&Ms behind an old box of oatmeal in the cabinet. Those colored chocolates must have been her saving grace after long days with us. Daddy would joke about her love of chocolate, and I'm pretty sure that she had no idea that I'd discovered her little secret.

I knew that a stack of money could be found in an empty coffee can on a shelf behind our boots in the garage. I never counted it. I found it when Daddy told me to go get a flashlight from the garage. I looked everywhere but never found a flashlight. I did find the can and its secret contents.

I knew that in the back of her underwear drawer, tucked behind her silk slip, was a black and white photograph of a baby. One baby.

In a white strip on the bottom of the faded photo: *My dearest Daniel.*

The words were in my mother's handwriting. Other than a boy named Danny in my third- grade class the previous year, I knew no one named Daniel. A brother? A friend? Who was Daniel? My heart ached a little when I looked at the faded photo. In all my snooping adventures, I had never come across any baby pictures of Frankie, Olivia, or me.

My dearest Daniel.

Who was this baby and why was he deserving of her loving reference?

Momma had her little secrets, and now she had a big one as she remained missing from my world. Secrets can be for goodness sake: Olivia should never be told that she is different. Secrets can be for protection: Nancy Krisco should never know our little family secret so she could blab to the other Busy Bodies and the entire world that our mother had abandoned us.

The day before our trip to Peony Park, I'd checked on all of Momma's secrets.

A bag of M&Ms with a clothespin holding it shut remained behind the oatmeal. The picture of a baby named Daniel was still in her drawer with all her underthings. The money in the coffee can in the garage: gone.

2

Katherine

1954

I was exhausted.

After five finals in three days with little to no sleep, I had nothing more to give. My roommate Carol offered me a ride to the airport, so I took her up on it.

"It's not a problem at all, Katherine. I need to head to that part of town anyway to pick up a few last-minute gifts for Christmas." Carol—her granny glasses halfway down her nose and frizzy hair that never moved—was the kind of person who always wanted to please people. "I'd be happy to get you to the airport."

I hadn't even given one thought to gifts for my family. I wasn't excited about seeing my parents and brother since the last time I had spoken to them, at Thanksgiving in Connecticut, had been anything but family-like. I slammed the car door on my mother as she dropped me off at the airport, and I hadn't talked to any member of my family since.

"Is your flight on time? Sometimes, they leave early, as crazy as that sounds." After spending the first day of my college experience in a tiny box called a dorm room at Santa Clara with the ever-loquacious Carol Cartwright from Idaho, I discovered that empty or quiet moments made her uncomfortable.

"I'll be good."

"Sure you're OK?"

"I'm fine."

"You look tired... and thin, very thin."

I looked up and saw my reflection in the window of the dorm building as we walked to Carol's car. I barely recognized myself. Carol was right. I'd always given time and energy to my looks, my make-up flawless, my short-bobbed hair styled. I'd always worn a skirt and sweater when I traveled; my mother brainwashed me on that habit. That day, in my jeans and pullover, I hadn't even run a brush through my hair, and I looked thin, very thin. I opened the door to Carol's old red Volkswagen Bug and got in.

"Just ready for a break, I guess."

A half-hour later, Carol nudged me. "Wake up, Sleepy Head. I'd park and walk in with you, but I have those errands and a paper to hand into my sociology professor, that needs to get to his office by 4:00 p.m. A minute later, he won't take it. No, we can't be late for Dr. Swann." I sat up and looked out at the Frontier sign at the Mineta San Jose International Airport. I handed Carol three dollars for gas as I grabbed my bag and opened the car door.

"No way, ma'am. Not taking a penny. Merry Christmas, Katherine."

"Thank you, Carol. Merry Christmas."

"See you after break," Carol yelled out. "Now get on that plane and sleep all the way back to Connecticut!"

The San Jose Airport, full of the beauty of the hustle and bustle of the holiday spirit, smelled like a freshly unwrapped candy cane. Stunning lights and gaudy garland draped the Frontier check-in desk as holiday music played overhead.

Though I usually drank in the spirit of the season, I sulked at the energy given to such a materialistic, emotional investment. Donald and Jan—as I liked to call my parents when they weren't in the hearing range—were the epitome of that self-indulgent existence. Our home was exquisite. Their holiday decorations: the best on the block.

From as early as I can remember, my parents paraded Howard and me as little accomplishment trophies to the neighbors and parents in my schools. My mother found the Christmas card to be the perfect platform to showcase the family as evidence to the world that Donald and Jan Wayman had it all figured out. My brother and I wore matching red and white outfits: me in a dress and Howie in a suit. My beautiful mother and tall, successful father towered behind us, hands on the shoulders of their perfect little Christmas treasures.

The world didn't see the whole picture though. My parents were financially strapped and living beyond their means—at least, that is what I surmised from the arguments between them late at night as they hovered over bills at the kitchen table. I'd never seen as big a smile on my mother's face as the day my Santa Clara scholarship announcement came in the mail. Santa Clara University, where the sun shines nearly three hundred days each year, would help the family and make my mother happy. I thought.

I walked up to a counter, looking for any information about my flight.

"Your flight is delayed an hour while the crew checks out a mechanical problem." The short woman, with hair, teased at least five inches above her head and eyes encased with smoky dark eyeliner, smiled and handed me a piece of paper. Her nametag read Vickie. "This here is information about an option we're offering for folks on this flight. We have a half-dozen people who'd like to move onto this flight. If you choose to wait for the flight tomorrow, Frontier will offer you a discount on a future flight."

"So... until then I just wait?" Sarcasm laced my words.

"That's right, hon. I'll make an announcement right before we board. Just settle down with a book or something. Sorry about the wait."

Thanks, Vickie. You're a doll. Even my thoughts were sarcastic.

I sat down at the closest seat to the check-in desk. I didn't want to go home, but I knew that I should get home on this flight. The discount on a future flight might please Donald and Jan Wayman. The longer I could put off the let's-pretend-we're-a-happy-family routine, the better. I didn't want to hear my mother scream as she opened the mail with my bad report card. I had tried to pull my grades up with a full-throttle effort during finals week, but I was almost certain that I'd lost my scholarship. There might not be a flight back to Santa Clara.

I looked out of the large airport windows at the overcast afternoon. It would be snowing in Connecticut. The house would smell like vanilla and cinnamon. Wizard, the family pug, would be underfoot the entire break, and that wouldn't bother me one bit. I was surprised at how much I missed my little brother Howie. The dull ache in my head and eyes got sharper as I held back my tears. Thoughts of home rushed over me, and I wasn't quite sure if I was hesitant about going home or if I might actually miss my family.

Resentment quickly flooded over the nostalgia in my heart. Thanksgiving break at home had not been a pleasant one. I was a freshman at Santa Clara with a 4.0 first quarter, and I still couldn't measure up to the goals of my parents. Howard was still the golden child who somehow had captured the hearts of my parents on day one of his life on earth. One more comment about the boys I was or wasn't dating or my lack of interest in planning my future, and I could have exploded.

Up until high school, I had played my mother's game very well. I'd succeeded and basked in my mother's salty praise for each report card, each honor, each leadership position. And the accolades lined up beautifully like compliant toy soldiers off to take on the world, in a battle that I soon learned I no longer wanted to be a part of after moving far away from my Connecticut childhood. Moving across the country to a world so different than my small, simple world of a protected private-school upbringing had frightened me at first. Alcohol, boys, and new attitudes came blasting at me, and I was both fearful and elated all at once.

The first taste of rebellion following the Thanksgiving altercation with my mom was intoxicating, and I soon found myself drowning in defiance of rules, with a blatant contempt for academic success. I went out during the week and found the exhilaration in flying from class to class with no preparation. I even skipped classes, something the old me would never have done. The pleasure that came from the new freedom and autonomy from my upbringing was more glorious to me than I had expected.

One man reinforced my exhilarating sovereignty: Paul Young. In 1954, while most of my professors were conservative and stodgy, Dr. Young, my young and handsome philosophy professor, stood out as he spoke to my classmates and me in a way we had never experienced.

"The United States has the most perfect government in the world." Dr. Young leaned back against his desk.

My fellow soldiers at the time and I wrote furiously in our notebooks.

"Stop!" Dr. Young pounded his hand on the desk of an unassuming and timid student, who sat in the first seat to be enlightened, not attacked. "Before you begin a life of acceptance, use your brains, people!"

I looked to my friend Wayne, who sat next to me. He looked as confused as I was.

"This isn't even a government class. My statement isn't about anything on the syllabus for today. You all just accept that what the adults in your life tell you is the truth and the law of the land. You just write it down and accept it. Do you believe that the United States has the most perfect government in the world?"

No one replied.

"Well, do you, Wayne?"

"Uh, I guess." Wayne looked at Dr. Young and then at me and shrugged.

"So, you just accept that statement as if anything I say is right?"

A student in the back cleared his throat and raised his hand.

"Yes, Ron?"

"Well, you are the teacher. Wouldn't it be considered disrespectful or… belligerent to question or challenge you?"

"If you were a child, probably. Are you a child, Ronald?"

Ron looked at the professor and then down.

"Are you?"

"What?"

"A child?"

"No."

"How about the rest of you?"

The professor's voice bounced off the walls. "You all are no longer children. You need to look at your world and question many of the things that you were fed to believe as a child. If not, this world will eat you up."

"Lost?"

A voice interrupted my memory, and I looked up at a man who was standing near the window. I saw first his silhouette only through the large airport windows as he stood against the light of the day. As my eyes adjusted to the light, I could see that he was very attractive. A pressed white shirt tucked into his khaki pants and his warm smile stood out in great contrast to the wave of confused emotions flooding my exhausted state. I looked around to see whom the man was addressing.

"Yes, you with the sad face. Are you lost?" The man's full head of dark hair framed his tan face, the white of his teeth popping against his skin, his eyes a bright grey.

"No." An eerie version of *Joy to the World* crooned overhead.

"I know this airport really well. I could guide you."

"I'm fine. Thank you." I pretended to adjust my bag and looked up at the check-in desk.

Tricky Vickie was no longer standing there.

"Can I buy you a cup of coffee while you wait for your flight?"

"I'm sorry. I don't even know you."

"So, not lost then, huh?"

I thought about the stranger's question, and the dam that had held back my tears for a long time broke. Lost. That's exactly how I felt. I moved my hand to cover my lips which were forming an ugly crying face. I looked down.

"What do you want?" the man asked.

"What do I want? What do you want?" I asked the nervy man.

"I don't want anything. Actually, my life is pretty incredible."

I sat up straight, took a deep breath, and cleared my throat. The man turned and walked away.

"Wait."

The man stopped, turned back to me, and flashed a smile.

"I didn't mean to come off sounding so rude," I said. "I'm just not myself right now."

"Who are you then? If you're not you."

"Tired."

"So, if you're not lost, and you're not *you*, any chance you're a coffee drinker?"

"I am." I wasn't, but I didn't want to come off as even more rude.

"There's a coffee shop down the next corridor that has coffee that isn't nasty—well, not too nasty. Best I could do nearby, until you board your plane. Will that work?"

I laughed. The first laugh in a long time. "I probably need a little caffeine…"

"I'm very disciplined when it comes to coffee. I only drink coffee on days that end in the letter *Y*. I'm Charles. Charles Armstrong."

The warm hands of Charles embraced my hand. "I'm Katherine. Where are you heading?"

"I just dropped a friend off for his flight." Charles picked up my bag and guided me toward the coffee shop. "I was heading home when I saw you. I just had to talk to you or meet you... sorry. I didn't mean that to sound so creepy."

"No, my mistake. Heading home to Connecticut. I just finished a semester at Santa Clara."

"Santa Clara. Impressive. What are you studying?"

"Well, my parents think I'm studying to be a nurse, but I really want to go into business. I guess you could say that I'm studying to understand this world."

"Totally get that. I came to California to be an actor... and get away from two alcoholic, abusive parents. I got away, but the dream of acting fell to the side. I never went home."

"Sorry."

"I'm not. I found a better place with a better mission. I've never been happier."

"Because?"

"Because I live where every person respects me. Respects my opinion. I live where I can be me."

"So, where's this place that sounds like heaven?"

"About a half hour from here. Not quite a town. A winery, actually. The vineyard is growing by leaps and bounds, and our brand is becoming known, even on the east coast. Are you a wine drinker?" Charles found a small table for two and he set my bag down.

"I thought the drink of the moment was coffee."

"We grow grapes for an amazing Cabernet. You may have seen our label—Celestial Way. We're working on developing merlots this season. Turns out coffee beans don't make great wine." Charles laughed a beautiful laugh and pulled a wallet from his pocket.

"My parents let us have wine at Thanksgiving and Christmas. Actually, it's legal for me to drink in Connecticut, but not here in California. Funny, right?" I was beginning to feel my spirits lift.

"I'm going to go get us two cups of coffee. Do you take anything in yours?"

"Everything. I hate the taste."

Charles grinned. "I'll be right back."

I smiled. I wanted to be happy. I really did. A woman and her little boy were sitting across the aisle. The boy was playing with toy cars on the table as the woman spoke in soft whispers to him.

"Here you go." Charles placed my coffee in front of me. "Loaded with cream and sugar and anything else sweet that I could find."

"Thank you."

"So, I take it you're twenty then?" Charles took a sip from his cup.

"Eighteen... and a half."

"Wow, I had you much older."

I was flattered but on guard. "So, Celestial Way."

"Yep." I tried to put an age on this strange man named Charles: twenty-seven, thirty?

"Sounds like a great concept." I looked at the second finger on the left hand of Charles: naked.

"It is." The laugh again, the beautiful laugh. "The labels on our bottles are light blue, like the sky. President Eisenhower bought several cases for his Christmas dinner next week. Dwight from the White – that's what we call him."

"You sell wine to the president?"

"Just this year. Captain, the owner of Celestial Way, bought an old monastery with the hopes of riding on the wine comeback train."

"Comeback?"

"Wine was a huge thing back before Prohibition. The number of California wineries diminished from over seven hundred to a little over two hundred. Captain says the demand and the resurgence of wine in America today is the best kept secret. Wine's going to be big in America in the next ten to twenty years. Big."

"So, I guess that makes you part of this secret."

"I guess it does." Charles looked at me with a grin like James Dean. A scream brought us both back to reality. The little boy across the aisle was throwing a tantrum, and the mother picked him up and looked at her watch.

I looked at my watch.

"Oh my gosh, I need to get to my gate." I stood up and looked for a clock in the airport. Maybe my watch was fast.

"I've got your bag," Charles said, as I ran out of the coffee shop. He was following close behind.

The corridor to my gate seemed longer than before, and I scanned the gate numbers. Gate 213 was two gates away. I got to the check-in desk as the boarding doors closed. "Wait! I need to get on that plane."

My good friend Vickie turned to me. "Sorry, but we can't open the door after it shuts."

"But I'm standing right here. You saw me coming."

"This flight is full now. We called your name earlier, and when you didn't come up, we gave your seat to a person on standby."

My heart pounded as I took a deep breath. My mother would be furious. "When's the next flight to New Haven? Do you know when the next flight to Connecticut is?"

"Ma'am, I'm going to need you and your husband to wait over there until I answer this woman's question." I had interrupted the woman when I ran to the gate.

I looked behind me, where Charles stood with my bag.

"Could you please wait until I call you up to check future flights?"

I took a deep breath. Charles stood patiently as I walked over to him and laughed. "I missed my flight."

"Saw that."

"I'm going to need to get my head around this." I looked down at the piece of paper with information about the option for a cheaper flight. Once Vickie was available, I walked up to her again. "Is there some kind of a deadline for when I need to reschedule my flight?"

"The sooner the better, hon." She was writing down information as she spoke. "The number to contact us is on the bottom of the sheet. Holiday flights are filling up. Christmas is in two days. Let us know soon."

I walked back to Charles and sighed. "You've been very kind."

"I'd be happy to drive you to a hotel on my way home." *Silent Night* played over our heads.

"I'd appreciate that." This was no time to be proud.

Charles picked up my bag, and we walked toward the exit near the baggage claim.

"I may have to visit your little vineyard town one of these days, Charles. I think I'd like your secret place."

"Any time."

We walked out to the end of the parking lot. Charles opened the passenger door of an old green Crosley station wagon for me and put my bag in the back seat. I yawned and looked out at the beautiful landscape. The sun sat on the California horizon like a big orange ball, peacefully perched.

As Charles drove out of the parking lot, he said, "There's a Motel 8 east of here and a Howard Johnson Motor Inn a little closer. You could probably take a cab to the airport in the morning."

"Sounds good."

The quiet in the car and the first moments of peace my body had felt for months filled me with hope and excitement that both intrigued and scared me. "Which direction is the vineyard?"

"Other way. It's north of here. About a thirty-minute drive."

Silence.

"You're welcome to stay at Celestial Way. We have plenty of room."

"I'd like that."

"So, we're turning left?"

"Sure."

I had one last thought before I fell asleep: snow falling outside my house in Connecticut. The Christmas lights on the house would frame the seemingly perfect home.

Home.

Oh, Katherine, you're not going home.

3

Esther

Day Two 1976

"What can we do now?" Frankie whined. "When's lunch?" The rain poured outside as the lure of *Candy Land* and *and Ladders* dwindled, and I was praying for a non-Junior-Mint moment. We stopped playing *Candy Land* after three games as I suspected that Frankie was stacking the deck. Who gets the Queen Frostine card every time? We played the *ABBA* album three times, both sides; Frankie and I danced as Olivia stared at the album cover. On the front, a man and a woman sat and stared out in front of them. On the back, another man and woman were kissing. Frankie thought it was silly. Olivia was obsessed with the pictures. Frankie and I then played three games of *Chutes and Ladders* as Olivia sat close to me, humming as she opened and closed my music box. *Somewhere Over the Rainbow* played as a tiny ballerina twirled around slowly in front of a glittering, colorful rainbow. Olivia loved the music box so much she thought it was hers. I know it connected her to Momma; she'd slept with the music box in the nights after Momma's great disappearing act.

Olivia's obsession was not surprising. The repeated song, the glittery ballerina, and the fact that she could keep the music box with her at all times transformed my gift from Momma into Olivia's security. I never complained, but Momma surprised me with a charm bracelet not long after we all realized that the musical present was no longer mine. I'm pretty sure Momma bought the piece of jewelry at Ben Franklin's Five and Dime. I had seen a similar bracelet in the costume jewelry aisle. The painted charms on the bracelet represented different pieces of Momma's favorite story: a tin man, a lion, a scarecrow, a white witch's hat, a black witch's hat, a dog that looked like Toto, and two shiny shoes that were painted ruby red. The little charms lined the bracelet, precariously tethered to the chain like a house to the ground during a tornado. I wore the bracelet so much that the paint on each of the charms wore thin, like the passing days of childhood, reminding me that I couldn't wear the bracelet forever.

The music box and the bracelet were both reminders of the special place in Momma's heart for *The Wizard of Oz*. Pictures from the movie filled a big book that Momma kept under the couch in the living room. Daddy said it was a coffee table book, which was funny since we didn't have a coffee table. The book's title: *The Story of MGM*. Momma would sit with us and look through the colored pictures in the hardcover book that was *bigger than Olivia*. Momma said that the letters MGM stood for the initials of the names of some big mucky-mucks— in Hollywood who all wanted a piece of themselves in the world of fame.

I still know the pictures by heart to this day. Pictures of the munchkins goofing around behind the scenes of *The Wizard of Oz* set. A two-page spread of a beautiful woman standing by the pool was my favorite. The name of the movie was *Million Dollar Mermaid*. Several pages included behind-the-scenes pictures from *Gone with the Wind*. The actors are drinking coffee and smiling at the camera in one picture. The big dresses of several women in another picture mesmerized Olivia. Momma knew the names of the actors and the characters they played. She'd say, more to herself than to the Junior Mints and me: *It was a magical time.*

The middle spread was a scene of Dorothy walking on the yellow brick road with Toto, the munchkins surrounding her as she started her journey. When Momma talked about *The Wizard of Oz*, she remembered watching the movie over and over again. In a blurry memory, I remember lying next to her as we watched the movie go from black and white to color. My mom knew the lines by heart, and told us that we all had the power, just like Dorothy with her shoes.

Her obsession, and, I suppose, our limited budget meant that the fall of my first-grade year, the Duvall children went trick-or-treating dressed as characters from the well-known movie. Momma bought material and sewed our costumes. I was Dorothy. Olivia was a munchkin ballerina, and Frankie was Toto. Momma braided my dark, long hair and found some red shoes at the thrift store that were a little too big, but I wore them with pride. Momma was delighted. I was too, until Kathy Krisco made fun of me at school on the day of the Halloween parade.

"Did your mom make your costume?" She rolled her eyes without even looking at me.

"She did."

"Thought so."

"I win. I win." Frankie screamed as his guy— what he chose to call the game tokens—landed on a box that sent him up a long ladder. He'd landed on a square, one of the hundred chancy boxes on the board that had a picture of a boy rescuing a cat from the tree. "Up, up, up!" Five minutes later, after landing on a box with a boy stealing cookies from the cookie jar, Frankie was in tears as the box directed him: down, down, down, to the bottom of the board. "I hate this stupid game." Frankie stood up and kicked the board.

My respect for my mother skyrocketed in those endless days as I wondered how she got everything done while keeping the three of us on task. Momma detested the television set, and she would do everything in her power to shoo the three of us outside to play. I'd wanted so badly to be like Momma and would hold off turning on the TV until I had no other options.

"How about another game of *Candy Land*?" I asked. The wind howled outside as the summer rainstorm refused to subside.

"I don't want to play games anymore. I want to go out in the rain and play with my truck." Frankie stomped to the kitchen with his yellow truck and moved the glass door open. I didn't see any harm if he stood out on the back porch while it rained. I could start making lunch until he got tired of getting wet and wanted to come back in. He'd be dry before Daddy got home.

"OK, but five minutes only. Dad said not to go outside."

Daddy hadn't gone to the store since Momma had left. Peanut butter sandwiches again. We had only a few handfuls of broken potato chips at the bottom of the bag, and I divided them on the three paper plates in front of me, giving myself the smallest amount. Water would have to do since we were also out of milk. On the kitchen counter, the digital clock read 12:01. Next to the clock was a stack of mail; on the top was a large envelope addressed to Tara Duvall. The envelope was much bigger than the envelopes under it holding bills and other boring-looking mail. My dad would pick up that big envelope every day and stare at Momma's name. I think he didn't open it because he was hoping she'd come back and open it. 12:02. I stood by the clock and waited.

12:03.

12:04.

12:05.

The phone rang.

"Hello?" I tried to sound responsible.

"Tara?"

Not Daddy's voice.

A man's voice had whispered my mother's name. At least it sounded like he'd said Tara. Or, maybe he had said 'terror', or maybe he had just said hello, and I wanted to hear her name. I froze.

"Where are you? Tara?"

I held my breath. Frankie walked back into the kitchen soaking wet, holding his truck, "I need a towel!"

Click.

I stood with the phone next to my head until the loud buzzing told me to hang up.

I hung up.

The phone rang again.

I hesitated but picked up the phone from the cradle on the kitchen wall. "Hello?"

"I thought I told you not to answer the phone, Esther. I just called and got a busy signal. Who were you talking to?"

"I don't know."

"Don't you remember that I told you not to answer the phone except when I called?" Daddy scolded me in a firm, quiet voice.

"Yes."

"Then who were you talking to?"

"I don't know."

"You don't know? Didn't they say?"

"No."

"Esther." My dad's words came in a crisp whisper. "It's important that people don't know that you're home alone. I can't be two places at once… Esther?"

"Yah."

Frankie yelled from the bathroom, "I'm hungry."

"Sorry, I yelled at you, Esther. I'll be home for dinner."

I knew that we didn't have anything for dinner. More peanut butter sandwiches? "I'll try and stop by the store on the way home."

"K."

"Be good."

I hung up and stared at the three sad lunches on the counter. Olivia and Frankie both grabbed a paper plate and sat at our card table. I filled three glasses with tap water.

"Why aren't you eating, Esther?" Frankie's mouth was full of peanut butter and bread.

"Not hungry." I could have thrown up.

After lunch, the wind and rain blew hard against our back window, attempting to match Frankie's earlier tantrum. The strange summer storm came in August, a month that was typically hot and humid.

"Can we watch TV?"

"Sure." I wasn't sure I could carry this responsibility until school started. If Momma didn't come back soon, I didn't know how Olivia could go to school. The adult worries were heavy, and I wanted my mother more than ever.

As the rain continued into the afternoon, Frankie fell asleep on the couch watching *Match Game 76* while Olivia colored in her favorite coloring book on the floor. On the TV screen, Gene Rayburn held a long microphone close to his mouth and looked into the camera: "James Bond went to an all-night restaurant. When the waitress told him that they were out of coffee, he ordered a blank." He then looked at the celebrities behind him. He walked up to Richard Dawson and moved the microphone to Dawson's face.

"A girl," Dawson said. "James Bond ordered a girl."

"Girl," Olivia mimicked as she colored. Daddy had bought three of the same *Barbie* coloring books from the clearance bin for Olivia. She sat for hours, covering everything on a page in one color, neatly inside the lines. Barbie's hair and her car, and a palm tree were all purple. Her strokes were smooth and calming, and I admired her ability to be peaceful in a huge storm of unknown. Around three o'clock the rain stopped, and the sun came out. A knock on the door startled all three of us. Frankie awoke and sat up. He and Olivia looked at me. I moved my finger to my mouth and shook my head no. The person knocked again at the door and stopped. A silhouette of a short thin man stood in front of the larger front window of our living room. He cupped his hands around his eyes and pressed closer to the window.

"Hey!" The man waved to me. The man was not a man. Marty Westerholt, our paper boy, knocked on the window as he looked at me sitting on the couch. Marty had a shock of dark brown hair and a delectable smile. "Collecting for the newspaper." His muffled voice was kind and guiltless. A known paper boy is better than the unknown voice of a strange man on the phone. "I stopped by last week, but no one was home," Marty said as he pointed to the front door.

I unlocked and opened the front door. I looked beyond the paper boy to see our neighbor-lady Tess standing on her porch watching us.

"Wow, you guys must have had the TV on super loud. I knocked a few times. I usually collect on the third Tuesday of the month. Is your mom home?"

"Our mom's visiting our grandmother... who's sick." The words came out as quickly as light moves on an oil slick. "I'm not sure when she'll be back." That quick. That slick. The lie was so smooth that it almost felt right. I'd never told such a bold lie in my life, and I knew at that moment just how easy a simple, slippery lie was. Olivia's big brown eyes stared at me. Frankie's jaw dropped. Our grandparents were no longer alive, and the Junior Mints knew that.

"So sorry." Marty's eyes searched the back of the house. Was my lie not convincing enough? "Well, when do you think would be a good time for me to come back?"

A new lie burst from me just as quick and slick as the first: "Probably next Tuesday. She should be back by then."

"Don't you go to Henderson Grade School? This coming year I'll be at the middle school, but I'm sure that I've seen you."

I'd thought I was invisible—just invisible Esther Duvall, the strange girl whom people overlooked, the girl with the unusual name. Mrs. Jereske used to call me Aster, like the star. Marty remembered me from school—a school whose walls surrounded mostly pretty girls with nice clothes. Marty remembered the girl in the K-Mart clothes and the homemade

Halloween costumes. With his beautiful crooked smile, he asked again. "Well, do you?"

"Do I?"

"Go to Henderson?"

"Yes."

"That's what I thought. I'll come back next week. See you then."

As Marty turned to leave, I looked at the clock near the front door: 4:45. Daddy would be home soon.

"Just tell her that Marty will be back." Marty smiled as he picked up his bag from the front porch and peered into the house again. "You sure you're all OK?"

"Yep. See you… later." I shut the door and took a deep breath.

"I thought he was that man." Frankie's voice interrupted my grumpy thoughts.

"What man?"

"The man in the store who hugged Momma. That Marty guy's too skinny and has lots of hair."

It'd been a long summer, and I had been with the Junior Mints and Momma every day. How could Frankie have a memory that I didn't have? I stared at Frankie in shock at what he was saying.

"When you and Olivia were with Miss Pringle," Frankie added.

"Pringle." Olivia was paying attention.

I'd blocked the meeting out of my mind. We'd met with Miss Pringle right before our mother disappeared. I knew that

Miss Pringle, Henderson Grade School's sole counselor, had asked Momma to set an appointment at which time she'd test both Olivia and me. At first, I wasn't happy. I knew Olivia struggled. She would be different than most kids in school. But I did well in school. Were they testing me because the school thought I was different?

"No, Esther." My mother's laughter had calmed me. "The school doesn't think you're challenged enough," Momma had told me the night before the test. "They think that you might do better in harder classes... maybe even the grade ahead."

"I don't want to change grades. That will make me even more... different."

"I didn't say we'd be doing that. We just want to find out our options."

Frankie ran to the back door and was about to slide it open.

"Wait, what man?" I said.

"He was way bigger than that guy. Way bigger. Momma bought me Juicy Fruit gum."

"Frankie, what man?"

"He wasn't bad. He just seemed..." Frankie searched for a word. "...sad."

On the island that was our family, I could think of no other man than our dad and the principal at Henderson whom my mother might know. She talked to the mailman and the grocery clerk, but she would not, should not, hug another man.

"Why didn't you tell me that, Frankie?"

"I forgot... hey, do you think that man in the store took Momma?"

Olivia winced.

37   MARY KAY LEATHERMAN

Daddy opened the front door before I could give it another thought. "Take the Junior Mints to the backyard, Esther."

There were no bags of groceries in his hands. Peanut butter sandwiches again.

"Why?"

"Just do it!"

Olivia and Frankie went to the back door as I glanced out the front door. Maybe Daddy left the food in the station wagon. I saw our station wagon parked in the driveway and three police cars pulling up to the curb on the street in front of our house.

"Go. Now."

Two Junior Mints and a Milky Way sat in the backyard for about a half hour. Olivia, who never complained, started whimpering. I knew she was upset and hungry. I looked through the sliding glass door to see Daddy in the kitchen at the card table with two policemen flanking him and another man in an important suit standing over him. In a moment of defiance and self-preservation, I opened the door and, herded the Junior Mints in and pointed to the ugly living room couch. We slinked in and sat down. An hour later, we were still sitting on the couch, still confused and hungry. Only now, a fat man with buttons holding tightly to a stretched work shirt was asking me strange questions. Dark rings of sweat crawled out from his armpits.

"Nine," Olivia said as a new tall man with an important looking uniform walked in the front door. Frankie, Olivia, and I sat on our couch and watched the man walk in without so much as a knock on the door. A short, pretty woman in a navy skirt and white blouse walked in behind him. "Ten."

Frankie pulled on my arm. "When are these people leaving?"

"It's all going to be fine," I said. That's what Momma would say.

"I'm going to ask you once again: has your dad ever hurt you or your brother or sister?" I was losing patience with the big man with a mustache who had pulled a chair from the card table to the living room next to us. Our mother would never have allowed us to take a chair from the kitchen out to the living room. We'd been trying to ignore him, but the old fart just wouldn't go away. He moved toward me and looked me in the eye, his face so close I could smell his breath. "Now listen here; if you cooperate with us, we won't have any problems." The heat and smell of his breath jolted me to another time.

Sweet and sour.

That's what I remembered. The sweet and sour smell of a man's breath. I was sitting on his lap. He rubbed my back as he laughed at a room full of people. I think Momma was in the room. He moved his face closer. Sweet and sour. He was singing with other people in the room. The man kept rubbing my back. I shared the vivid sweet-and-sour-breath memory with my parents.

"Wow. You remember that?" Daddy asked. Momma shook her head.

"I was in a white dress or shirt. His breath was awful."

"That was Whiskey Walt." Daddy knew exactly who I was talking about.

"Who's Whiskey Walt?"

"It doesn't matter." Momma looked at me. "He's dead now."

"Yeah, Walt liked to drink whiskey all day long." My dad winked.

"What's whiskey?"

"Something you shouldn't drink all day long," my mom said as she left the room.

The mean officer questioning me smelled like Whiskey Walt.

"Get out of my face," I said to him in the meanest voice I could muster. The big man backed up. "Don't you have any other questions on your sheet there?"

"Well, this question happens to be an important one."

"No. My daddy never hurt any of us. I already told you that," I said. Olivia pushed her face into my sleeve and whimpered.

"Hey!" The woman who'd just entered our house moved toward us. She had dark smooth hair that stopped at her shoulders and wore a navy skirt that fit her petite figure well. "Kemper, could you give the kids a little break?" The smell of a peeled orange hovered over us as the woman sat next to Frankie and smiled at us. "You guys like McDonald's?"

"Yah!" Frankie yelled. We had been to McDonald's once, on Momma's birthday.

"My name's Ramona. What do you say we take a little ride and get a Happy Meal?"

"Can Daddy come?" Frankie asked.

I looked in the kitchen. My dad's head was in his hands as a room full of adults stared at him. One man—he was taller and younger than the others—pointed his finger at our dad as he spoke. "...never called 911... do you know where she is... where were you..."

"I think we'll just stay here, ma'am," I said. I would make peanut butter sandwiches as soon as all these people in our house left. "Do you know when you all are leaving?"

Ramona's dark hair shimmered as she looked at Kemper. "Well, it won't be for a while. I think we could get some fresh air and some food and ..." Kemper got up from the chair and walked into the kitchen. I looked beyond Daddy's head and saw several men in the backyard. One had a dog on a leash. "I'm not sure if you three will be staying here tonight. Your neighbor, Tess Folten, said that you could stay with her tonight."

"Eleven," Olivia said as another man in a uniform walked through the front door. Didn't even knock. Wasn't even invited.

"Mrs. Folten told me that you've stayed at her house before, when your parents went on trips."

Lie.

Tess was a liar, and probably she was the tattletale who had called the police about my mom. Why was it her business if our mom took a long way home from the store? True, we had been to Tess's house before, maybe a hundred times or so with our mom, but we'd never spent the night. And my parents had never been on one trip away from us. We usually went over to Tess's house with Momma in the day when Daddy was at work. Momma and Tess would have coffee in her little kitchen, which was a country kitchen museum decorated with wooden roosters and chickens and blue and yellow wallpaper that wrapped around the crowded room with a parade of animated hens running after their baby chicks. Olivia was mesmerized by the pattern and would count the hens and chicks until Momma would shoo us all out to the backyard on nice days and the living room on rainy days.

Tess may have looked like a harmless old lady, but she was all sass and what Momma would never say but probably knew as well as I did: a big know-it-all. The age difference between Momma and Tess was pretty big, and I think now, as I did back then, that our mother found the mother that she no longer had in Tess. On rainy days at Tess's house, we would play in the living room making up games. We were good at making up games. The *Who Am I* game was a favorite. We'd look at all the pictures on the walls and tables and make up stories about the people in the pictures. Frankie was the best at the *Who Am I* game.

"Who Am I?" I announced as I pointed to a man in a picture.

"Hi. I'm George, and I'm a banker." Frankie's voice was deep and goofy. "I want all of your money."

Olivia giggled.

"What about this lady?" I asked as I pointed to the picture of a beautiful woman in a wedding gown. The black and white picture of the woman on an altar with a bouquet of roses was the first of many pictures that lined the staircase going up to the bedrooms.

"That lady… let me think." Frankie continued in a silly, high-pitched voice. "Hi, I'm a lady who just decided not to get married. I'm going to run as fast as I can to the North Pole and become an elf." I always marveled at the number of pictures and frames. Did Tess Folten really have this many people in her world? Where were they? And how could she afford all the frames?

I squinted my eyes and tilted my head as I moved closer to the bride in the wedding picture. "Hey, is that Tess?"

Olivia and Frankie moved closer to the picture.

"Boy, did she get fat," Frankie said.

"Frankie! Don't say that."

"Fat," Olivia whispered.

The truth.

Later, I told my mom that I didn't think any man would want to marry grumpy, old Tess. Momma told me that the wedding picture was 'evidence' that, in fact, a man did want to marry Tess and have two sons with her. Her husband had died years ago, and now Tess was just an interesting old lady with time on her hands.

Where was the evidence of our childhood, of Momma and Daddy's wedding? We had only one picture on the wall in our living room. It was a painting of a bunch of trees behind a lake. The colors were orange and yellow and brown and ugly. Momma said that my dad had bought it at a sale at a gas station. I used to pretend that it was the view from the house my mom and dad lived in before we were born. A long time ago.

My own lie.

In place of pictures were the stories that we embraced when we went to bed. Our mother would talk about Princess Esther being born in Cincinnati and the Amazing Junior Mints taking over the world after we moved to Omaha. We heard those stories so many times, they played like a movie in our minds as we drifted off to sleep.

No, we had never spent the night at Tess Folten's house.

"We're just fine staying here, ma'am."

"Well, your father may not be staying here tonight. He might be coming down to the station for some more questions."

A half-hour later, we were sitting at McDonald's with the lady who smelled like orange peels. Ramona talked non-stop about silly things like our favorite food and color and what we wanted to be when we grew up as she played with her necklace. I didn't answer. Olivia didn't answer. Frankie answered and ate his Happy Meal and most of mine.

"Home," Olivia said, rolling her Happy Meal Ronald McDonald eraser back and forth on the table.

"I want to go home, too," Frankie said. "Thanks for taking us here, Miss..."

"Ramona. Please call me Ramona. We can head back now."

When we got home, Daddy was gone.

I was angry.

"If you want to help your brother and sister pack an overnight bag, that would be super helpful, Esther."

"Overnight bag?"

"A suitcase? For your pajamas."

I grabbed a grocery sack from behind the fridge and helped Olivia and Frankie find their pajamas and toothbrushes. I found Frankie's favorite match car and a rainbow pinwheel and put them in the bag with our pajamas. Frankie insisted we take the MGM coffee table book. He carried the big book across the street. I held the paper sack and Olivia's hand. Olivia had an old bag with a handle over her arm with the music box, and we followed Ramona to the house across the street.

Tess was waiting in her doorway as we walked across the street with Ramona. I thought I'd be more excited about my first sleepover. Instead, I was mad. Frankie and Olivia walked beside me, Olivia holding my hand.

"Come on in." Tess held the door open for us and put on a big, fake smile. "You guys hungry?"

"Nope," I said.

"We went to McDonald's," Frankie announced.

"McDonald's?" Tess said. "Wow, that must have been fun." Tess had an apron on over her dress. Big surprise: it was covered in chickens.

"Here's my phone number," Ramona said as she handed our grocery sack and a card over to Tess. "I'll be back tomorrow to take the children to see Dr. Vaughn… who has some questions for the children."

"Thank you, now." I think Tess had tears in her eyes as Ramona walked to her car.

"Where are we going to sleep?" Frankie asked. "On the floor?"

Tess motioned for us to follow her upstairs. "No, I have beds for each of you."

"I can take the sack."

"Why, thank you, Esther. If you want to help the Junior Mints get ready for bed, I'll be up in a bit to tuck you in." I didn't appreciate Tess using our chocolate nicknames. She had, after all started all the problems that day. Later, Tess came up and turned the light off in our room, and before she shut the door said in a sugary, sweet voice, "Sweet dreams." Tess closed the door but left it open just a bit.

"How are we supposed to have sweet dreams without Momma and Daddy?" Frankie was facing the wall as he spoke. "The sheets smell funny." He was crying.

"They'll both be back soon. I promise." I stroked Olivia's hair as I spoke. "It's kind of fun having a sleepover, right?"

Frankie said nothing. Olivia sobbed.

In my most Momma-like voice, I whispered, "Little angels, let's shut off the day."

When I could hear both Olivia and Frankie breathing heavily, I slowly moved my arms around Olivia and sat up. The closing music to the show *M*A*S*H* was playing from the television downstairs. Voices from the TV floated to my ears, and I got up and slowly opened the door. I knew the music to the ten o'clock news. "Channel Seven is there for you each day." Daddy used to let me sit with him and watch the first ten minutes if I couldn't sleep.

I couldn't sleep.

"Our top story tonight: a local Omaha woman has been missing for several days, according to individuals who reported the news to the authorities."

I moved down the hallway and sat on the top steps.

"Police are questioning the husband. Clark Duvall is a person of interest, but authorities are not disclosing if he is a suspect. Even without a body, it looks like they have enough reason to investigate."

Without a body?

My mom wasn't dead. The man on the television had twisted his words to sound as if Momma had run away from Daddy. That Daddy was bad. That Daddy had even killed her.

ALL THE LOVELY LIES 46

"Several people have called authorities with their concerns. While the authorities are not saying who had tried to contact Tara Duvall for the past week, authorities are confirming that they went to the Duvall home and could not find Mrs. Duvall. The couple's three children are now staying with relatives until further information is available. Channel Seven attempted to reach Child Protective Services, but no one would talk about the case."

Tess Folten was not our relative. She was a nosy, old lady who just might have tattled on us.

"In other news, the President honored that petite young lady from Russia at a dinner at the White House this evening. Nadia is still winning the hearts of the world after her perfect tens in the Olympic gymnastics competition several weeks ago. Americans are talking about the tiny fifteen-year-old from Russia. We just can't get enough of the golden girl."

A month earlier, Frankie and I had turned questionable cartwheels in our living room as Nadia Comaneci scored a perfect ten on her uneven bars routine. My parents were ecstatic as we cheered on a little girl from a smaller country who threw off a scoreboard that was not programmed for a perfect score. Momma was addicted to the anticipation surrounding the Summer Olympics, and I thought that we were at the most exciting place in the world, watching the Summer Olympics in our living room.

I got up to go back to my bed, and the stairs creaked.

"Esther? Is that you?" Tess called from the living room below. I ran back to the room and shut my door. I put my face in my pillow and sobbed.

4

Katherine

1954

The first night I spent at the vineyard was the best night's sleep I'd had in a long time.

Charles had me set up in a suite in the main stone building of the estate, a big bell tower above the main building reminded those who viewed the space that it had once housed monks. He called it the Mother House. Ten years earlier, the monks moved north when the order decided that a vineyard was not the right fit— apparently this order was not good with grapes—and Captain had purchased the whole acreage with the beautiful stone building for a good price. "For a song and a prayer," Charles said.

A small knock drew me from my sleep. "Good morning, Santa Clara."

I sat up, still wearing the clothes from the day before. Charles opened the door and entered with a tray of breakfast. A rose in a vase. A glass of orange juice. A plate with toast, two eggs, and a vine of fresh grapes.

"Did you sleep well?"

"I did. What time is it?"

"Time? You have a plane to catch or something? I hoped I could change your mind, if even for a few days."

I looked over at the piece of paper on the side table with the rescheduled flight information and a phone number to call. Christmas was in two days, and my parents were probably up in arms about me not getting off the plane I had been scheduled to take. I dreaded the call to say what: *I'm going to be late? I lost my scholarship? I let you down again?*

Charles set the tray on the bed next to me. "I mean, I'd be happy to take you back to that airport and put you on a plane, but I think you'd be happy hanging out here for a while. Think of it as a vacation."

"Hanging out?" If it could be that easy. I picked up a piece of toast and smiled at Charles. He walked back to the door and leaned against the frame of the doorway to the room, khakis again, this time with a light blue shirt untucked and sandals replacing his dress shoes. He was slightly unshaven and absolutely amazing.

"Captain wants to meet you. That is if you have the time. I told him all about you. Eat a little breakfast, and I'll be back in about a half hour."

After Charles left, I ate one bite of toast and looked out the window of my room. The window was wide open with no screen, so the smell of the fresh land and air swept over me as I took a deep breath. The landscape outside was vast and full of green growth, a steep hill beyond the living quarters of the abbey was lined with rows of vines. The rows were neat and consistent, unlike my life, and I drank in the beauty of the order. Speckled among the vines were men and women pruning the plants with such slow and delicate grace that I admired their devotion. The workers, moved in union, in different sizes and clothing—one woman in a loose skirt, a man in jeans, an older man in overalls— created a quilted design on the knoll that held me mesmerized.

When Charles returned, I was still undecided about what I would do the next day, let alone the next moment. "How about a walk?" Charles said from the partially opened door. "Maybe clear your head or at least see the grounds before you head back."

"I'd like that." I followed Charles down the cool hallway to a door that took us the back way toward the vineyard. Now that I could see the immense land that framed the hill behind the abbey, I saw even more men and women working on the vines, row after row. The pattern of the rows had direction and rhythm, and there was something both pacifying and perplexing about the repetition of the rows. The punchline to the paradox: rich and crisp grapes that created wine.

"They're trimming and pruning, the most time-consuming yet most important work we'll do until May when we start our new cycle for next year's crop. We've got the best team in California, in my opinion, right here in Alameda County." Charles placed his hand on the small of my back as we walked further toward the hill where the vines were.

"Like bees in a hive," I said.

Charles tilted his head and laughed. "You should see the busy bees in the Mother House making the wine. The vintners are working on making our Cabernet from the most recent crop back on the other end of this main building where you stayed last night. Right now, they are busy fermenting and bottling. Some of the workers are dealing with wine in the tanks. When the monks flew north, they left everything behind. We used their equipment for the first few years but have just recently replaced their old catalyst fermenter with two new ones."

Charles stopped and pointed to the farthest part of the land at the base of the hill.

"That area's where we built the cottages for the newest group of people who joined us."

"It just goes on and on," I said as I cupped my eyes from the sun. "Where did all these people come from?"

"From all over. Roy over there, carrying boxes of bottles, he lost his wife to cancer. Miss Rosalie, that woman over there is a single retired teacher. And we're not quite sure of Arty's story. The tall guy with the wild hair. He doesn't talk much, but the hardest-working guy on that hill. All different stories. Now, one big family is making wine."

"And what's going on back there?" I pointed to the farthest part of the campus, where men were moving wood off a truck.

"Growth."

A man on a horse yelled to Charles, "Captain approved the plans for the barn. Would you have had anything to do with moving him in that direction?"

"I may have had something to do with it, but let's keep that little nugget of information between you and me, Gregory," Charles yelled back at the man.

"What nugget?" Gregory yelled and smiled as he rode back on the path toward the new development.

"I'm telling you, Katherine. You want to be a part of this ride."

"Horses?" I asked.

"The horses help us get out to the rougher terrain. Rainy days are tough on cars and trucks out here. The men preparing the land for the barn are using dynamite to blow up the rough terrain. We even make our own dynamite. All you need is a bottle of glycerin oil, some nitric acid, and a few pounds of sawdust. Who knew? Wait, there's the main man." I looked back to the door of the Mother House, where two men stood in the furthest archway of the stone building. "Captain!" The shorter man waved back and motioned us to the Mother House. Seven archways lined the front of the main house, with the bell tower topping the middle archway. The warm golden color on the surface of the structure had stucco accents and rusty-colored shingles on the roof that gave a true Southwest adobe feel to this structure with such a rich history.

"I guess we've been summoned." Charles winked as we walked back to the Mother House.

"So, this is the beautiful woman I've heard so much about? Lovely to meet you, Miss Katherine." I couldn't decipher the slight accent of the man as Captain took my hand and kissed it. "And smart, too, from what I've been told." Grey laced the full head of dark wavy hair in an attractive pattern that made the patriarch look more regal than old. The larger man stood behind him with arms crossed. His sunglasses hid his eyes but not his demeanor.

"Thank you, but I'm not sure how Charles surmised my intelligence in a car ride. It really was kind of him to help me out on a bad day." I tried to block out the memory in my head of how rude I had been to him at the airport. "Your winery is incredible. Or do I say vineyard? Winery or vineyard? Guess I'm not as smart as Charles said."

"A perfectly good question, and the answer is both. Celestial Way is a vineyard, which is just a plantation of grape-bearing vines which are destined for the bottle. Celestial Way is also a winery. A winery is a property licensed to produce wine. I'm not sure if Charles has shown you the facility in the Mother House where we make our wine."

"We were just about to head in there, Captain. And, Katherine, this is Eugene, Captain's assistant."

I put out my hand toward Eugene, but the nod of his head suggested his greeting. I smiled and said, "Nice to meet you." Eugene might have needed a reminder of the definition of an assistant; he had apparently applied for the role of bodyguard. Maybe the two were synonymous here. Eugene's arm muscles flexed, and I sensed a warning: Keep your distance from Captain.

Two young women came up behind us from the direction of the cottages. One was tall and thin with long, wavy strawberry blond hair. The tall woman wore sandals and a man's dress shirt, which bellowed over her jeans. The shorter woman wore a prairie dress, and her short dark hair appeared to have been cut by a child or maybe a drunk person. Captain called out to the two.

"Ladies, please come and meet our guest, Katherine. Katherine, this is Miss Mary Ellen and… wait a minute, Miss London."

"Nice to meet you two." I held my hand out. Miss Mary Ellen shook my hand.

Miss London, the woman with the short, choppy hair, would not make eye contact.

"Are you two ladies heading to the kitchen?" Captain asked. "I know the kitchen team is preparing for the noon meal."

"Yes," Mary Ellen replied as she touched her stomach, which now revealed the swelling of her abdomen, which the big shirt had covered. "We don't want to be late." The two moved past the group and toward the door. "Enjoy your visit, ma'am."

As soon as the two ladies were in the building, Charles cleared his throat. "London's new here. Actually, she picked the name London. She was a runaway from LA, who had more than her fair share of bad experiences. She came here to start over. Reinvent herself."

Reinvent.

"She's a charming young lady," Captain added. "Just a little skittish for now." German or Scandinavian. I was still working on his accent. Captain, Charles, and I moved in through the breezeway and into a big dining hall with Bodyguard close behind.

"You OK?" Charles touched my arm as he leaned into me. He smelled clean and innocent.

"I'm fine."

"Please join us for lunch, Katherine," Captain said, once we entered the coolness of the dining hall. His voice bounced off the high ceilings and walls. I tried to imagine the room filled with monks. They must have had a large community to have had such a big facility. I wondered where those non-wine-making monks had landed after the Grape Exodus.

"Children?" I asked.

Captain turned around and looked at me.

"It's just that I haven't seen any children yet."

"Oh, children are here, and they are the most important piece of the pie. They are the future of the Celestial Way. As we speak, the mothers are taking all the young ones out to play beyond the vines. They should be heading this way for the noon meal any time now." Sounds of clamoring plates and the clanging of silverware slowly took over the room, along with warm and pleasing smells. I'd barely touched my breakfast, so my stomach begged me to stay for lunch. We moved swiftly through the large dining hall to the kitchen.

From the wide-open window, a plump woman with voluminous curly red hair framing the upper half of her body yelled out, "Looks like we've got company, Captain."

"Yes, indeed, Lottie, my dream. What smells so divine?" Captain replied.

"One of your favorites: Shepherd's Pie. I'm Charlotte Tuttle, ma'am. Call me Lottie. They keep me way back here so I don't mess up the wine." Lottie winked at Captain and held her hand out to me through the window. Finally, a hand to shake.

"This one," Captain said, "is as fiery as her hair. Eugene and I will be lunching in my quarters."

"Give me ten minutes, and I'll have Mary Ellen bring a tray with your meals." Lottie smiled as she answered Captain and adjusted her black apron.

"That would be great, Lottie," Captain said. "After lunch, we're heading out to test the soil and check the vines. Enjoy your visit, Katherine."

"Thank you, Captain. Nice to meet you, Lottie." I wished I had more time with the warm lady in charge of the kitchen.

"It was a pleasure to meet you, Miss Katherine." The captain once again took my hand and kissed it. The bodyguard nodded, his sunglasses still framing his face inside the dining hall.

Charles motioned to me to follow him. "Get thee to the winery, young lady."

Charles held my hand as he led me through the kitchen to a big door and down a long, wide hallway, sconces on the walls lighting the path to a set of large double doors. Charles opened the doors to a room about twenty-by-twenty feet that then opened to a room nearly as tall as an airplane hangar, but half the size of one.

"Wow, was this all here when Captain bought the place?" I asked. The size of the Mother House was deceiving. It seemed to go on and on.

"The smaller area here was the original winery, pretty tight quarters. We added the warehouse to this main area this past spring," Charles said as he guided me to the center of the room, his hand on my arm as we moved into an area where over forty people were busy in different areas, oblivious to our entry. "Over there are two new catalyst fermenters. The revenues from this season's crop will allow us to buy more. We've got to fill this large room." Barrels of wine lined the back of the room. A large entrance that looked like a barn door opened out to the hills where more people worked the vines. Strong smells overtook me. I looked around the large area as a palpable hum of activity vibrated.

"We'll be bottling that batch of Cabernet tomorrow. We do it all here. Except for the label. We still outsource the label making, but we hope someday to bring that in-house as well."

The loud laughter of a large man back toward the kegs filled my heart with happiness. He was a head taller than everyone and his body was as large around as the kegs. People gathered around as he said something I couldn't hear and he laughed again, the sound booming out and hitting the ceiling and coming back down like beautiful rain.

"And that is Dorian. Dorian is what makes this part of Celestial Way run like a machine. Everybody loves Dorian. Loud and robust, and he makes the best Pinot Noir ever."

"Oh, the Doctor is in!" Dorian's loud voice echoed off every wall. We walked toward Dorian and the crowd around him.

"I'm just taking this lovely woman on a tour of the place. Dorian, this is Katherine. Katherine, this is Dorian and his team."

Dorian took my hand and kissed it. "Katherine, you're lovely. The Doctor is never wrong. Welcome to Celestial Way."

"Why, thank you." I'm sure I blushed. "This place is amazing. I hear you are the one who makes this place work so well."

"I assure you, this team is the reason we make the best wine in the area."

"We didn't mean to interrupt you," Charles said.

Dorian clapped his hands. "Time to get back to our barrels and tanks, people." And more laughter rained down on us.

Charles cupped his arm through mine as we moved back to the long hallway. "We can head back to get some lunch if that works for you."

"So much to take in," I said.

"I remember when I first came here, I'd never even had a glass of wine."

As we walked down the wide hallway back to the kitchen, I saw a large door in the middle of the hallway. "Where does that lead to?"

"The Gathering Hall. Where we have meetings. I'll show you." Charles moved the big door, and as he did, a bell above the door rang.

A bell.

Like the sound of bells at mass. Like the sound of jingle bells.

A bell.

I froze.

"Katherine, are you alright?" Charles said as he turned to me.

Christmas in two days, and my parents had to be worried sick. My father had probably called my roommate, the police, and the CIA.

"Katherine?"

"Sorry." I put my hand on the back of the wall to steady myself. I'd been so enamored by the novelty of Celestial Way that I had forgotten about the world beyond the vineyard. The bell took me back to my mother's favorite movie, *It's a Wonderful Life*. We watched it every year after Christmas dinner. *Every time a bell rings, an angel gets its wings.*

"Are you feeling sick?" Charles asked as he guided me into a room that felt like a chapel. He moved me to the pew to sit as I caught my breath and put my head in my hands. Charles rubbed my back as I relaxed. The line from the movie came from the mouth of the little girl Zuzu. Jimmy Stewart, in the role of George Bailey, is holding the little girl who announces *Teacher says, every time a bell rings, an angel gets its wings.* And we all knew that Clarence, the affable Angel Second Class, finally had gotten his wings. My mother always cried.

Charles pulled something out of his pocket— two green apple Jolly Ranchers. He unwrapped one and handed me the candy. I sat up and took it and put it in my mouth as he unwrapped the second piece and put it in his mouth. "You're going to be alright, Katherine. I promise." I moved the candy around my mouth as I took a deep breath and looked around. The pews were clearly from an old chapel for the monks who had been here before, but there was not any other hint of a church or religion in the open space with tall windows on both sides, framing the artwork that was a vineyard. No evidence of statues or religious pictures.

"We meet here twice a week. Captain updates the community." Charles was still rubbing my back.

"Where are the statues?"

"The monks took all their religious items when they moved. Let's get you some food." Charles stood up, the sunlight from outside shining in on his twinkling grey eyes. I got up and put my hand on his arm to anchor me. We walked slowly out of the Gathering Hall and down the wide hallway. Charles opened the big door to the kitchen; the noise from the dining hall was deafening in contrast to the quiet of the long-ago chapel. Adults and children filled every table. The acoustics of the big dining hall with the high ceiling were probably more fitting for the silent monk types. Lottie stood with several children near the sink in the kitchen and motioned for me to come near her. Charles was overtaken by women and children who swarmed around him like flies on a sticky child and pulled him out into the dining hall.

"He's a regular Cary Grant. His fans await him," Lottie said. "Captain is the captain: in charge. But Charles, well, he's the fixer. Broken people are drawn to him. His presence kind of makes you feel healed, as strange as that sounds. Captain is the captain, and Charles is the doctor. You don't need anything more than that." Lottie laughed at herself as she turned to look at me. "Oh, dear. Are you alright?"

"I'm fine…"

Lottie turned and grabbed a plate of food. "I just put this plate together for you. It's still warm. Eat up before you waste away to nothing."

I took the plate and looked around the kitchen for a place to sit down.

"Right, here, Miss Katherine." Lottie pulled a chair up to the counter and handed me a fork. "Please, eat." Lottie set her renowned Shepherd's Pie in front of me with a fork.

"Mommy, I won!" A small boy with red hair and freckles ran into the kitchen and pulled on Lottie's apron. "I jumped all the way up to the sky!"

"Oh, you did, now, did you?" Lottie winked at me and crouched down to the boy. "Are you sure about that? To the sky?"

"Well, not to the sky, but… to this high." The boy held his hand as high as he could. He might have been six.

"And you won, did you?" Lottie prodded.

"Uh, not won, but… I jumped real high."

"That's wonderful, my little ball of light. Dylan, I want you to meet Miss Katherine. She's a guest to the Way." Lottie moved the boy's body toward me.

"Pleased to meet you, Miss Lady."

Lottie belted out an Irish laugh that warmed my soul.

"Pleased to meet you, Mr. Dylan." I shook the boy's hand.

"Now, go out to the grounds to play until rest time. I'll meet you after we finish the lunch dishes." Dylan ran out of the kitchen, and then, I'm pretty sure he ran wherever he wanted. "That one will be the death of me."

"He looks just like you," I said. I didn't hesitate to pick up my fork and start digging away at the Shepherd's Pie.

"Yes. The one and only Dylan Michael Tuttle. He's a force to be reckoned with. Full of big stories. He thinks a big story is a wonderful thing. I think he's full of the dickens. We're working on his naughty little habit." Lottie's red curls reflected every light in the room. "I'm not going to go all wild on this, but I need to call him out. On the fibs and all."

"Fibs?"

"Harmless, for the most part. He's just a child, but he's my big fibber. I tell him that fibs are not good. Children who tell little fibs grow up to be adults who tell big fibs. People fib for two reasons: to cover up a truth that is just too painful or to make the truth more interesting because it's just too boring. He's just trying to make every story more interesting, and I'm trying to break him of the habit."

I looked over Lottie's shoulder into the big dining hall and saw Charles moving from table to table, people smiling at him and moving toward him.

"But he's a good boy, really. He's taken to this place really well."

"How long have you been here?" I asked. Everybody in the room had a different story of what had brought them to Celestial Way.

"Three years. A higher power saved us. That's all I can say. Dylan and I were living in my car for a few months when Rocco stumbled upon us. Literally, he knew we were down on our luck, but we were temporarily safe from Dylan's father. Dylan's father would've killed us both if he'd ever stumbled upon us."

"Rocco?"

"There." Lottie pointed to a tall man with longer blonde hair. He was talking to Charles. "Rocco brought us back here three years ago, and we've never looked back."

"Does your son miss his father?"

"Dylan doesn't remember his father much, just the good stories I tell him, most of them aren't real. I guess I'm a regular fibber myself, but for good reason. No good would come from me telling him how his father used to beat me. Dylan actually talks about the stories to others as if they are his own true stories. It makes me realize how much of our lives are just made-up stories."

Lottie wiped down the counter as I took my dish over to the sink to rinse.

"Silly question," I ventured.

Lottie stopped, her blue eyes sparkling at me, "No such thing."

"Where are the decorations? I mean, it's almost Christmas, and I haven't seen one ornament or tree or even mistletoe." The tree would be up and decorated at my home back in Connecticut. I also knew my parents were probably livid with me at the moment.

"Oh, you won't find Christmas here. Or any other holiday, for that matter. Holidays bring up too many bad memories for most of these folks. Religion too. That's what most of these folks are running from: the prisons of structured goodness. The children don't know anything different. Instead, we celebrate life every day. It's best to leave the past in the past if we're going to find peace. That's what Captain says. To find our true selves, we need to let go of all the bad and focus on our present truth. Past in the past."

"Past in the past..." I was starting to feel a little better.

Lottie broke into an awkward German accent, mimicking Captain: "If you think of the past, you will be despondent. If you think of tomorrow, you will fret. Where you are at this moment. That is peace. Wherever you are in goodness. Dismiss the rest." Charles was moving back toward us. He winked at me as Lottie continued in the accent of the Captain. "You can fib to the world, but you must be honest with yourself to find peace."

5

Esther

Day Three 1976

As promised, Ramona arrived at Tess's house the next day with smiles and hugs.

She wore grey slacks and a white blouse. Her hair was pulled back, her beautiful face glowed with a smile. Girls like me looked at young women like Ramona and wished they could be them someday. "Are you ready for a busy day? We're meeting with a doctor who's very good at helping kids just like you."

Kids like us. Already labeled.

Tess responded before we could. "They've all eaten a big breakfast and are more than ready for the day."

I refused to partake in the effervescent discussion about going to talk to some adult who was going to ask us probably the same questions again, over and over. I wouldn't even admit that the breakfast of bacon, eggs, and the most amazing French toast I'd ever eaten was a nice change from our limited menu in the past weeks. I was still mad.

"We had lots and lots of syrup," Frankie told Ramona.

"What about you, Miss Olivia?" Ramona bent down toward Olivia. Olivia moved her head away and held tightly to her bag with the music box. Olivia may have liked Ramona, but she would not engage.

"She's fine," I said.

"Esther, I forgot to thank you for being so helpful last night. You seem pretty mature for your age."

I liked Ramona but didn't like it when adults talked down to me. Ramona took my hand. "Are you alright with going first to talk to Dr. Vaughn?"

"Yes, ma'am."

"You have nothing to worry about. Just be honest."

"You kids be good," Tess advised. "I'll see you when you get back here around...?" Tess looked at Ramona.

"Before 3:00. Thanks, Tess."

Frankie talked non-stop on the ride to see Dr. Vaughn. Ramona replaced, if only for a moment, the hole where Momma fit into his life. I wished I could have felt as good about the day. Olivia's head leaned on my shoulder on the drive. We'd never been to the part of Omaha where we were driving. Big trees and buildings I'd never seen before flew past us as we moved toward the office, and I felt like a lamb to slaughter. We got to the big gray building that looked like a doctor's office. A sour pit in my stomach reminded me that I had no control of the world. On the second floor of the building was a long hallway with glass doors off to the right: *Smith and Jensen Law Firm, Eyes/Ears/Nose and Throat Specialist, Tim Fletcher, and Orthodontist, Meier*. And then there was the door that we entered, a glass door but with no writing on it. The small room we entered served as a waiting area. The words Dr. K. Vaughn were on a small sign fixed to the only door in the waiting room. A woman walked through the door.

"Esther, this is Dr. Vaughn. She just wants to talk to you a little bit. I'll sit here with Frankie and Olivia. I promise that I'll be here the whole time."

Dr. Vaughn was not at all what I expected. Instead of an old frumpy man with very little hair, a tall, thin woman with a full head of long, curly brown hair filled the doorway. She was older than Momma and Ramona, and she was very pretty. "Hi, Esther. How're you doing today?" She opened the door more as we both moved into her office.

"Well, not so good, I guess." I knew that most adults wanted children to say only the niceties, but I thought that if Doctor Vaughn wanted honest answers, I would comply.

"I can only imagine." Doctor Vaughn shut the door. "Please sit down here on the couch with me. Would you like something to drink? I have 7-Up in my little fridge." The fish tank behind Dr. Vaughn's desk encased several big orange fish. Some moved slowly; some didn't move at all. I knew Momma and Daddy wouldn't approve of me saying yes to the 7-Up. After all, Dr. Vaughn was just being nice, but today was about the truth.

"Sure."

The tab popped as Doctor Vaughn opened the can of 7-Up. Rather than pour a small amount into a kid's cup, Doctor Vaughn handed the entire can to me. I'd never had a full can of pop in my short life, ever. A trick? A bribe? I still wasn't sure who the good guys were.

"Thank you." I sat down on one end of the brown leather couch.

Dr. Vaughn sat in the middle of the couch and moved her body to face me. "So I can get to know you, Esther, why don't you share three things about yourself that you know to be true?"

"Well," I had to think about this one. What in my life was true? "I'm almost ten. I have brown hair. And I love my family. Three things. All true."

"Great. Esther, with most of the children I talk to, I use props to ask questions." The *S*'s in Dr. Vaughn's words were sharp as she spoke, in a good way. "It helps them to understand the sometimes 'unpleasant' topics I'm addressing. I use puppets or magic wands. With your brother and sister, I will use those puppets, and I may ask them to draw pictures for me. I don't think that I need any props with you. Do you agree?"

"Yes, ma'am." The bubbles from my first sip felt cold and stimulating in my mouth. My sour stomach was feeling better. I wondered if the fish that didn't move in the tank were dead.

"I thought so. Rather than wave a wand, I want to ask, if you could have three wishes granted today, what would they be?"

"Wishes?"

Would my wishes tell her something about me?

"Yes."

"Three?"

"Yes."

"Well, I think you know what the number one wish would be."

"I want to hear you say it."

"I wish my mom and dad were home. I wish I could go back to two weeks ago when everything was perfect." My voice trembled, and I quickly took another sip. Dr. Vaughn said nothing. "Does that count as one or two wishes?"

Dr. Vaughn laughed a warm, beautiful laugh. "Let's say that it counts as one."

"OK, then... I wish the girls at Hamilton Grade School weren't so mean." I'd been drinking the pop so fast, I felt a burp in my throat.

Dr. Vaughn wrote something down. *Did I say something wrong?* "Are the girls at Hamilton Grade School mean to you, Esther?"

"They're mean to everyone, ma'am."

"Help me understand. Are all the girls at Hamilton Grade School mean to everyone?"

I giggled at her question, and a burp slipped from my throat. Dr. Vaughn laughed. "I meant a few girls at Hamilton are mean to everyone."

"I wish I could tell you that when you grow up, Esther, everyone will be nice to everyone. Unfortunately, some older men or women are still unkind to others. I understand."

I liked Dr. Vaughn.

"Do you want to hear my last wish?"

"I do." Dr. Vaughn moved her body closer to mine.

"I wish that adults didn't lie so much."

Dr. Vaughn smiled and wrote something down on her tablet.

"Was that a bad answer?"

"What do you mean by bad answer, Esther?"

"Was it wrong?"

"Your thoughts can't be wrong. Your thoughts are your thoughts."

"Well, when I took a test at school a few weeks ago, I could tell that the teacher was looking for the right answer."

ALL THE LOVELY LIES 68

"You mean like a math test."

"An IQ test. I could tell the man giving me the test was looking for the right answer."

"You took an IQ test, Esther? At your school?"

"Yes."

Doctor Vaughn scribbled on her pad again.

"Wait!" I said.

"For what, Esther?"

"Can I change one of my wishes?"

"In my world of wishes, it is more than alright to change your wishes. Which one do you want to change?"

"The one about the stupid girls at school. I mean, the mean girls."

"What do you want to change it to?"

"My last wish is that Olivia and Frankie are OK… I mean, with all of this… I know that Frankie will be OK. I just worry about Olivia. She's different, but she's perfect. When you talk to her, I want you to know that she has the biggest heart in the world."

"What about you, Esther?"

"Me?"

"Don't you wish that you will be OK?"

"I'll be fine. I just hope I can take care of them."

"That's a pretty big responsibility for a ten-year-old girl. Don't you think?"

"Well, I'm not ten until next week. I just hope that… can I ask you a question, Dr. Vaughn?"

"Certainly."

"If you could have three wishes granted, what would you want?"

"Wow." Dr. Vaughn pulled at the string of pearls around her neck. "Well, that's funny. I guess you turned the tables on me. I just... I haven't thought about it."

"Be honest, please. Not like the other adults."

"Well, let's see." Doctor Vaughn cleared her throat and sat up straight. "Esther, because you've been so honest with me, I will be honest with you."

"OK."

"I wish." Dr. Vaughn took a breath and cleared her throat. "I wish that my baby had not died a day after she was born." She cleared her throat. "Her name was Amy."

I sat still. The cold can in my hand started to sweat beads of water.

"And I wish I had handled... her death, and, um, my husband leaving me, after the sad days... better."

The fish tank behind Dr. Vaughn's desk made a funny noise. One of the orange, allegedly dead fish moved.

"I guess I have one more wish left." Doctor Vaughn cleared her throat. "I wish that more people in the world were like you, Esther."

"I wasn't fishin' for a compliment, ma'am." Daddy used that expression for people who wanted attention.

"Well, I see people all the time, and I want you to know that I know you will be fine. I guess you know that too."

"Am I done now?"

Dr. Vaughn looked down at her watch. "Yes, you're done."

While Olivia was in with Dr. Vaughn, Frankie and Ramona played checkers. I worried about Olivia as I watched Ramona let Frankie win, three times. I knew that Olivia wouldn't look at or talk to Dr. Vaughn because when she was in new places, she depended on Momma and me. How would she answer her or tell Dr. Vaughn that she's fine and that she doesn't need to go away from us for help? I looked at the door until it opened. Olivia ran to me as Dr. Vaughn spoke to Frankie.

"Frankie, I'd love to spend some time with you now. Did you know that I have some very interesting fish? And they each have a funny name?"

Frankie ran from the checkerboard to Dr. Vaughn. "How many fish?"

"Seven. Come on in." Dr. Vaughn shut the door.

I put my hand into Olivia's and squeezed. Olivia looked around for her music box. "It's right here where you left it." Ramona handed Olivia the treasure. Olivia took the box over to a corner in the room where the sun showered an area just big enough for her to sit in.

"Can we go back to our house after Frankie's done?" I asked.

"Probably not right away… but I do have a surprise for you three."

"Surprise?"

"Yep, I can't tell you." Ramona cleared her throat. "While we're sitting here, would you be comfortable if I asked you something, Esther?"

"I already told that man Kemper that Daddy never hurt us."

"Not about your dad. About your mom."

"What about her?"

"Well." Ramona looked over at Olivia as she spoke. "Do you remember anything about the day that your mom vanished? Anything at all?"

"She didn't leave in the day. She left at night. While we were sleeping."

"You know that for sure. Did you hear her?"

"No. She read to us and tucked us in. And… the next morning, she was gone."

"Did your dad hear her leave?"

"He didn't say. He just said that Momma was gone. He's not a big talker."

Ramona smiled. "No, it doesn't seem like it. Do you think she was taken?"

"Taken? No."

Weird question.

"Do you think your dad knows where she is?"

I was floored by the question. "Don't you think he would go and get her if he knew where she was?"

"I guess so. I'm sorry to upset you, Esther."

"I'm not upset. I'm confused. Why's my dad in trouble? It's not a crime for a mom to walk away from her home. It's not a crime to be left behind. So, why's Daddy in trouble? If he's guilty of being unlovable by my mother, then shouldn't we be in jail too?"

"People are just talking to him."

"About what?

"It's complicated."

I knew what complicated meant, and I didn't understand what was so complicated about a man who was sad that his wife left him.

It wasn't complicated. It was sad.

"What about the days before she left? Do you remember anything that seemed different? Anything at all?"

"I don't think so."

Ramona picked up on the fact that I didn't want to talk about my parents anymore. She had exhausted all the boring adult questions that she had asked at McDonald's the night before, so she asked me if I liked to read. Do I like to read? *Are the Kennedys gun-shy*? Our mom had taken us to the library every week for as long as I could remember. I was in heaven as I picked different books each week, and a favorite series of mine was also a favorite of Ramona: the *Nancy Drew* books. I knew she wasn't just blowing smoke as she and I talked about our favorite books.

"*The Clue of Broken Locket* and *The Hidden Staircase* are the best Nancy Drew books." Ramona played with her hair as she spoke, and for a moment I tried to imagine what she looked like at my age. Was she popular, or was she like me? Was she nice or mean?

"Did Nancy Drew ever get married?" I asked.

"Not in any of the books I've read. She seems to stay the same age forever."

"Are you married, Ramona?" I asked.

Ramona stopped and pulled at her necklace. "Well, not now. But someday."

"Did a man give you that necklace?"

"My boyfriend did."

"What's on the chain?"

"Two hearts. See?" Ramona bent down and showed me the two hearts.

"Do you want to marry your boyfriend?"

"Of course. He's really a great guy."

"Then why doesn't he ask you to marry him? Or why don't you ask him?"

The door from Dr. Vaughn's office opened, and Frankie flew out of the room. "Wow, that was like the coolest office ever. Way better than the dentist."

"Ramona, do you have a minute?" Dr. Vaughn's voice was soothing and kind.

"Sure. I'll be right back. And then the surprise," Ramona said to us.

The door shut on the two adults. "Surprise," Olivia whispered.

"Do you think we're going to McDonald's again?" Frankie asked. "Or maybe Peony Park. What do you think, Esther?"

The door from the hallway opened as not-my-favorite Officer Kemper interrupted us.

"This place is not easy to find." Kemper pulled a handkerchief and wiped the sweat from his red face as he looked around the room. "Where's Ramona?"

"In the office with Dr. Vaughn," Frankie answered.

"What is she doing?"

"What do you think?" The words were out of my mouth before I could stop them.

Kemper looked at me and squinted. He moved toward me and pointed a finger at me. "A little respect, young lady. Is that how you talk to adults?"

I moved toward Kemper and pointed at him. "Only adults I don't like."

Kemper moved close to me with his hot, sweet, and sour breath. "You think you're pretty smart, do you?"

"I know a secret about you," I whispered back to him. Kemper's eyes widened. "I know what makes your breath smell the way it does."

Kemper backed up and tucked his shirt in. He moved to the office door, opened it, and slammed it shut.

"I don't like that man," Frankie said as he picked up a *Highlights* magazine and sat down in a big orange chair. "I like Dr. Vaughn."

Olivia wound the music box and placed it in the center of the sun circle. I watched her look at the ballerina moving around in front of the sparkly rainbow. The upper right edge of the sparkly material was looking ragged. Movement through the glass door to the hallway caught my attention. A tall, thin man with an overcoat and big hat that were both out of season and out of date opened the door and stood with his body holding the door open.

"Looks like you're ready." The man was too young to wear the dated hat and too thin to wear the out-of-season coat. Was he one of the many men that Olivia had counted coming into our house the night before?

"For our surprise?" Frankie got up from his chair and ran to the door.

"That's right. A surprise. Let's get going." The young man opened the hall door again.

"Are we going to Peony Park?" Frankie asked as Olivia and I stood up.

"Daddy." Olivia's voice was loud as she put the music box in her bag and slung it around her shoulder.

"Give that girl a prize. You get to see your father for just a little bit." Frankie ran past the man and out into the hallway. He was racing down the hall like he had just landed on a good square on the *Chutes and Ladders* board.

Up, up, up.

Olivia was not far behind as the man held the door for me. "Shouldn't we wait for Ramona?" I asked.

"She's going to meet us there. At the surprise."

Frankie and Olivia were out the front door before the man and I got to the bottom of the staircase.

"Wait!" I yelled.

The man moved out the door after the Junior Mints. I ran out, following the three, this time the man leading. He moved toward a brown car parked in the lot behind the building. The car looked new, but it had a dent in the back with a broken taillight.

"Wait," I yelled. "We don't even know your name."

"Jacob." The man's voice cracked as he said his name. His hat was crooked. "I'm Jacob, and I need to get you three to your surprise. Hurry up."

Frankie opened the door to the backseat of the car and jumped in, Olivia not far behind. "Why didn't Ramona tell us you were taking us to our dad?"

"We only have a little time to visit with your father, so hurry and get in." Jacob motioned toward the backseat.

"Where's our dad?" I asked.

"It wouldn't be a surprise if I told you. Right?"

Frankie yelled, "Come on, Esther. You're taking forever."

I moved into the back seat with the Junior Mints. As the car started, I took a deep breath. I was excited to see Daddy. I wanted to find out from him what was so complicated. Our life was so simple and so good. We were not the complicated type.

Jacob drove in silence for about fifteen minutes, his oversized hat slanted to the right on his head. The smells of old french fries and dirty socks overtook us as we looked at the fast food wrappers on the floors in both the front and backseats. An empty plastic cup with a lid and a straw and the words *Jack in the Box* rolled back and forth on the floor as Jacob drove. Jacob took a turn and cussed under his breath. Jacob then turned on the radio. The ABBA song *Mamma Mia* blared from the car radio as the car turned into the parking lot of a shopping center. *We are not mall people.* That's what Daddy would always say. Too many strange people are wandering around a mall. We can get what we need at the regular stores. Jacob parked the car and took a deep breath.

"What are we doing here?" I asked.

The man in the hat had pulled out a map from the glove compartment and turned it around several times. "What the...?"

"Is Daddy here?" Frankie asked.

Jacob got out of the car, shut his front door and opened our back door. "Get out."

"Why are we here?" I was starting to lose my patience with Jacob.

"I told you. It's a surprise." Jacob slammed our door and took Frankie's hand. "Let's go."

"But…" Frankie whined.

"But what? You want to see your dad, right? Come on."

Jacob walked fast, and Frankie tried to keep up. Olivia and I were about five feet behind them when we got to the door of the mall. The man in the hat opened the door. "Come on. Hurry up."

The mall was packed. On a hot, humid day at the end of the summer, people tired of the pools and the heat were shoulder to shoulder in the Westroads Mall. Worn-out mothers with bags of school shoes and grumpy children trailing behind could be seen in every direction. Jacob moved to a pay phone in an alcove area near the restrooms.

"I need to make a call. Stand right here. Don't move." The man in the hat no longer had that fun 'let's go to your surprise' voice. "Renee should be here to meet us soon."

"Renee?" I asked.

"The lady you were talking about." The man turned to the phone and pulled some change from his coat pocket.

Renee?

Lady we were talking about?

Meeting our dad in a mall?

I'd never even heard of a fast-food place called *Jack in the Box*.

Lie.

Lie.

Lie.

Jacob was a liar. The man in the hat, who at first came across as young, green, and not-as-polished-as-the-older-officers, now appeared as though he had either shown up late to the party without enough details or was not even connected to Ramona and Kemper and the men who had invaded our home the night before. I was not a fan of the stranger danger movies we watched in school; I always found them condescending and flooded with bad actors. But now I felt a moment of panic ballooning in the center of my chest.

As Jacob dialed a number on the phone, I took Olivia and Frankie by the hand and ran. Both of their hands held tightly to mine as we serpentined through the crowd of summer strangers. Adults looked down at us as we bumped into bags and arms. I didn't know where we were going; I just knew away from the man. We had landed on a bad square on the game board of life, and we were sentenced to fly down the chute.

Down, down, down.

"Hey. Quit shoving," a large woman yelled.

"Damn kids," an older man said as we moved our way quickly through the sea of bodies, hoping to put great distance and major obstacles between Stranger Jacob and a place of safety. My stomachache was back, and I pulled the Junior Mints closer to me. The crowd loomed over us like a wave in a petulant ocean, and that ocean felt much safer than the man in the hat. I wanted to be in my backyard on the picnic table, wondering about the moon. I wanted to be anywhere but in a mall packed with grumpy people and a stranger chasing us. I realized then and there that I liked order. Momma put the order in our life: routine, fun, and lots of love. I felt none of that at the moment. Up ahead, the crowded hall separated into lines of people who were waiting to get into a movie complex with many little theaters. I ran with the Junior Mints and cut in line, a felony I'd never have attempted at Henderson Grade School. I glanced back to look for any hats in the crowd.

"Hey!"

An usher in a red sport jacket and little black bow tie taking tickets was ready to scold me and direct me to the end of the line when I squealed, "My brother's going to throw up!"

I pulled Frankie and Olivia into the lobby of the theater, past the concession stand, and down a hallway of theaters. Three doors down, I pulled my brother and sister into a dark theater, which smelled of overly buttered popcorn and momentary safety. I squinted as my eyes adjusted to the dark theater with a big screen displaying two kids' baseball teams facing each other on the baseball diamond, a kid from each team holding a trophy, the closing scene of the movie. I could see two empty seats near the screen, and we moved down the slanted aisle lined with lights on a red carpet covered with speckles of popcorn. Olivia, Frankie, and I squeezed past four people in the row to get to the empty seats. I liked that the seats were not on the aisle in case the usher in the red jacket decided to look for us. With the huge lines in the mall hallway as big as they were, I hoped that three little kids sneaking into a movie was the least of his worries. As soon as I relaxed, I heard and felt Olivia's sobs. My little sister was in meltdown mode, and I didn't know what to do. I moved closer to her face and put my arms around her.

"We're OK. We are OK." I whispered the words over and over and tried to rock her. Frankie, on the other side of Olivia, patted her back. I didn't see as much as feel the eyes of people around us looking at three children huddled together in a dark theater. The effect of the rocking, along with the dark and cool theater, wooed the over-stimulated Olivia—still holding tightly to her bag with the music box—into a sweet sleep. Music played as the credits to the movie *The Bad News Bears* started rolling, the lights of the theater growing brighter. I'd seen commercials for the movie and wondered if I, ever in my life, would get the chance to watch the movie that was gaining national attention from every preteen in America in 1976. Frankie and I sat, still glued to our fragile sister, as people funneled out of the theater.

"Enjoy the show?" The voice behind me was young and familiar. Marty, our newspaper boy, put his hands on the seat behind us. "You didn't get to see the best parts. Oh..." Marty saw Olivia. "Everybody OK?"

"Our newspaper guy!" Frankie said.

I knew so few people in the great metropolis of Omaha. How, when I was hoping to disappear, much like my mother, did I run into someone I knew in my hiding place?

"We're good." I tried to appear interested in the credits rolling on the big screen. Frankie looked to the back of the theater.

"I'll be right back." Marty left, and I thought about waking Olivia and running out the door near the screen, but to where?

"I have an idea." Marty was back.

"Really, we're fine."

"My dad has an office just across the street. We can run over there and give your sister a place to feel better."

"She's not sick. She'll be fine."

"Alright then… why don't you let me show you where my dad works and also the place where I work on Saturday mornings?" Marty was the first non-adult that we'd seen in two days. Since I could think of no other place to go, I obeyed. I wondered if Jacob might be in the parking lot, waiting to pounce on us.

"OK. Where are your friends?"

"We met here. I told them I had to head home. Why don't we go the back way? If we leave here, we can walk in the neighborhood behind the mall and go in the back door of his office… if that works for you."

"That'd be great," I said as Olivia sat up. "We're OK, Olivia. See? We're OK," I whispered.

For once, Frankie didn't question our next move. He grabbed my other hand as the three of us followed Marty to the door near the screen. We walked down a long, narrow corridor to a door that opened to the outside.

"Follow me," Marty said as he opened the door to a spray of hot, humid air and blaring sunshine. We walked away from the parking lot to a neighborhood behind the building. I scanned the area for a man in a brown hat. We walked one block and moved toward the back area of a strip mall. Marty took a key out of his pocket as we moved toward the center of the long building with only one level. I saw a bright blue ten-speed bicycle locked next to a trash bin near the back door of Marty's father's office.

"Dad's an accountant, which translated means boring and boring." He opened the door and turned on a light. "He makes a good living, but I know what I don't want to be when I grow up: an accountant." The tiny back room of the office had a small area rug. A green couch and a small TV on a short table were the only pieces of furniture in the room. Marty then opened a door to the front part of the office, a room with two desks and big windows facing the busy street out front. "This is where all the fun begins! Just kidding. I clean the main office, back room, and bathroom every Saturday morning and meet my friends at the mall after. I get paid good money since Dad avoids taxes in paying his son. You don't need to be telling anyone that little secret. This gig and my job as a paper boy mean that I'm living the dream." Frankie looked out the front window as did I.

When I thought of the man in the hat, I remembered the book that Momma had read to me in my younger years: *Curious George.* George the monkey would always refer to the man in the yellow hat who had lured George with his hat and taken him from Africa to America. The man never had a name, just the man or the man in the yellow hat. In all the books that Momma read, the man seemed like a father to George in all the silly predicaments that George got himself into. Our man in the hat had lured us into his trap with the enticement of a visit with our father. We'd fallen for the trap only to discover that our man was not a father-figure. I'm not even sure what or who he was.

"We can go into the back room if you'd like," Marty said. "Take a seat. Relax a little. I can turn on the TV if you want." Olivia and Frankie sat down. I could tell that they were tired and scared, but I had no idea what our next step would be in the nightmare that had taken over our lives since Momma disappeared.

"TV would be great." I knew the numbing effect of TV might calm the Junior Mints.

Marty turned on the small TV atop a rickety stand; a commercial for *H.R. Pufnstuf* was on. Olivia and Frankie sat on the couch next to each other. Marty motioned for me to come into the front office. He shut the door and pointed to the floor behind the desk.

"Your parents let you come here by yourself?" I asked.

"It's just me and my dad. He trusts me a lot. It's cool."

Marty and I sat on the floor against the wall behind the desk. I guessed that Marty and I had the absent mother deal in common. In this big world, the Duvall kids might not be the only kids whose mother had walked away.

"I need you to be honest with me, Esther." Marty looked down at his hands. "I've got to ask: is your dad chasing you right now?"

"My dad?" Marty clearly had not read the newspapers he delivered. "No, my dad is... I'm not sure where he is, but he's not chasing us."

"Then who are you three running from?"

"I don't know."

"Then why are you running?"

"I don't know what else to do." My lower lip trembled, and I bit my lip, which didn't keep the tears from pouring from my eyes. I sobbed. I'd only cried in front of my mom. Marty put his hand on my knee. I took a deep breath. "Sorry."

"Don't apologize. I just don't know how I can help you if you can't explain what's going on. I can call my dad..."

"No."

"What do you want me to do?"

"I'm sure that your dad is a nice guy, but I'm so tired of not being able to trust adults."

"Do you trust your mom and dad?"

"I trusted them. Momma disappeared, and they took Daddy from us. And no one else seems to be able to explain to me just what's going on." I looked around the room and saw a framed picture of a young couple with a little boy in red overalls on the desk we were hiding behind. "Is that you?"

"A very chubby me. I think I was two."

"Is that your mom before she left?"

"Before she died."

I couldn't reply.

"I don't really remember her. I was so young. I look at pictures of her and me together, and I make up little memories of what we might have done. The only connection I have to her is my name. Her last name before she married my dad was Martin. Camilla Martin."

"I'm sorry."

"Don't be. I wish I could say I'm sad. It's kind of hard to be sad about or miss someone you don't remember. Does that make sense? I know she was a great person. From what I hear. My dad… well, he's still sad. She got really sick. I don't know much else." Marty stood up and moved toward the front windows. "So, who or what am I looking for? A big hairy monster?"

"A man. In a hat."

"A man in a hat. That narrows it down." Marty spoke in a silly accent.

"Young. Tall. Thin. Driving a brown car. The car had a broken taillight. He took us from an office. We were there with the officers."

"Officers? Like police officers?"

"More like investigators. Like on *Barney Miller* or *Columbo*. They don't wear police uniforms. The kind that just take over your house, ask a ton of questions and then take your dad away."

"Is the man in the hat an officer?"

"I don't know. He said his name was Jacob, but now I don't even believe that. I think he was going to take us away. I'm not sure why. The worst part of it all," I said, "is that I don't trust any of the adults. And I feel like my brother and sister and I are just so, so…"

"You feel like you're fish in a barrel, and people are shooting at you."

"I guess."

"If you were shooting at fish in a barrel, you'd probably get a few. It would be extremely easy."

"I have never heard that, but, yah, that's how I feel."

"Esther, Omaha may not be New York, but it's a pretty big place. They won't find you. I promise."

"They?"

"The bad guys."

"The hardest part of this shooting fish game was that we still didn't know who was shooting at us and why."

"You'll need to eat. I'll run over to the bakery next door. Betsy always throws out bread at the end of the day, which is still pretty good. Betsy, the owner, loves me. She likes to save me things, so I usually stop by on days I clean the office. When I get back, we'll make a plan."

"Right."

"Don't worry, Esther." I liked the way he said my name. "I'll keep you safe." Marty opened the door to the back room, his shaggy dark hair spraying out in all directions from his head. I wanted to trust someone. I really did.

"Are we going home soon?" Frankie looked like someone who had just been hit in the head by a board game of *Chutes and Ladders*.

Marty walked out the back door. "Go ahead and lock it behind me. I'll be right back."

"We can't go home right now. Jacob will probably go to find us there."

"Is Jacob a bad guy?" Frankie asked as I turned down the volume of the TV as a little man with an Alka-Seltzer tab as a hat on his head sang *Plop, plop, fizz, fizz, oh what a relief it is.*

"I don't know, Frankie. I don't think he had permission to take us. We're going to wait for Marty to come back with some food."

"Are both the front and back doors to the office locked right now?"

"Yes. Marty has a key."

"Key." Olivia walked into the front office.

"Are you doing better, Liv?"

Olivia wouldn't look at me.

Twenty minutes later, Marty unlocked the back door and came in with a sack. "We've got more than bread, people. Pretty excited here." He placed food on the couch since we didn't have a table. "Bread, bagels, and two pink cupcakes."

"Cupcakes?" Frankie's spirits were lifted by pink frosting and sprinkles.

"I sweet-talked Betsy into some cream cheese for the bagels. I have a few paper cups for water in the closet. We're set." Marty looked up at the clock.

"Do we need to get out of here, Marty?"

Marty motioned for me to move to the front office. He shut the door, and we both sat down on the floor again. "You can stay for now. It's Saturday, and Dad won't be here until early Monday morning. I have to get going, though. My dad won't be happy if I get home after the sun sets since I'm riding my bike. The couch is a rollaway bed. My dad stays here during tax season, sometimes. You can noodle on what you want to do. A good night's sleep will help you figure things out."

"Why are you being so nice to us, Marty? You barely know us." My voice cracked again. I would not cry again.

"Seems like you guys are in a bad place right now. I just want to help."

I had my parents. I had my little brother and sister. I can honestly say that I didn't have a friend until that moment. "Olivia and Frankie love the cupcakes. Thank you."

"I'll be back early tomorrow." Marty handed me a small piece of paper with his home phone number on it. My new friend Marty had been gone for several hours, and the Junior Mints were fast asleep on the roll-out bed as I sat on the chair next to them. Before she finally calmed down, Olivia had wound the music box three times to play *Somewhere Over the Rainbow* as I blew her pinwheel to spin her into relaxation. Frankie didn't complain as I think we all were thinking of Momma as the music played. After they both fell asleep, I tried to noodle on where we would go after leaving the office. Nothing. I couldn't think of anywhere and anyone that I could trust. I liked Ramona, but I had no way of contacting her. I still wasn't sure if she was a good witch or a bad witch.

Ramona had asked me to think of anything out of place the few days before. I squinted my eyes and tried to go back to the days before Momma had left. Momma had taken Olivia and me to Henderson Grade School a few days before she disappeared. That's when Frankie saw Momma hug the strange man. The day before she disappeared, I'm pretty sure that Momma had taken us to Tess's house so that she could have coffee with her— nothing out of the norm. But when we had gone home, I could tell that Momma had been crying. The tears were not normal. Other than that, nothing. I could think of nothing else that would hint at her leaving.

I had the TV on and turned down as the Junior Mints slept. I saw the opening of the ten o'clock news on the TV. My school picture from the past year filled the screen. I moved quickly to the TV and turned it up just loud enough to hear. A man reported from a desk, my face displayed behind him. My hair was plain, my clothes homemade, my smile simple. I was still taking in the fact that I was on the ten o'clock news as the man spoke. "Our top story tonight has authorities asking for your help. The three children of a missing Omaha mother and their father, who was arrested early this morning for kidnapping, are now also missing. Chief Kemper of the Omaha police force spoke with us earlier this evening with this request."

The footage of Kemper in front of our house was clear and brief. "We're asking all Omaha citizens to be on the lookout for Esther Duvall, a nine-year-old girl, and her two younger siblings, Frankie and Olivia, who went missing today. Please contact us if you see them alone or with any other adults." There were no pictures of Frankie and Olivia.

The reporter continued with more of the story. "Authorities say the missing mother, Tara Duvall, is also a suspect in the kidnapping of a baby with her husband, Clark Duvall. Please contact authorities if you see her." The pictures of my mother and father were the ones I had seen on their driver's licenses.

"We interviewed parents from the school where the oldest Duvall child was in attendance this past year." The reporter held a microphone in front of a pudgy woman.

"I'm not surprised." Nancy Krisco stood outside Henderson Grade School in an ugly green pantsuit and a scarf around her neck. I wondered how many large pantsuits filled the closet of Queen Krisco. "The Duvalls were never involved and seemed standoffish to other parents. I just hope they find those darling children soon."

I turned down the volume on the TV and took a deep breath. My parents kidnapped a baby? The picture from Momma's drawer popped into my head: *My dearest Daniel*. I tried as hard as I could to piece together the words I'd just heard when it occurred to me that Mrs. Krisco might be the tattletale. Maybe she had called the police after we saw her at Peony Park. Still, why would the officers question a man whose wife didn't go to PTA meetings at the school or answer her telephone? Why would they need to question Daddy at all? As far as a kidnapped baby was concerned, Momma and Daddy couldn't have hidden something like that from us.

The office phone rang.

I let the phone ring. It stopped. I wasn't sure if people called accountants late at night. It started to ring again. I didn't want the ringing to wake up Olivia and Frankie, so I moved into the front office and picked up the phone.

I said nothing.

"Esther? It's Marty."

"Marty?"

"You're famous. Did you know that your picture was on the ten o'clock news tonight?"

"I just saw it."

"So did my dad."

"Oh."

"You've got quite a lot going on in your life right now."

"It's not... the news is not the truth."

"We need a plan, lady. Any ideas yet?"

"Still noodling."

I could hear Marty grin through the phone.

"I'll ride my bike to the office early tomorrow. We'll figure it out."

"Thank you."

"You have my number, so call if you need me. My dad never answers the home phone. Sweet dreams, Esther. Oh, and Esther, you looked pretty in your picture." I hung up and smiled as I watched the end of the news. As I sat on the only chair in the room, I dozed off into a restless night of sleep.

The dream I had in an office at the end of Omaha is one I will never forget:

I walk into a big kitchen, and I see the silhouette of a woman standing by the counter. The room is grey, and we are alone. The woman has on an apron over a long skirt. I go to her, and she picks me up and puts me on the counter. She smells like cinnamon rolls. As if she hears my thoughts, she gives me a cinnamon roll bigger than any cinnamon roll I've ever seen.

I point to the window to show her that there is a tornado outside. She turns to the sink and turns back to me and is no longer the woman.

She is the man in the hat.

I jump from the counter and see Olivia and Frankie in the doorway. "Run," I scream.

I grab their hands, and we run from the kitchen and the man in the hat.

Ahead, I see a yellow brick road. It is bright and colorful. I tell Olivia and Frankie that we must follow the road to find Momma and Daddy.

I look back and see the man in the hat riding a bicycle, still chasing us. We run through a field of poppies. We get to the yellow brick road and Tess is standing on the road waving to us. I look down and Olivia and Frankie are not with me. I look back and see that the man in the hat has Frankie and Olivia and is running away from me.

I woke up.

A staticky sound came from the television, and the light from the screen glowed on the clock on the wall. Even though it wasn't a digital clock, I could tell the time: 4:05 a.m.

Tess.

Momma had cried to Tess. Momma had me memorize Tess's phone number as the just-in-case number: just in case I call home from school and Momma doesn't answer, just in case I can't find Momma, just in case a strange man is after us. Tonight was certainly a just-in-case case. Momma trusted Tess. If you had asked me three days earlier whom I could trust, I didn't think that it would ever be the old lady across the street and our newspaper boy. I opened the door to the front office and slowly shut it. I picked up the phone and dialed.

One ring only.

"Hello?" Tess sounded serious.

Words wouldn't come out of my mouth.

"The shop is closed," Tess said without emotion.

"What?" I asked.

"Esther? Is that you, honey?"

"Yes."

"Where are you? Are you alright? Are you with Olivia and Frankie?"

"Yes. They're safe. They're sleeping. What shop is closed, Tess?"

"Where are you, Esther? I'll come and get you right now."

"We can't go home, Tess. There's a strange man chasing us, and I don't know who to trust."

"Your mother is my dear friend, Esther. You can trust me. Where are you?"

"I'm not sure." I looked at the desk. With light from the big storefront windows, I saw an envelope and picked it up.

"You're safe, but you don't know where you are? Who are you with?"

I read aloud the words on the envelope under the name *Howard Westerholt. "Liberty Tax Service. 10214 Westchester Road."*

Laughter through the phone confused me. "You're hiding in a tax office?"

"My friend took us here. It's his dad's office. Across from the mall."

"I'm heading there now. Can you have the Junior Mints up and ready in fifteen minutes?"

"Sure. Tess, pick us up behind the building, please."

"See you soon, Sweetie."

"Tess, remember, we can't go home."

"Oh, Esther, you're not going home."

6
Katherine

1962

*E*rnest Hemingway once said, "Wine is the most civilized thing in the world."

That being said, the salvation of the civilized world evidently lies in the hillsides and soil of the Celestial Way plantation.

I can't remember the moment I decided not to get on a plane to go home to Connecticut. I really don't know if I ever spoke the words.

I just stayed.

One night turned into two, and two nights turned into two weeks after Christmas. Two weeks turned into two years, and two years to four, and four years to eight.

With eight full cycles of the vineyard seasons passed, I no longer marked my years by a calendar. I embraced the change of the seasons at Celestial Way as the vines lived, died, thrived, and changed colors in the California sun. The fruits of the crops grew larger and larger each year as the Celestial Way label and its specialty wines grew more and more popular.

I looked out of the large window in my office toward the hills filled with vines. Several workers were already working the vines, and the sun was coming up on the horizon. Strangely, the moon was still resting in the sky, almost as if he was defying the sun. You can't take over my reign. The fragrance of the vineyard blew into my window and was warm against my face. This time of year, the vines were green and hopeful, and I was busy making the weekly order for Celestial Way.

My business office was off the big kitchen where the community ate in shifts each day. The small office was the picture of efficiency as I organized files, sent out orders, and paid bills. I had always been a natural with numbers and money, and Captain was relieved to hand over the books and the job of placing and monitoring orders for the winery, vineyard, and kitchen to the young woman who had always wanted to go into business. While Charles worked on the operations of the entire campus, Captain worked closely with me to maintain the flow of the campus management.

Captain's vision and knowledge of the formulaic vineyard conditions for wine grapes and his research on improving the process of making the best bottle of wine paid off for the gamble he'd taken twenty years before in the land thirty minutes from San Jose. A saying in the world of vineyards and winemakers is that "the worse the soil, the better the wine." Vineyards are commonly set on hillsides and on soil of little value to other plants. The hillside of Celestial Way faced south to maximize the amount of sunlight that showered the precious plants as Captain fostered his plan.

The plan included Charles. And in time, the plan included me.

Charles and I married.

Back in the spring of 1955, under a brilliant moon out near the steep hills covered in vines, Captain stood before us and pronounced our union. I stood barefoot in a yellow sundress loaned to me by a woman who worked the fields, little flowers in my hair. Charles looked into my eyes the entire ceremony. I had never imagined the freedom I felt in the early years, and I soon felt myself escaping into the unfathomable green, gold, and rose hues of the Celestial Way landscape, plunging into the canvas of a new life. Nine months later, Maureen Renee was our blessing, born the day before Christmas of 1955, almost a year to the day I'd found the vineyard, or the vineyard had found me.

"These are the last boxes for your supply order." A tall man with blue smiling eyes leaned against the frame of the door to my office. "Tomorrow, we'll have the frozen foods, and you can get me your updated equipment order." PIE truck lines moved our wine freight across the country, but Mick Sullivan delivered the personal supplies and food to Celestial Way, mostly from local vendors. Mick could not be more Irish and could not look less so. At least of the stereotype. While visions of red-headed, ruddy-complected, short, and stocky leprechauns scream of the Irish look, Mick's tall, trim body and full head of dark hair looked nothing like the stock Irishman. Only the twinkle in his bright blue eyes hinted at his heritage. His name confirmed the genealogy.

"I'm sorry, Mick, I don't have that order today. We're waiting for our winery team to let us know if they fixed the temperature-controlled fermenter. Fingers crossed. I don't want to pay for that and all the new wine racks that we so desperately need. I promise I'll have it tomorrow." I held my hand out to shake Mick's hand. "Will a handshake do for my word?"

"Your word is gold, Kat. We can order the racks now and hold off until you know for sure about the fermenter." Mick still shook my hand. His warm hands were the only link I had to a world beyond the plantation.

For as long as I could remember, Mick was one of the only people with the unique honor of being allowed onto our grounds, other than the bigger trucks that shipped the wine across the country. Mick and Captain's bodyguard Eugene had served two tours of duty in the Korean War. They had memories neither would share about some bad days in the battle at the Chosin Reservoir and the Pusan Perimeter. Their shared traumatic experiences built an iron shell around the two, so I quit asking about the Korean years after a while. I knew that an unwritten trust agreement also rested between Captain and Mick. Mick knew of our regular orders—the food, the equipment, the supplies for the cottages—but he also knew of the unusual orders at Celestial Way. He knew of the medical treatments for the community members with cancer, diabetes, and other health concerns. He knew that these items were important since we were a self-sufficient place. No one ever went to the hospital. Captain didn't trust hospitals and believed we could take better care of our people than anyone else. Mick also knew of the expensive cigars shipped in for the men's evenings in the Big Barn. He knew of Captain's unique obsession with and compulsion for Jameson's Irish Whiskey.

"It looks like your extra help is having fun with my Maureen," I said as I laughed at Mick's son Levi, who had stopped helping Mick and begun helping Maureen move the tables of the big dining hall out of the Mother House for a Celestial Way Gala that evening, a yearly event at which Captain gave out awards to exemplary family members and celebrated the goodness of the vineyard. Levi was only ten but could pass for much older and he helped his dad on days when school was out. My beautiful Maureen, with her long dark hair in braids and her green eyes darting to keep up with Levi, was seven going on forty. Most people on the plantation said that Maureen was a beautiful blend of Charles and me. "Perfect."

Lottie had said. "But how could Maureen not be perfect? She has the genes of the chosen couple." I blushed and brushed off the comment. On the one hand, Charles and I had been chosen by Captain to be second in command to his leadership of the community, which now held over 300 individuals; on the other hand, I was not always comfortable with the adulations I'd receive from other members of the community.

"Levi's just now starting to be more help than a pain in the butt." Mick laughed as he went back to his truck for the last few boxes. "Still loses his focus around a pretty girl, though."

As I pulled out my file with the orders for the next week, I smiled. I loved my order and my system, and I'm not going to lie: I loved the control I had. No doubt, I'd never have had the position I held at Celestial Way in the outer world.

"Is now a bad time?" London peeked around the doorframe as she spoke. "I'm a little early."

"Any time is a good time for you," I said. London was going to help me set up for the big event.

London had come a long way from her chopped hair and fearful presence on the first day I had met her. Her hair had grown out, still curly and unkempt, but all other aspects of her appearance were clean and neat. I had never seen London in anything but a prairie skirt and a long-sleeved buttoned shirt. Her horn-rimmed glasses both framed and hid her beautiful features, which I suppose was her goal as she got herself ready every day.

"I have something." London shuffled into my office, showing me a white bag.

"Let's see, it's not my birthday, so I'm guessing you are bringing me a bag filled with money."

London pushed her glasses up on her nose and stared at me.

"Kidding, London. Have a seat." I pointed to the large brown leather couch under the window to the vineyard. "What do you have?"

"Could we shut your office door?" London stopped to see me several times a week, and I suspected that I replaced the mother, who had been one big disappointment to her.

"Sure," I said as I shut the door. I could see Maureen and Levi running through the aisles of the long tables in the dining area. "Is everything alright, London?"

"Yes. Well, no." London opened the bag and pulled out a yearbook. The raised numbers *1953* stood out in silver against the black leather binding and anchored the title of the book: *Forester High School, Home of the Fighting Spartans.*

"Your yearbook, London?"

London shook her head yes as she looked down.

"You do know that you're not supposed to have it, right?"

Again, she acknowledged.

When Captain welcomed newcomers to Celestial Way, he held a ceremony where the community welcomed the newest members to the plantation as each new member released their previous life. My fondest memories from the previous eight years were tagged with the lineage of Releasing Ceremonies. A beautiful ceremony, really. Our community welcomed a new life, and the new life let go of the old life, of all the material objects and the bad things from the previous years. The community had to live in a Pure Presence. That cathartic act was the most altruistic thing I had done in my life, and my ceremony was a week after I arrived at the vineyard in 1954. In releasing the physical and emotional baggage of my Before life,

I enabled the community to maintain the peace that made Celestial Way so different. Change yourself and change the world.

"Close your eyes," Captain called to new members. "Think of your pain and suffering from your past as black balloons with long strings that you are holding onto."

I could feel those strings. I could see those black balloons in my mind. Anger. Resentment. Confusion. I didn't want any of those things in my heart anymore.

"Release!" Captain's beautiful voice would ring through the dining hall.

"Release!" The Celestial Way community repeated.

"Release! Release!"

Tears had rolled down my face into a warm blanket. London had been standing right beside me that night. She was releasing her horrific childhood right beside me. Our balloons raced away from us as we willed them away. London knew more than anyone that she shouldn't have the yearbook with her. She should have given that to the Convivial Committee years ago. Ramifications of holding were never known but feared. Two years earlier, a truck driver named Carl, who had been with the group for a few months, was found with a photo album from his previous life. The community gossip later alluded to a punishment of some kind, but what had disturbed me more than a penalty was the fact that Carl didn't show up for breakfast in the dining hall the next day and was never seen again. I'm not sure who first coined the phrase, but we all knew that people at the Way who messed up would be *unfamilied*. To be unfamilied was one of the worst fates I could imagine. Celestial Way cut off Carl like a big black balloon, never to return.

"Anyone else know that you have it?" I asked.

"Yes."

"Who?"

"Captain."

"Captain?"

"I begged him to allow me to keep it. It was the only thing I asked. Inside this yearbook are pictures of my brother and sister."

"And Captain allowed you to keep it?"

"Not at first. But after I begged, he said that I could keep it in his office and only look at it there." London cleaned Captain's office twice a week. I think Captain felt sorry for her.

"Wow, and you have it here?"

"I do. I need your help."

"I'd be happy to help you, London. I just don't want you to get in trouble for having this…"

"My brother's dead."

I knew that London had a bad childhood, and I suspected she was hiding scars on her arms or, worse, on her wrists. I just never knew what had happened.

"He died years ago. The three of us—Stacie, Eddie, and I—well, we were all tossed out into different foster homes after my dad killed my mom."

"I'm so sorry."

"I'm not. Only time Dad ever helped us out. My mom was abusive. My dad was abusive. The night he shot her, he killed two birds with one stone. She was gone, and he was sent to prison."

"Wow."

London brushed off the fate of her father. "We would've been better off on our own, but we were all under eighteen, so we were sent to three different foster homes. Eddie didn't get along with his foster father, and the only way he knew how to react was with violence. He went to jail, a different one than the old man's prison. I stayed in touch... he died in prison. I never knew the details. I never asked. I was pretty sure he died in a fight. That's all he knew."

I could hear laughter echo out in the dining hall.

"But Stacie, I don't know where she is. The last few nights, I've been having really terrible dreams, and I feel like something bad has happened to her. She and I were always so close; we would finish each other's sentences. I could feel things about her when we weren't together. I just wish I could go look for her and bring her here."

"Do you know where she was when you first came here?"

"With her foster family in south Los Angeles. I was about five miles north with my foster family. Once I heard about Eddie, I walked all the way to her house. Her family said she had left; I wasn't surprised she left, but I had no idea where she went."

"And you somehow ended up here?"

"I hitch-hiked. I wanted to get as far away from LA as possible. It took several weeks to move up Highway 101. Rocco was the last one to pick me up. When he told me about the vineyard, I realized that I had nowhere else to go. This place saved my life."

"I still can't get over the fact that Captain let you keep this book." I ran my finger over the raised silver numbers, 1953."

"It's actually Eddie's yearbook. He was a senior. I was a sophomore, and Stacie was a freshman." London opened the book to a page she had memorized. She pointed to a picture. "There. What a sad, pathetic girl."

A young London frowned from the square school picture. The name beside it: Stephanie Gates.

"London, you look so young."

"In the Before, I was Stephanie. That name is definitely one black balloon I let go of."

"Why'd you pick the name London?"

"When I was little, the popular girls would sing *London Bridge is Falling Down* as they jumped rope. I sat on the side of the playground and could hear their voices, almost taunting the song, almost as if they were laughing that the bridge had fallen down. I don't ever want to fall down again. And, London is as far from LA as I could think. I liked the name."

London turned the pages back several times. "There. That's Stacie."

A strikingly beautiful girl with big brown eyes smiled up at me. I could see a small resemblance to London. For the most part, Stacie was the girl whose beauty grabbed your attention and drew you to her picture on the page first.

"You must really miss her."

"I do."

"I'm not sure how I can help you."

"Maybe not you, but what about your guy?" London, in her simple manner, was sometimes slow with words. I sensed that she had struggled in school, and I think that she had no interest beyond high school.

"I'm not sure I'd want to include Charles in this search." Charles had been critical of Captain's drinking lately and was not always happy with some of his decisions. Charles wouldn't be happy that Captain had allowed London to keep a Before item at all.

"Not Charles. Your guy out there who helps with orders and stuff."

"Mick?"

"Yah, he drives a truck around, right?"

"Yes."

"Could he put up pictures at stops and on his truck?" London was smarter than I thought. "I just can't think of anything else to do other than leave and find her." London knew that if she left, she wouldn't be allowed back at Celestial Way. "So, you think that he could use her yearbook picture as the one to make copies of?" London pushed her glasses up her nose and cleared her throat. "It's all I have left of her."

I placed the yearbook in the white bag and put the white bag in a drawer on my desk. "I'll take care of this, London." I turned to her as she came toward me and hugged me. "I can't make any promises, but I think your plan is a good one. I'll talk to Mick. Let's keep all of this between just the two of us. Deal?"

"Deal." The rare smile on London's face was my answer. She looked as if she wanted to hug me. She moved her glasses up her nose and walked out of the room and turned. "Thank you, Katherine."

London passed Mick as she left my office. Mick stuck his head into the room and whispered, "Almost forgot to tell you…A man is orbiting the earth in a rocket as we speak." Mick kept me updated on the news from the outside of the vineyard.

With no television or newspaper, members of Celestial Way remained in the fifties as the rocky sixties roared into the century.

"He actually left the earth?"

"Yep. NASA wanted to see how a person would react to the pressure and speed. His name's John Glenn. My sister thinks he's handsome." From our surface discussions, I surmised that Mick's wife had either died or left Mick and Levi. Mick's older sister lived with them.

"Amazing."

I found a strange ease in the tether to the outside world I had in Mick. While I adored our peaceful plantation—my entire world was the vineyard and the winery community—I was well aware of a bigger world beyond the road out of the campus. Mick would feed me tidbits of information about the world and even smuggle in a newspaper occasionally. I always hid the forbidden contraband and only looked at the newspapers when Charles was away. The idea of the U.S. involvement in a war in a small country far from America called Vietnam intrigued me. I looked through magazines and newspapers Mick brought me and took in changes from just eight years ago; the cars in the advertisements looked almost futuristic, and the fashions and hairstyles of the men and women outside of Celestial Way were funny yet fascinating.

"One more thing." Mick stepped into my office and pulled out his wallet. "Here." Mick showed me a picture of a woman cut from a magazine or book.

"Someone you know?" I asked.

"Seriously? It's Natalie Wood."

"The little girl from the Santa movie? *Miracle on 34th Street*. That's her?"

"All grown up now. She's in a movie called *Westside Story*. And she looks like you. Replace her brown eyes with your green eyes. You're a movie star, Kat. I had to do a double-take when I saw the picture."

A loud bang interrupted us as it echoed in the main dining hall. A table on the far side of the large dining hall was on its side, and two very guilty faces looked across the room at us.

"My fault," Levi lifted both arms. "I did it."

"No, I did it." Maureen argued. "I knocked it over."

I looked back to Maureen and Levi, neither looking childlike anymore. It didn't seem that long ago that Levi and Maureen were running around these same tables, playing hide and seek while Mick made deliveries. Levi grinned at Maureen as he pushed the table back upright. Maureen pouted her lips and pushed her hair from her face as she smiled and moved toward the kitchen.

"No worries," I said. "Just turn it over and go grab a cinnamon roll and milk. Those tables are hard to move around."

"Thanks for the offer," Mick said, "but Levi needs to help me finish unloading this shipment so we're not late to the next stop."

"Maureen, why don't you go pack up a dozen cinnamon rolls for the Sullivans to take.

Thanks again for your patience, Mick. I'll have everything in order by tomorrow."

"No worries."

"London!" I called to London in the kitchen. "Could you help Maureen get a box of rolls for Mick and Levi?"

"Just one box?"

"Yes, that would be great."

"And do you need me to tape it shut?"

"Great idea. They're traveling home."

London moved toward the kitchen to help Maureen.

Mick jumped up into the back of his truck. "Most people here can function only in the lower levels of Kohlberg's stages of moral development."

I stopped. I hadn't heard the term moral development since my sociology class at Santa Clara over a decade before.

"You know, it's almost like they're comfortable with the simple existence of someone telling them what to do. It's almost lazy, moral laziness.... in my opinion." At that moment, Mick went beyond nice guy/delivery person to an intelligent being, and I realized that I hadn't had an intelligent conversation in years. Charles traveled all the time, and most conversations in my day were about the functioning of the vineyard. I found Mick's words enticing and frightening at the same time. I must have been staring since Mick stood up and looked at me.

"Not you, Kat. I'm sorry if you... that's not what I meant. You make this place run. I mean, it works for the system you all have going on here. Everybody has a part in the play that is a functioning winery. People have their roles and do these roles well, but if you ask them to go beyond their duty or make a decision outside of their boxes, well, they zone out. Like your little London there. No offense meant. I need to learn to keep my thoughts inside my head."

"No, you're probably right. I guess when you have so many people living together…"

Mick interrupted, "No need to defend. It wasn't nice of me to say. I was just talking to myself. This place works so well, you could be the model for companies and big businesses."

"Dad," Levi yelled from the room. "Can we give Maureen her surprise now?" Levi's big blue eyes matched his father's. He was a smaller version of Mick.

"I need to make sure Maureen's mother is alright with it." Mick moved to the back of his truck, bent down and picked up something from inside a box. A beautiful fox-red puppy whimpered and wiggled in his arms. "We found him on a side road early this morning. We're never home that much so…"

"We thought he could protect you!" Levi said as Maureen arrived at the truck with a box of cinnamon rolls.

"He's so cute!" Maureen gave the box to me and ran to the small creature.

"Hope you're not mad at me," Mick whispered.

"Can we keep him, Mom?"

"We do take in lost souls," I said, shaking my head.

"We can visit him when we make deliveries," Levi said, petting the head of the pup that now squirmed in Maureen's arms."

"Merlot," I said.

Mick, Levi, and Maureen all stared at me.

"If we're keeping the pup, I get to name him. This little guy's name is Merlot."

"Works for me. Come on, kid. We've got more orders to deliver before sundown." Mick turned to me. "Call me if you get an update on your order. See you next week, Movie Star."

Mick was my connection to the outside world, but Charles tethered me to the vineyard.

That night, Charles came home from a long trip. We lay in bed with the moonlight pouring into our room and across the bed, Maureen asleep in the other room.

"I missed you so much." Charles was behind me as he took his fingers and moved them up and down my side. "How many days was I gone this time?"

"Thirteen," I mumbled.

"But who's counting? I promise I'll be home for a while."

"Or at least until the nineteenth, when you're gone again."

Charles had been marketing our newest merlot to old vendors and new vendors on the east coast. He'd spent a week in New York, and another in Washington, D.C. He, Rocco, and a few others from the Direction Team were traveling more than ever, and while I kept myself busy at all times, I was starting to resent the time he spent away from Maureen and our marriage. More than anything, I'd hoped for another baby, but two miscarriages and an absentee husband were making me more and more aware of the women with swollen bellies that surrounded me daily.

"I'm here now." Charles moved his hands up to my hair and moved several strands from my face.

"I know. Will the traveling ever stop?"

"Katherine," Charles whispered, "the life we have here is so blessed, and the reason we can enjoy it is the success of our wine. People here are dependent on me. You know that more than anyone."

"I think I just have too much time to think. When you're gone. Late at night."

Was I really opening my Honesty Box? I had shared with no one, not even Charles, the corner of my mind that I could never deny. While I had surrendered almost all the black balloons of my life years ago, I held some back but never forgot them. I knew that I'd have lost myself if I had not kept, hidden, and secured the part of me that was honest about everything. My Honesty Box was getting more and more crowded as I dared to think what I really felt.

"I miss my family." My words were soft and hesitant. Charles was rubbing my arm. "I think about things."

"About what?"

"Home."

"We're blessed."

"My home in Connecticut." Charles stopped moving my hair.

"I think about them. My parents. My brother. What they must be thinking. If I'm dead. If my family stopped looking for me. Are they angry or..."

Charles sat up and moved his legs to the side of the bed. "We've had this discussion before, Katherine. Those people are your Fallen Family. You're hurting yourself and our community when you even think of them."

"Hear me out. I mean, my parents were strict and direct and... I just think my parents are probably good people who worked hard but made mistakes."

Charles said nothing.

"Doesn't it make sense to forgive others? That's what Captain always tells us. I mean, I'm not sure what I'd even forgive. Sometimes to live in the Pure Present, we also need to let go and forgive. My parents took care of me and sometimes even told me things I disagreed with. Families don't always agree."

"What are you talking about?" Charles stood up and turned to me. "I'm your family, Katherine. Maureen is your family. The Way is your family." Charles turned back to me. "You haven't been talking to those people, have you?"

"No, nothing like that." I put my hand on Charles. "I just wonder about them. Sometimes. I still love it here, but…those people were once all I had. Don't you ever just wonder?"

"Never. You don't mean any of those words. You remember how much of your freedom they took from you. They never understood your dreams or respected your ideas."

"Charles, I was a self-absorbed college student who didn't understand the struggles of my parents. I thought about no one but myself. Captain even says that being selfish opens up all sorts of Bad Boxes."

"I think you're forgetting some important facts about the people who raised you, Katherine. You never would have amounted to anything in their eyes. You were always the 'never enough' daughter. You said that, remember?"

"I know I said that, but now I'm not sure if they really said those exact words… or if I just thought that's what they might say."

"You know that by even thinking of those people, you're shutting out the sunshine from the highest goodness. You are intentionally turning away from... I can't even believe you're saying this to me. What's making you think these things? You said you were happy. You said you missed me."

Shut it.

I'd made a mistake. I knew that I could never go there again with Charles, and I knew that I could never share the other thoughts: the outside world looked fascinating, the big world seemed full of dreams, and especially, that I might want more than Celestial Way, and I didn't want for that to be wrong or bad.

Charles went to the top drawer of his desk in our room and pulled out several Jolly Ranchers. He said nothing as he unwrapped one and put it in his mouth. He laid the handful on his desk, pulled his pants from the back of the chair, and put them on.

"I'm sorry. I don't know what got into me," I said as I sat up in bed. "Forget I ever said any of it."

Charles grabbed a shirt and put one arm in a sleeve.

"I promise I won't talk about it again."

He put his other arm in the other sleeve.

"Charles?"

"It hurts us all." The hard candy clicked on his teeth as he spoke. "It hurts the Way when you regret the family that was not there for you, when Celestial Way has showered you with goodness."

"But they weren't all bad..."

"Stop. Those thoughts insult the world here. We can't connect to or even think about the past we left behind."

Charles buttoned his shirt and slipped on his shoes. He picked up a set of keys from his desktop and moved toward the window, the moonlight hitting his face, his eyes squinting. He stood there for several long minutes. I thought he was going to continue scolding me. "They need me. They all need me." Charles moved directly in front of the window, his silhouetted body dark against the moonlight. He took a deep breath and was silent for what seemed like an eternity.

"Charles?"

Charles turned back to me with an expression of surprise, as if he'd forgotten I was in the room. "I'm heading out."

"Out? Where are you going?"

"To clear my head." Charles moved to the door and turned the knob. He stopped, looked back at me, and opened the door and left.

I looked out the window at the big, round harvest moon showering the bedroom. I thought about the man orbiting Earth as I lay there. The man who was now tethered to nothing. Outside of the vineyard. Outside of this world.

THE REVEALING

Toto, I have a feeling we're not in Kansas anymore.

Dorothy

7

Esther

DAY FOUR 1976

I trusted Tess 97%.

We'd just learned fractions and percentages in math during fifth grade. I knew what a piece of a pie looked like, and out of a big pie of trust, I still had a sliver of doubt about Tess. Justified, I believed, because, in those days of adult lies, Tess was still an adult.

Around 5:45 a.m., I peeked out the door. Tess stood behind Marty's dad's accounting office in front of a white car, which I'd never seen before. It was still dark outside, but I could see her face. The car had four doors, a dent on the passenger side, and a round yellow styrofoam smiley face on the tip of the antennae sprouting from the hood. Tess looked older and tired; her hair was messed up on the top. She may have missed Marcia's Beauty Box appointment that week. She wore a faded blue leisure suit that I had never seen her wear. She waved. I nudged the Junior Mints to move with me past the dumpster in the back parking lot of the strip mall.

Tess opened the back door of the car, and we all funneled in. The smell of cigarettes and a pine tree air freshener hanging from the mirror flooded our senses as I noticed the driver: a big, bald man who didn't look back at us. "Settle in, guys," Tess said. She closed our door and opened the front passenger door to get in.

97% turned into 84%. A numbers game.

"Where are we going?" I asked, as Olivia and Frankie leaned into me, both still groggy with the residue of sleep.

"A safe place." Tess and big, bald guy looked forward in silence for the next half hour. The black vest over the driver's T-shirt looked like leather in the morning light. A tattoo of a woman stretched across his muscular right arm. I think she was naked.

75%.

A splinter of light on the horizon hinted at the new day. I'd never seen a sunrise, and here it was, without any sentimental moment to mark it. The drive to safety didn't look familiar. The Duvall kids were getting to see parts of the city we'd never seen before in the summer of 1976. Summer camp or a crawl through the city in strange, smelly cars? I have never been to camp, but I bet, bugs and dirt included, I'd rather be a camper. We stopped at a red light, and even though no other cars were in the intersection, we sat. On the right corner of the intersection was a church, several older people moving slowly toward its front door.

It was Sunday.

A day when people all over the world went to worship. A day when people gathered in a feeling of community in their best clothes. A day when families made a statement about their faith.

Sunday was not a church day in the home of the Duvall family. My parents spoke of a higher power regularly, but not of a church or any organized religion for that matter. Rather than getting dressed up to sit in pews like most kids in my school did weekly before the school week began, the Duvall children put on their God shoes every day. Momma had said that if we love each other and are good to others, we are putting on our God shoes every day. "You all have the power with your God shoes." At night, after we washed our faces and brushed our teeth, after we turned off the day, Momma would kiss our foreheads and tell us that goodness was in our hearts, a nice thing to hear if you're a child drifting off to sleep.

Eventually, the big white car was covered by shadows. We moved through downtown as big buildings that almost touched the sky on each side of the car made it feel as though we were being swallowed. Not long after we entered the tunnel of the giant buildings, we were heading out of the tunnel and out of town.

"I have to go to the bathroom," Frankie whined.

"Almost there, kiddo. Hang on a bit." Tess didn't look back.

Olivia looked out the window and whimpered.

"What's that?" Frankie pointed to a big group of buildings isolated from the main road. "That's the airport. See the planes?"

As soon as Tess said planes, a large plane came into view as it took off.

"Wow! It's so big." Frankie was distracted from his urgent bladder.

The white car moved past the airport and drove for several miles and turned down a long road to a wooded area where a white building sat beside a tree near a big sign: Shamrock Motel. I had a feeling that we weren't in Omaha anymore, Toto. The letter "R" was not lit up, but the remaining letters of the Shamrock Motel sign were, and the daylight competed with the lights for dominance. The white car drove around to the side of the building, and the man driving the car looked to Tess and spoke the first words we had heard from the anomaly. "I'll be right back."

"We'll be right here," Tess replied.

After the man had moved into the front office of the motel, Frankie whispered to me, "That's the guy."

"What guy?" I asked.

"The one Momma hugged in the store," he whispered.

"Yes, Frankie," Tess said, "Stav is the man you saw with your mother in the store." I wasn't sure if I was relieved or unnerved by the fact that Tess saw this man as safe or that the man who hugged my mother in a grocery store had a naked lady on his arm.

"Who's Stav?" I demanded.

"Stav is an angel," Tess answered without looking back at me.

"Suave," Olivia said. This dubious angel's name rhymed with the name of the strawberry shampoo that Olivia recognized.

Frankie snickered. "He doesn't look like an angel."

"Stav helps people and guides them to safety."

"From what?" I asked. "What's he saving us from and why are we here? What's so great about this stupid place?"

Olivia gasped. Stupid was a bad word at our house.

"Answers in good time, Esther."

"I really have to go." Frankie had his hand on the door handle.

"Run off behind that tree, Frankie. Quick, like a bunny now."

I fumed after Tess clipped my questions. I had been very patient. I was no longer feeling patient. Olivia and I got out of the car, and we leaned against the car as we waited for Frankie. I looked around the area and had a strange feeling as if I'd been here before. Off from the parking spot was a big, round piece of earth where shrapnel of dead firecrackers and other fire displays littered the area. The nation's big bicentennial celebration had gone on for weeks earlier in the summer of 1976, and my mother had not been happy the non-stop late-night fireworks kept Olivia upset and sleepless.

"When do we stop celebrating?" Momma had said. "Happy birthday. Now move on."

Daddy had bought a few small fireworks, and of course, the sparklers were a hit with his young audience. Frankie and I had loved the celebration, but Momma and Olivia had stayed inside on the fourth.

"Do another one!" Frankie had encouraged Daddy.

"Step back now." Daddy had been patient with us as he moved to the end of our driveway. "One more, and then we're done."

"Two hundred years is pretty old," I'd said as I covered my ears and ran back toward the house.

The last display was the best, and Frankie had clapped and cheered when it was done. Daddy had put the dead remnants into a bucket of water and looked at me. "You think America's old, Esther?"

"Sure do."

"We're a baby as a country compared to other countries. We're the babies in the world of ancient lands."

"But we're a great country," I had insisted.

"Sure, the powerhouse for the most part. Ironic. I guess you could say that America is precocious."

Precocious.

My dad knew I was a collector of words, and here was a new one. I had only heard the word in the song from Mary Poppins. For as long as I could remember, I could feel words. Momma always said that I loved tasting them. I loved hearing new words, and while I may have heard the word precocious before, it was one that needed clarification.

"Precocious," I'd said slowly. "Something good, right?"

"Right," Daddy encouraged.

"From the song, it seems like it also means smart. Right?"

"Sure, and in the case of America, advanced. Beyond what is expected. So, a baby country that rules the world."

"Daddy," Frankie tugged at my Dad's shirt. "Are you sure we don't have any more crackers?"

"Firecrackers are all done, and so are you, Frankie. Time for bed."

Stav whistled from the motel door and motioned back to a long row of rooms in a building separate from the one with the sign. He held up seven fingers for Tess, and she opened her door and yelled to Frankie, "Room seven. Come on this way, guys. Grab something from the trunk."

Olivia and I got out and moved to the trunk where Tess handed us bags and boxes of food to take to room seven. She took out a jug of milk from the trunk and shut the trunk. "Follow me." We complied. What choice did we have? Stav met us at room number seven, turned the key, and opened the door. A lamp on a desk was the only light in the room containing two beds with gold and rust-striped bedspreads. The room smelled of musty old cigarettes and apple juice. "Just set everything down over on the table." Tess pulled out bowls and spoons from a bag and set them on the table. "How about some Lucky Charms? Breakfast time."

I knew that the Junior Mints were hungry, and so was I, for that matter. I helped Tess get the cereal for us as Stav turned on the small TV in the corner of the room.

"The rain is gone for now, and the heat is settling in on us," The man from Channel Seven warned his viewing audience. "Look for temperatures to hit that hundred-degree mark today. Pay special attention to pets and the elderly during this Omaha heat wave."

"We're keeping the curtains shut today and lying low," Tess said.

"Breaking news on the story of the missing Duvall children."

I looked to the television set which displayed a scene of several flashing lights from police cars behind the strip mall where Marty's father's office was. Reporters were holding a microphone in front of a woman in an apron.

"Betsy Milano of the Cherub Delights Bakery called authorities early this morning to report what she thought was a sighting of the Duvall children."

Betsy spoke into the microphones as she told reporters, "I saw the picture of the older girl on the news last night. I noticed a girl who looked similar with two younger children walking just past the dumpster at about 5:30 this morning from the bakery window by our sink. By the time I moved outside, they were gone. I'm not one hundred percent sure, but I knew I should call."

The reporter on the scene looked into the camera, "Authorities are still asking the city to be on the lookout for the three missing Duvall children."

"Thank you, Tanya. Channel Seven wants to note that you should also be on alert for the mother of the children, who may or may not be with them. Mrs. Duvall may be armed and dangerous."

Stav turned off the television and looked at Tess. I broke the silence. "Armed? What does that mean? Momma's not dangerous. What are they talking about?" I could feel the tears fighting to come out.

"They don't know what they're talking about," Stav said through a thick mustache. "Tara's the kindest soul I know." The new man in our world walked out of the hotel room. Tess moved to the door and shut it.

"Esther, you don't want to get the Junior Mints upset." Olivia and Frankie were finishing their cereal and looking in the box of toys that Tess had brought from our house before it was turned into a crime scene. Frankie pulled out a G.I. Joe. Olivia found her favorite paper dolls. "What you heard on the news isn't true about your mother."

"So how can they even say those things if they aren't true? Everybody watching thinks that they're telling the truth."

"I know," Tess said quietly as she motioned me into the bathroom. "I'm so sorry, Esther." Tess shut the door and pulled me into her, hugging me tightly. I started to cry. "Esther, the news is not always the truth. It is what it is. It's what will make the big story."

"Did Daddy and Momma kidnap a baby, Tess?" I spoke into the shoulder of my nosy neighbor lady as I stared at the pale pink tile of the motel bathroom behind her, sniffling and following the pattern of the tiles: pink, pink, black, pink, pink, black.

Tess said nothing.

"Was it Daniel? Is Daniel the baby they took?" I asked.

Tess pulled back from the hug and looked at me. "Goodness sake, child. How do you know about Daniel?"

"Momma had a picture of the baby in her drawer. I shouldn't have..."

"Of course she did." Tess took a deep breath and seemed to be talking to herself.

"Who's Daniel, Tess?"

"Well... let's see. I think it's best if you hear it from your mother, Esther." Tess stumbled on her words.

"Well, in case you haven't noticed, Momma's missing. So, I can't really ask her."

My point seemed to register as Tess looked at me and laughed. My intention was not to be funny.

"Tess," Frankie said as he knocked on the door. "Did you bring my yoyo? The green one."

"I think so, Frankie. I'll be out in a second."

I put my hands in my pockets in a statement of frustration as Tess opened the door to help Frankie. I felt the piece of paper with Marty's number on it. The sheet read:

402-921-2130

Call me! Marty

Marty. I had almost forgotten to call Marty. I wondered if he'd seen the news.

"Tess?"

"Yes, hon." Tess was helping Frankie pull the knots out of his yoyo string.

"Can I call a friend?"

"I don't think that's such a good idea right now, Esther. I brought a few Nancy Drew books for you."

"He's the friend who protected us from the man at the mall. Please." I moved into the main room and sat on one of the two beds.

"Bad," Olivia spoke as she sorted her paper dolls.

"He's the one who took us to the place to stay last night."

Tess moved over from the table and sat on the bed with me. "Esther, we don't want people knowing where we are."

"He would want to know that we're alright. He gave us food and was real nice."

"Sure." Tess moved toward the phone on the side of the bed. "Would you like me to dial the phone for you?"

"Sure."

90%.

Tess was good.

Tess dialed Marty's number and sat and watched as I pulled the phone to my ear. Three rings. Someone picked up the phone. My heart pounded.

"Hello."

It was Marty.

"Marty?

"Oh, wow. Am I ever glad to hear your voice. Are you all alright?"

"We are."

"Where are you?"

Tess looked at me as I spoke. "I can't say. We're safe though."

"Who are you with?"

"My neighbor, but we are not in our neighborhood. We're in a safe place. She's a good friend of my mom."

"You're sure?"

"Yes."

"Good. Get a piece of paper."

"What?"

"I need you to write something down. So that we both have it, just in case. You can show it to your neighbor lady."

"OK." I looked at Tess. "He wants me to write something down."

Tess turned over the paper with Marty's phone number and pulled a pen from her pocket. "Marty, I'm sorry that I didn't lock the door. I didn't have a key."

"Key," Olivia said from behind me.

"No problem, Esther. I set my alarm for super early and rode my bike to check on you all. When I saw you were gone, I locked the door."

"Oh, good."

"After that, the police and the reporters came. Other cars came too. I hid in the trees behind the strip mall during all the craziness."

"Wow."

"It was like a circus. Anyways, I saw a brown car."

"OK."

"A brown car with a man in a hat. And the kicker: a broken taillight. Pretty sure it was your creepy guy."

By now, Tess was moving her head in to hear what my friend had to say.

"The man in the hat?"

"I'm pretty sure. He was trying not to be seen. Like me. Only he wasn't hiding in the trees, and he wasn't alone. He was with another man, a shorter, heavier guy."

"What do you want me to write down, Marty?"

"His license plate number. I thought you might be interested to know that the guy's not from Omaha or even Nebraska. The plates were California plates."

"California?"

"Do you want the number?"

"Sure."

Tess wrote the letters and numbers down as Marty read them to me. I held the receiver out so that she could hear.

"Hold on a minute, Marty."

I put my hand on the bottom end of the telephone. "Tess, can I give him this number?" Tess moved her mouth into a twisted pose. "Sure."

"Marty, I'm going to give you this number. Promise not to tell anyone?"

"Scout's honor. Even though I've never been a scout."

After I hung up with Marty, I felt tired. Tess had brought us our toothbrushes, and I had never been happier to brush my teeth.

"Tess, what are we going to do with the number you wrote down from the car?" I asked.

"I was thinking about calling Ramona. I still have her number on the card she gave me. She's the only one I trusted in that whole bunch."

I looked through the box of things Tess had gotten from our house. I saw several Nancy Drew books and the MGM coffee table book. I picked up *The Haunted Bridge* Nancy Drew book and lay back on one of the beds. I opened chapter one and started to read. Tess picked up the phone and dialed a number.

"Uh, yes, the shop is open. I have three patterns to sell you if you're interested in sewing anything this afternoon. Would you be able to sew through the night?"

There was a pause.

"Yes, 3:30 would be lovely. Thank you for your business."

Tess hung up. "Alice will be coming by this afternoon to be with you through the night. You can trust her. She's another angel. There are still several cars patrolling your house, and mine too, I'm pretty sure. I need to be home so that they don't suspect me... being with you..."

"Patterns?"

"Yep, today you're each a pattern in a sewing shop. You're all beautiful patterns who need protection while we get this whole thing sorted out."

"Just what are we sorting out?"

Serious question.

"Plenty."

Stupid answer.

Tess grabbed a Dr. Seuss book from her box and got on the bed with the Junior Mints. She started reading about different colored fish as the sleep monster jumped on my back; I fought the heaviness of sleep with a book in my hand. The long night before with little sleep and a nightmare sent me into a several-hour nap that day in the Shamrock Motel somewhere outside of Omaha. Along with Frankie and Olivia, I napped.

Alice, or, as Frankie called her in the years following that summer, Crazy Alice, showed up with long, frizzy blonde hair and a fiery spirit to match. Her flowing colorful skirt and white t-shirt against her tanned skin were accented with a fringed belt and all sorts of beaded jewelry. Her shirt had large cursive letters: *Love Child.*

"You're up!" Alice's big blue eyes batted at me no less than six inches from my face. "You're the ringleader, right? You look like you're large and in charge."

Frankie and Olivia both woke from their naps to the loud voice of yet another new adult in our world. "Who are you?" Frankie asked.

"I'm Alice, and I'm here to help y'all have fun. But don't tell Tess." If Crazy Alice said, "Don't tell Tess" once, she said it a hundred times in the hours that she stayed with us. "We're going to play games and have root beer floats and A&W burgers and watch all the TV you want. You're just the cutest little patterns I've worked with in a long time."

Olivia and Frankie stared at Alice, mesmerized by her aura.

"You're not really patterns. I'm just talking shop. No more sad faces. Before we play games, let's jump on the bed." Alice kicked off her sandals and hopped up on the bed. "Just don't tell Tess."

I sat with Olivia while Frankie and Alice jumped on the bed, singing a song that Frankie had never heard before.

Ten little monkeys jumping on the bed, one fell off and bumped his head.

Frankie jumped and giggled. Olivia whimpered.

Momma called the doctor, and the doctor said: No more monkeys jumping on the bed.

True to her word, Alice had brought root beer floats and dinner from A&W. I'd never had a root beer float, and Frankie thought he'd died and gone to heaven. We ate our dinners on the floor in front of the small TV, watching *Sonny and Cher*.

"OK, so I once saw Cher in L.A. She's even prettier in person. And Sonny, why he's just this little toad next to her. A cute toad."

"Are you from Omaha?" I asked Alice.

"Now I am. Not originally." Alice took a big slurp from her root beer float and made a loud, funny noise. Frankie belted out a laugh. "I'm from all over, I guess. You want to learn a trick, Ringleader?"

I realized she was talking to me. I nodded.

"OK, so when a person's talking to you, you can tell if they're lying or not." I usually could tell if a person was being honest. I just felt it in my gut.

"So, first," Alice said slowly, "you ask a person a question. Like, why did you get home late?"

Sounded like Alice had experience on this one.

"When the person answers," Alice continued, "you watch their eyes as they answer the question." Alice's big blue eyes sparkled as she revealed her magic. "If the eyes of the person answering you look up to their left, they are looking to their memory bank. Remember their left would be your right. Got it?"

"Sure." I'm not sure I wanted it, but I got it.

"But," Alice looked to Frankie and Olivia as she continued, "if that person looks to his right—the creative side of the brain—he's making up a story."

We all sat and waited for the punch line.

"They're lying! Don't you get it!"

Frankie giggled.

Alice explained. "So, let's say, for the sake of argument, that the person looks right and says, I'm late because the person driving me home had to drop off a meal for his sick mother... Lie!"

"So what's the truth?" Frankie asked.

"Well, maybe he was having so much fun at a party that he lost track of time. I don't know. It was just an example."

"What if," Frankie grinned and spoke to Alice, "the person's eyes are crossed?" Frankie fell on the floor laughing.

Olivia giggled and moved closer to Alice, holding her arms out to her as if she was reaching for something. "What do you need, Baby Doll?" Alice cooed. "What can I do for you?"

Olivia moved closer to Alice, and Frankie looked at me, confused. Olivia didn't like to be held. Olivia did not like direct eye contact. And she most definitely didn't like people new to her world. Momma once told us to respect the bubble around Olivia and respect her space. "If you put a hula hoop around her, that would be her bubble. Just stay out of the hula hoop unless she comes toward you." Alice was new and, in my opinion, kind of different. Either Tess told Alice about Olivia, or Alice must have sensed the invisible hula hoop as she sat still and waited. Olivia moved closer to Alice and moved her hand up to Alice's earrings. The big red and yellow earrings moved back and forth even as Alice sat still. Olivia touched the earrings.

Olivia spoke: "Pretty."

I think I forgot to breathe as the entire Olivia episode transpired. A tickle in my throat made me cough loudly, and Olivia pulled back from Alice. Alice took off her earrings. "You like the pretty colors? Here you go, Baby Doll. They're yours. I made them myself."

"She loves colors and rainbows and stuff," Frankie said, as he picked up her pinwheel and showed Alice the music box with the rainbow ballerina.

"Key," Olivia said as she held up the earrings and moved the beads back and forth.

Magical Alice had been accepted into the rarely visited inner circle of Olivia Duvall. Olivia played with the earrings right next to Alice as we watched *Kojak*. Alice looked through the MGM coffee table book as the music to the Channel Seven ten o'clock news came on. For once, the Duvall family was not the top story of the night.

"Dangerously hot temperatures in Omaha today sent most to the pool or at least the basement to cool down. Andrea Teller is live on the scene at Memorial Park where entire families are camping out in the night air on blankets to sleep in the park in an unusual effort to fight the heat." The film footage showed a hill at Memorial Park in the darkness of the night with blankets everywhere. Maybe the Duvall family would have camped out on the hill, if the Duvall family were at home. We would all line up our blankets next to each other and be like any other regular family on an abnormally hot night in the Midwest. We would be normal.

"This book is freakin' amazing," Alice said, leafing through the big book. "I remember watching *The Wizard of Oz* on TV every Thanksgiving. Those weird monkeys used to give me nightmares. I saw *Gone with the Wind* once in the movie theater. In that entire movie, everyone was trying to save Tara. It was amazing."

The man reading the news story then transitioned. "On this hot night, authorities are still searching for the Duvall children and any leads to their whereabouts. Please call the number on the screen if you have any information."

Alice jumped up and turned off the television set. "OK, so are you all ready to go swimming? What do you say, Ringleader?" Alice looked at me and swirled around to Frankie. "And you, young man, I think I'm gonna have to call you Wise Guy. What's up, Wise Guy?" Alice used a funny voice and pretended to hold a cigar.

Frankie looked at Alice and said, "We don't have our swimsuits, and Olivia's afraid of the water." I hadn't seen a motel pool when we parked.

"Well, we're gonna swim in our dirty clothes and tell Tess that we washed them. Baby Doll can sit on the side of the pool and watch our towels." Olivia grinned as she looked away. "What do you say, Ringleader?" Alice was letting me make the call.

"Sounds good to me," I said. I was excited to not think about bad things or lying adults.

"OK, then let's go. Wise Guy?"

Frankie looked at Alice.

"When I say your name, you say here. Wise Guy?"

"Here!" Frankie shouted.

"Ringleader?"

"Here," I said.

"Baby Doll?"

We all looked at Olivia, and Olivia smiled and looked down. "Here," she whispered.

The Shamrock Motel pool was behind the long row of motel rooms. The lack of lighting and the dirt and leaves in the bottom of the deep end did not even bother us. We had run through the sprinkler in our backyard, but we'd never been in a real swimming pool. Olivia sat by the towels near the end of the pool and smiled. Alice, who had changed into shorts and a T-shirt, jumped in. Frankie and I jumped in behind her. Alice caught Frankie as he jumped in again and again, and she complimented me on my jumps. Alice sang the ABBA song *Waterloo* as we swam. Frankie chimed in, and I thought Alice was going to lose it over the fact that a six-year-old knew all the words to ABBA's *Waterloo*.

"We know the words to all of them," Frankie shouted, as he jumped into Alice's arms.

"I'm not sure that I know all of the words. I'm impressed."

"We know the words," Frankie said, "But I don't know what they mean. What's a Waterloo?"

"Waterloo is a battle. And the woman singing the song is basically saying, well, she's saying that she's a prisoner to this guy."

"Prisoner?" Frankie asked, as he got ready to jump in the pool again. "Then why does she sound so happy?"

"I know. That part's weird to me, too," Alice looked at me. "Don't you think that's weird, Ringleader?"

I thought about it. "I guess. Why would you feel like you win, when you lose?"

Alice said, more serious than she had been all night, "I guess the girl feels like she can't leave him." Alice paused. "But she should! Leave Waterloo. Walk away from the battle! Be a prisoner no more. That's my vote. Make a big splash this time, Wise Guy. Let's get Baby Doll wet!"

Olivia giggled and moved away from the pool.

That night in a pool behind a motel that no longer exists is one of the most vivid memories I have to this day. Smells. Sounds. Colors. The moon glowing over us. My dad was in a jail cell, alone and probably worried about us. I had no idea where my mom was. In retrospect, as an adult looking back at the pool, I know that we were in a dirty old motel pool behind a rundown motel, but at the time, I found it to be a moment of heaven in a really bad summer.

Olivia handed out towels after Alice whistled. "That marks the end of the Duvall Swimming Olympics."

"Do we have dry clothes?" Frankie asked.

I don't think that Alice ever thought about the small detail of dry clothes. She looked at me: "Ringleader?" We found clothes in the bottom of the box on the table. An outfit I hated, but I wore that night to bed. Alice slept with Olivia. I lay with Frankie in the other bed. The Junior Mints were quickly asleep as I sorted through the past few days in my head.

"You OK, Ringleader?" I gathered that Alice, whose frizzy blonde curls were now wet, dark and straight from the pool, was struggling with getting to sleep as well. "I'm sorry about getting your clothes wet. They should be dry by tomorrow."

"I don't care about wet clothes."

"What do you care about, Esther?"

I looked up at the moonlight streaming against the ceiling in our room. "My family."

"You're good stuff, Ringleader."

The shadow of a tree branch moved around on the ceiling.

"Esther, I wish I could tell you that everything will be alright, but I don't know that to be true. I do know that you will always have the angels to protect you. That I guarantee."

"I just don't get it all. Angels and patterns with a shop. What does it have to do with my parents? I know that my dad's in jail and my mother disappeared. Nothing else." My voice cracked on the word else.

Alice spoke after a long silence. "It's a long story."

"I'm listening."

"Well, first you need to know that Tara is about the nicest woman on this planet. We went through some really tough times together."

I had never once heard Momma mention an Alice.

"Wow, where to start. I guess I have to ask you: if something has goodness when it starts, and then it turns bad, is the goodness still inside?"

"I guess so." I started to think that I'd never hear what had happened to Momma. Alice hadn't answered my question about the angels.

"Ringleader, have you ever been a part of group that started out great?"

"Sure." My family. My classes at school. The Daisy Troop.

"And then it went really bad."

The Daisy Troop.

"Tara and I were at a bad place that had once been a good place. And then bad things started to happen to us. Really bad things."

"Alice, did my dad hurt my mom?"

"No. Goodness no. That man adores her. He would die for her."

"Did my parents kidnap a baby?"

There was a pause and then: The truth. "Yes."

"Was it Daniel?"

"Daniel? You know about Daniel?"

"Was it?"

"No."

"Then who was it? Will anybody give me an answer?"

The trees were moving back and forth in quick movements as what felt like a storm was brewing. I thought about the families sleeping at Memorial Park.

"Baby Doll."

"What?"

Alice's silence was her answer.

"That doesn't even make any sense."

"It's true."

"But Olivia is Frankie's twin, so how is that kidnapping?"

"Because Olivia isn't Frankie's twin."

I took a deep breath. Through the sheer curtain of the only window, I saw movement. "Sorry, Esther. Have you ever looked at the two of them? They are day and night."

"That's because Olivia's different…"

"Not how Olivia is, how Olivia looks. Olivia has blonde hair and brown eyes. Frankie has blue eyes and curly dark hair."

"Momma and Daddy kidnapped Olivia?"

"Yes, but not in a bad way. They were helping her."

And just like that, I was scared to death to hear any more truth about what was going on. "Sorry, Esther. I knew that you were about to find that out, and well, to hear it now."

Hurt like hell.

"Baby Doll, well, she had a mom that was unstable. Do you know what I mean by unstable?"

I did.

"Baby Doll's mother couldn't take care of her, so, Tara and Clark took her to help her." Frankie said something in his sleep that sounded like *run* and rolled over.

"You need to get to sleep, Esther. Sorry to hit you with so much, uh…" Probably for the first time in her life, Alice was at a loss for words.

"Truth?" I said.

"Yah, truth."

"So, Daddy's not in jail for hurting Momma?"

"Right."

"They really did kidnap a baby."

"Yes, ma'am."

"And Momma's not dead."

"Right. Tara's with other angels. She didn't want to put you all in danger with the people who were part of the bad place. From what I heard, one of them found you three the other day."

"Alice," I whispered. "I think someone's outside our door."

Alice yawned. "That's just Stav, sweetie. He's guarding us. If you look close enough at the silhouette of his big body out there, you can see his wings."

I looked at the angel outside of our window. I looked over at Alice, whose eyes were now closed. Alice was sparkly. Alice was fun.

Alice was the truth.

8
Katherine

1966

The edges of the 8" by 10" picture of Stacie's freshman class photo were torn and ragged, and her likeness was blurry, both from the weather and the fact that the enlarged photo made her face indistinct.

But from a good ten feet, you could still see who had been smiling at a camera over ten years ago. At least, that's what her ex-boyfriend said after he saw the picture on the back of Mick's truck parked on the side of Thai Pepper House in San Francisco.

"Hell, anyone would know that's Stormy. You can't hide her beauty."

"You think you know the girl in this picture?" Mick stopped and asked the man who was standing on the curb, his long hair unkempt and his bare feet dirty.

"Know her? I love her. Wish she still loved me, but that ship has sailed, my man." The young shoeless man moved closer to the photo and back again. "Shit, that picture's just like that Jesus picture. You know, the one where the eyes follow you wherever you go. It's like Stormy is watching over me. Even if she doesn't love me anymore."

Enticing smells poured out of the side door of Thai Pepper House as Mick put down a large box of take-out containers he was carrying into the kitchen door by the alley and zoned in on the young man staring at the picture on his truck. The strange man didn't carry much integrity with his appearance, but his insistence that he knew the girl in the picture—a picture that had been on Mick's truck for almost four years with not one nod of recognition—made Mick want to question the man more.

"Would you have seen this Stormy recently?"

"Every day. That's why it's so hard to get over her, man. She's into loving everyone, and I just hate watching that. You know what I mean? Stormy told me she needed to be free."

"I'm Mick. And you are?"

"River. Always moving. Always changing. River."

"OK, River, I know someone who would very much like to find the woman in this picture. She's been hoping to find her for a long time."

"Find her? Stormy's not lost. She's found. Floating in her freedom."

"Any chance you could take me to her, River? After I drop off a few more boxes, I could give you a ride to where Stormy's floating. Would that work for you?"

"Sure."

Good news, bad news.

Mick told me that the good news was that River helped him find London's sister. The bad news was she was not in a good place, physically or emotionally. They drove to the heart of the city at that time: Haight-Ashbury, an intersection on a two-way street where young and high dreamers congregated by the thousands in 1966. Initially, Mick thought it would be impossible to find Stacie in the sea of psychedelic love, but

Mick's new waterway friend led him right to River's ex-love. In a stairwell outside of a dry cleaner, Stacie—or Stormy— was making out with a tall man, not unlike River, though she obviously thought so.

"See what I mean?" River pointed to the busy couple in a stairwell of an old hotel. "She's killing me, man."

"You're sure that's her?" Mick still wasn't convinced.

"Stormy!" River called out. The woman broke from her kiss. Her eyes were glazed as she tried to focus on River, but Mick could see the resemblance to the school picture. "Stormy, someone's looking for you," he shouted. River had said that Stormy was floating in freedom, but she looked like she was drowning in a drug haze.

"What the hell?" The man with Stormy moved up the stairs. "I told you to leave her alone." Stormy's new love was a good head taller than River. Perhaps his name was Mountain.

"I'm talking about this man here." River ignored the mountain man, looked at Stormy, and pointed to Mick. "He has your picture on his truck. I'm serious, man. He knows someone who's looking for you, Stormy."

A woman with long, curly blonde hair moved toward the stairs. "Who's looking for Stormy?"

"I am," Mick said. "Actually, her sister is. I'm helping her out."

Stormy turned around and sat on the top step of the stairwell. She put her hands over her face and began to cry. The man who had been kissing her walked up the steps and past the group, tired of the conversation, on to the next person to love. The woman with the long blonde hair turned to Mick. "You've made her sad." She bent down and put her arms around the woman on the step, who looked like a little girl sobbing.

"Her sister's been very worried about her," Mick said, still not sure if this was London's sister or just a doppelganger. Maybe some real names would divulge the truth. "Stacie, your sister wants to help you. Stephanie. Do you remember Stephanie?"

Stormy stopped crying. Her eyes were still glazed as she looked up at him. "Stephanie?"

"I can take you to her."

River bent down to rub Stormy's back. "You should go, Storm."

"She's alive?" Stormy looked at Mick. "She's OK?"

"She's doing great," Mick, told her. "She misses you."

Stormy stared at Mick as though she were trying to find her sister in his eyes. "Who are you?"

"I'm Mick. I deliver food and supplies to the place where your sister lives. I can take you there."

"Can I go with you if you take her?" the blonde woman said. "I'm Blaze. Stormy and I've been together for a long time."

"I need to see her," Stormy said.

"I can take you to the place where she is. But no drugs. They don't allow drugs."

Stormy mumbled as she stood up. "I'm so tired."

Mick wasn't sure if she was tired of drugs or just tired, but he told the girls to get in his truck. He shook River's hand before climbing into the cab of his truck. "Sorry, River, I guess she really is moving on."

"Noted," River, said as he shook back. "Noted, man."

"Be good," Mick called out as he got in the driver's side.

"That's the plan." River sat on the stairs and waved.

Mick and his new cargo drove away from a river with a fiery storm. He told me that the cab of his truck smelled like sweet tarts and marijuana on the trip to Celestial Way, a paradox of innocence and frightening adulthood. The smell changed after Stormy threw up. I had mixed emotions when Mick showed up on a day when he wasn't scheduled to make deliveries to Celestial Way with two wayward girls, one extremely out of it.

"I found London's sister."

My heart skipped a beat. I hadn't once—in all the time we'd been waiting for news of the lost sister of London—thought that London's sister would be found. I hadn't thought about how Charles would react to the arrival of someone through Mick.

"She's kind of a mess, but here she is."

Mick walked the thin and dirty girls from the dock behind the kitchen on a late, windy afternoon. Lottie helped me move the girls to the kitchen as she gave me a look over their heads. "Welcome, ladies." Lottie's voice boomed against the walls of the empty dining hall. Adults and kids would be filling the room within the hour. "I'll put together two plates for you. Looks like you could both put some meat on your bones."

"That'd be great." Blaze held Stormy's arm as they walked to a chair in the kitchen. Stormy's denim sun dress looked as though she had worn it for several days.

"I've got these two covered. Dylan, would you go and set up the small cottage, #14. I think we sent fresh bedding out there just yesterday."

I hadn't seen Dylan move into the room. Dylan, now a pudgy, surly twelve-year-old, stood back from the discussion, his arms crossed, his face pouting. "I don't want to get the cottage ready."

Lottie moved toward Dylan and whispered loudly, "I'm very sure I didn't hear you speak. Get to the cottage now."

Dylan's eyes grew large, and his fair cheeks grew red. He stormed out of the dining hall. "Thanks for your help!" I yelled to him. Lottie and I knew that Dylan, who pouted on a daily basis, was even more bad-tempered since he had not been chosen to be on the Youth Committee. Both Dylan and Maureen had been in the group for younger kids: the Strong Seeds, which met weekly with Captain. The Direction Team had not selected Dylan to be a part of the Youth Committee—teenagers being trained for leadership at Celestial Way in the years to come. Maureen was in the select group, which met daily and reminded the unchosen of their blatant rejection. I felt for Dylan and Lottie, but Lottie and I both knew that Dylan got along with very few kids and adults.

"I'm putting food together for the two." Lottie pulled out two plates and grabbed a big spoon. "Mick said he had questions about the next order after you're done here."

"It was kind of Dylan to help."

"That kid will be the death of me yet," Lottie mumbled, as she scooped stew into the bowls. "Does London know yet? About her sister being here?"

"I sent Maureen to go get her."

As Lottie put together the food for the girls, I moved them to a table in the kitchen, away from any of the lunch traffic. "How was the ride here?" I asked the girls, trying to focus on everyday normal activities.

"I'm Blaze." Stormy's friend threw out her hand. I shook the dirty hand of Blaze.

"Well, let's get you some food and a good night's sleep," I said. Stormy held her sides as she rocked back and forth. I suddenly had a head rush from sitting for the first time all day.

"I can't thank you enough," Blaze said. "It was like that guy in the truck was an angel. I don't think I could have carried her much longer. Stormy just needs to get away from, you know, all the influences. She's so strong in so many ways." Stormy looked anything but strong as she started to shake. I went into my office to grab her a blanket and saw London in the door to the back kitchen when I got back to the table.

"Stacie?" London moved as quickly as I'd ever seen, running toward her sister. "It's really you? Stormy sobbed as London hugged her. The two rocked together as Lottie put two plates of food on the table.

"Lottie, could you send Tina to help the girls get settled?" I asked, as I put on my sweater to go see Mick out by the loading dock.

"I'll make sure she stays the night with them." Lottie headed toward our new blazing storm.

"I'm not going to lie. I guess I kind of thought the girl in the faded high school picture was a myth." Mick pulled a clipboard from the back of his truck.

"Agree," I said. "I felt like we were supporting London through you keeping a picture on your truck."

"Hey, are you alright? You look… washed out."

"Just a little tired. One of those long days, you know, when everyone needs something right now. Who's the other girl? With London's sister."

"Blaze. At least, that's what she wants to be called today. Pick a part of nature or a silly reference and you've got a new identity. By the way, river has already been taken."

"What?"

"I'm a hundred percent sure that Blaze isn't the real name of the friend of London's sister. It's like, these people think that by changing their names, they're automatically someone else. You can't run from yourself."

"Stormy?"

"Stormy is Stacie, and Stacie or Stormy has a huge problem with drugs. And now, she's your problem."

"I'm just not sure how to do this." I said, more to myself than anyone else.

"You do this all the time. Take in lost souls. Isn't that what Celestial Way's about?"

"I guess we just set them up…" Charles would be home from New York in a day or two. Would he find out that London had kept her yearbook and that Captain had let her? Warm tears filled my eyes.

"Kat." Mick gently touched my arm. "It's a good thing. You're a good person to take care of these girls." Mick knew me more than most. I never showed my vulnerable side to anyone, not even Charles. As Charles traveled more and more, I found that I couldn't turn to anyone at the Way. The others looked to me as a leader. Mick was my rock. He'd sometimes stop by at the end of his shift and take me for a ride in his truck after the people of the vineyard had all settled in for the night. We'd drive the back roads beyond the rough areas of the vines, Mick playing the radio with the latest music I'd never heard. Mick was my only friend.

"Thank you for finding her." I couldn't look at Mick.

"I'm behind on my schedule. Get some rest now. I'll see you next week, Movie Star."

I finished the latest order and paid several bills long after the dinner team had finished dishes and wiped down tables in the dining hall. I planned on going to cottage #14 to check on the girls after I finished my business agenda for the next day. I took the time to straighten everything on my desk as a light January wind blew against my office window. My rituals helped me to believe that there was still an order and a purpose in my world, the only true purpose being Maureen. She was the reason I held tight to the routine.

I moved a folder on the top of my desk, and the corner of an envelope caught my eye. I thought I had gone through all the mail: bills and orders, requests for Celestial Way to advertise, and all the daily correspondence. I had missed this one envelope. There was a return address but no name. The mailing and return address were both in handwriting, and the mailing address was to me. My heart skipped a beat, but I took a deep breath, as I knew I didn't recognize the handwriting to be anyone from my past family. I grabbed the letter opener as a wave of nausea took over my body.

I read the letter written on cream stationery.

Dear Katherine,

My wife and I wanted to thank you again for yet another amazing weekend at Celestial Way last month. We love the getaways, spending time in your cottages, and taking in the beauty of your beautiful vineyard.

On another note, separate from our wine orders and weekends at Celestial Way, I wanted to request a business partnership with you and your amazing cinnamon rolls: Celestial Cinnamon. My company's expanding, and I sense a successful business venture in such a partnership. Please consider my request.

Sincerely, Bernard Cutler

Not a note from my Fallen Family. Not a message from my past.

But a nice note, nonetheless.

Celestial Cinnamon.

It had a nice ring to it. My recipe—or my mother's recipe—had been a staple of the daily menu for the past ten years, Lottie making dozens each morning. The wealthy visitors to our cottages would have a plate of them on the tables in their cottages right next to fresh flowers. It had always been the nice touch that made them want to come back for another visit. It was actually my idea to have guests, Charles placing parameters around the price and time of visits. The lucrative measure had meant that I found a true friend in Bernie Cutler, one of the wealthiest men in Houston, a self-made man who owned several classy restaurants downtown and in the growing metropolis. He ordered hundreds of Celestial Way bottles yearly for his restaurant and personal use. He was the first visitor to the weekend cottages, not even blinking at the asking price for the chance to spend a getaway weekend with his wife in a California vineyard.

Footsteps down the hallway startled me. I got up to see if Lottie was still working in the kitchen. It was very late. I saw a man run by my door toward the kitchen area. When I moved out of my office toward the kitchen, Eugene was running water in the sink.

"Everything alright?" My voice echoed against all the walls of the empty dining hall.

Eugene stopped and looked at me. "Miss Katherine." Relief covered his face. "You have a minute?" Eugene had grown on me. His serious and intimidating "bodyguard" first impression soon evolved into a solid reputation of honesty and loyalty, just with a very dry nature. After several encounters with Captain's personal assistant, I realized that he was a caretaker more than the muscle to fight off bad guys. You couldn't find a better guy if you tried. Mick's words.

"Sure." I moved quickly toward the sink and saw that he was running water over several kitchen towels.

"Captain. He's just not doing well." Eugene made no eye contact as he gathered the wet towels.

Not doing well.

Code for Captain was drinking heavily. During the most recent years, the episodes only worsened. The irony: a man with a thick German accent drinking Irish whiskey at a place that made California wines. The irony: the man who was supposed to be in charge never helped with any of the heavy lifting. When Charles and Rocco were on wine trips, I was the one who handled the problems and made the big decisions. The irony.

"Is he in his room?" I grabbed a few more towels and followed Eugene, who was already running back down the hallway to their quarters. Our footsteps echoed down the long corridor. I saw a light coming from Captain's door to his room. Eugene pushed it open with his hip and ran to Captain, who was lying on the floor. Blood was everywhere. I felt the little food I had eaten during the day move up to my throat. Captain was lying on the floor, moaning.

"You'll be okay, sir. Walter, look at me." Eugene spoke softly as he had Captain move to his side, covering the back of his head with one of the wet kitchen cloths. "It's just one of those head wounds that bleeds like crazy. You're going to be okay."

"What happened?" I asked, praying my food would stay down. I stepped around the blood on the floor and placed my kitchen towels on the puddles of blood. Though I didn't see any, I could smell vomit. I took a deep breath.

"Took a spin."

"Spin." The word slurred out of Captain's mouth; his eyes glazed not unlike those of Stormy.

"That's right." Eugene moved Captain to sit up. "We've got to get you feeling better, Walter. Charles will be home soon."

"Hmmm?" Captain's word was inaudible.

"Charles. The Doctor will be back to the Way, maybe even tomorrow, and we can't have him seeing you like this."

"Yah, soon." The larger-than-life man who had led the beautiful Releasing Ceremonies, so big in my first memories of Celestial Way, was little and pathetic.

"Let's move you to your bed, sir. You'll feel better after I bandage your head and get you some aspirin." Eugene, his muscular arms bigger than the legs on most men, flexed as he lifted the ragdoll Captain and carried him to his bed.

"I'll get some aspirin," I offered, as I hurried away from the smells of the room. I went back to my office and opened my drawers with the medical orders and special medicines. I grabbed the aspirin, moved to the hallway, and stalled for a moment. I was tired and nauseated, not ready to go back to the room where I hoped Eugene was cleaning the blood before I returned. I looked down the corridor from my office to the Main Office, the biggest office at the end of the corridor with beautiful wood trim and plush furniture. The Main Office. That's what we called it. London cleaned it every day. When it was in use, either Captain or Charles was in the room, leading a meeting or a Revealing Session. I believed it originally was the main Abbot's office when it was owned by the monks. It was stately, manly and intimidating—deliberate and intentional on all counts.

The Revealing Sessions.

The Revealing Sessions were intended to be an extension of the Releasing Ceremonies. They were to cleanse our soul of the last and darkest spot, the most secret piece of our previous life that might be holding us back from the beauty of the perfect existence. Our community's purpose depended upon each member's complete surrender to the mission of Celestial Way.

"We must separate ourselves completely from our past," Captain would say. "We must detach ourselves entirely from our Fallen Family. You must divide yourself from The Before so that we may all enter into The After. The Rapture. And if you are ever to reach the Rapture, the ultimate peace, complete union with our higher power, you will need to get there through the Way: the Releasing and the Revealing are the only way to the Rapture."

My vivid memory of my Revealing included the long walk down this hallway, the entrance into the Main Office, and the invitation to a big chair across from a desk, where Captain, Charles and Rocco sat.

"It is time to take the demon from your past, the biggest secret that haunts you, and reveal it to the Way. We are united in our sharing of that which darkens our souls." Captain's accent became rich and powerful when he preached about Celestial Way. "In keeping those confidences close to our home here, we are made stronger as a community. If you don't see yourself for who you really are—the good and the bad—how can you help Celestial Way?"

When I thought of that day, I acknowledged that my concerns for my Fallen Family, and my speculation about their lives and if they think of me—all neat and quiet in my Honesty Box—have always been exempt from Celestial Way's request. But people kept secrets at Celestial Way. Captain allowed London to keep her brother's yearbook. Eugene didn't want Charles to find out how bad Captain got during his traveling days. I could only imagine the other secrets that hid in the shadows of everyday life at the Way.

That day of my Revealing, only a week after I first arrived at the winery, an angsty college student ready for something beautiful, I gave Captain one, and only one, haunting secret, the one that, even though it was revealed to the Way, still haunted me today.

"My father…" I lost my voice and cleared my throat. "My father took money."

"Your father."

"Yes. From his company. The place where he worked for as long as I can remember."

"And?"

How did he know there was more?

"And," I hesitated, "And he took care of both my family and another…"

"Another?"

"Woman. He took care of us and this person."

"Did the company know about the money?"

I didn't answer.

"Did your mother know about the woman?" Captain's voice got louder and his accent richer.

I didn't answer.

"And you know this how?"

"I know this because I heard my father on the telephone one night, the night before I graduated from high school. I heard him talking to her. The woman."

Captain said nothing.

"He called her Rita. My precious Rita. Not my mother's name."

The room was silent. Why was the Revealing so painful when the Releasing was so peaceful? Rocco cleared his throat. Charles moved in his chair.

"He told her that he was taking the money from Province Bank. That he…" I stopped.

"That he what?" This time, Captain's voice was soft and encouraging.

"He told her that no one would know that he took it. That he had taken little amounts, over time. Something like that."

I could hear the ticking of the clock.

"He told her that he would always take care of her." I looked down as I spoke. I wanted to leave the room. "That he loved her."

Charles looked as though he were moving to comfort me. He stopped.

"You are free, Miss Katherine," Captain announced.

I felt terrible.

"You are free of the darkest part of your past."

I did not feel free. I felt bad. Really bad.

"You'll always have the Way to guide you toward the greatest peace. To the Rapture. We are your family now. We are your Forever Family."

Captain, the man who organized and led the Revealing Sessions in the past years, was no longer a leader. He was a little old German drunk. At that moment, just like the bile coming up my throat, my anger toward both my father and my mother reared its ugly head.

My mother was demanding to my father, never in public, always at home. She berated him daily, saying how we never had enough and how we should be living a better life. My father, who I had always assumed was the strong, patient, silent type, was none of those things. He was weak. I'd always admired how he tried to please my mother, but that night, I could see that he had his own vices. And the foundation that had always felt so secure and right disintegrated as I listened to a phone call, my brother and mother both sleeping upstairs, my father whispering in the living room.

My precious Rita.

That night, any fear or anxiety I had previously felt about leaving home, going so far, being away from family, had evaporated. I wanted out. I was glad to go.

Inaudible voices. Voices from men outside of the door to the loading dock near my business office erased the memory.

"Can... always."

Laughter.

"I've got it..."

I recognized the second voice: Charles. Charles was back early.

And Captain was not in a good place.

The door from the dock opened, and Charles and Rocco, both holding boxes, moved into the kitchen area. Rocco flicked on the light. I stood holding a bottle of aspirin and the secret of Captain.

"Katherine," Rocco yelled. "You're still up."

"It's late, Katherine. You should be in bed." Charles set down a large box on the kitchen counter.

I felt guilty about my little secret, but Charles looked like he was hiding something as well.

"I'm taking aspirin to two ladies that joined us today. What are you two doing home early?" I tried to manipulate my voice to sound curious instead of suspicious. It didn't work.

"We finished up with a deal and decided to cut short the RD and head back home," Rocco said, also unsuccessful in sounding innocent.

RD.

I had seen the initials before. On bills, on letters. RD.

"What's in the box?" I moved toward the box which Charles was standing in front of by now. "It must have been a good trip to finish so early." I looked toward the corridor that led to the living quarters.

"We received gifts." Charles moved to hug me. "How's my little gift?" Odd expression for a man who usually refrained from such endearing terms.

"She's in bed and doing well."

"Is she liking the Youth Committee?"

"She is." I peered over the top of the box.

Charles lifted the top of the box and pulled out what looked like a big camera. "We received a few new gadgets from Alex Corbin in New York. He's the guy who bought most of this month's Cabernet batch. This camera spits out the picture as soon as you take it. Here, Rocco, take our picture." Charles handed the camera to Rocco who looked at the camera with mystery. "That button, the black one." Charles pointed and put his arms around me. I could smell his cologne, still strong at 10:30 at night. The days upon days, sometimes weeks went 'for the sake of the community' and the fun that Rocco and Charles were having.

"I missed you, Katherine." Lie. "Now look at Rocco and smile."

We both looked at the camera, Charles leaning into me.

"Look!" Rocco sounded like a kid at a circus.

A piece of thick white paper spit out of the front of the camera. Charles grabbed it. "Now, just wait." He started shaking the paper. "It's called a Polaroid camera. The film is being processed as we speak. The processing chemicals are in the camera."

I could smell the chemicals. I also could see Eugene peek his head around the corridor wall. Eugene and I made eye contact, he nodded, and he disappeared.

"When you snap a shot, the hole of the camera here opens briefly to let in the pattern of light reflected from whatever you are taking a picture of." Charles was as excited to share his knowledge of the camera as he was fascinated with the gadget. "The reflected pattern of light hits the film, which absorbs different colors."

"Magic." Rocco was mesmerized at the picture forming in front of our eyes. I could make out a blurry image of Charles and me.

"Chemistry." Charles held out the photograph that was now fully developed. The image on the paper was of a handsome man dressed in expensive clothes standing next to a woman in an old blouse and skirt. The woman looked tired. The man smiled as he leaned into the woman.

"Wait," Rocco said, as he pulled a pen from the box. "We need to document this moment."

On the bottom of the picture was a white space. In childlike writing, Rocco wrote.

Charles and Katherine

January 30th, 1966

The camera had captured a moment that had just happened, and the moment had been documented. My grandmother, who never liked having her picture taken, had told me that some cultures believed that if someone took your picture, they were taking a piece of your soul. I didn't see my soul in the photograph. I saw a lie.

I looked at Charles. He looked disappointed at my reaction, as though he could hear my thoughts. These "gadgets" went against every philosophy that he preached to the members of Celestial Way. Charles was becoming more and more selective in his participation in the directives of wisdom on the path to peace.

"They're gifts, Katherine. We had no choice but to take them, to acknowledge the gesture. It's business. We won't let the community know about them. It's too much information for the group to take in."

"Just like the gift you brought to Maureen last month?"

Charles had given Maureen a view-master for her birthday. She loved it. She played with it every night before she went to bed. She had five reels. Her favorite was something called *Family Affair,* based on a TV show that was popular in the outer world—a world against which Charles preached in the Releasing Ceremonies and the Revealing Sessions. Charles told her that she was not to tell the other children about the gift. It was a special gift from him to her only.

"Any other 'gifts' in your box?" I asked.

Rocco pulled out another gadget. Charles looked uncomfortable. "Plenty. This one captures your voice. We could use it at our meetings. You push this button and talk. 'This is Rocco and Charles and Katherine. Katherine, say something.'" A reel of brown ribbon moved as another received it.

"I, no..." I didn't want to play with the toys.

"OK, now wait. Here ya go: *This is Rocco and Charles, and Katherine. Katherine, say something... I, no...* Isn't that amazing?"

The technology was amazing. The deceit was not. I looked at Charles. He wouldn't look at me.

"I'm heading to check on the new girls that arrived today." I shook the aspirin bottle, a helpful prop for my own lie. I no longer felt bad about Mick's role in getting the girls to Celestial Way.

"I'll come with you." Charles grabbed my arm. "Rocco, why don't you take the... boxes back to the Main Office."

"Yes sir, Doc."

"I can walk to the girls by myself."

"Katherine, I'm with you." He grabbed my arm and hooked my hand in his arm as I moved out into the chilly night air. "So, tell me about these new people who arrived."

"One has a drug problem."

"Where are they from?"

"They came in from San Francisco this afternoon." I conveniently left the part of Mick out.

"We'll welcome them as we always do." He was trying hard to make up for the gadgets.

"One happens to be London's sister."

"Strange coincidence."

"Yes, strange."

We were about five or six cottages from cottage fourteen. Charles knew I was not happy with him. "Any other news from the time we were away?" He pulled a Jolly Rancher from his pocket.

"Well, Bernie Cutler wants to work with me selling my cinnamon rolls. We sell wine. We could sell pastries."

Charles stopped and bristled. "You spoke to Bernie?"

"No, he sent me a note."

"Bernie should talk to me first. What was he thinking?" Charles' body was a silhouette against the moon. I couldn't see his eyes, but I knew he was glaring.

"Charles, I work with Bernie all of the time with orders. There's no reason he shouldn't have reached out to me. It's my cinnamon roll recipe. It's not a big deal."

"Why wouldn't he contact me?"

"Bernie and I have worked together on the booking of the cottages for his friends. I've brought in a good deal of money of renting out our Wine Weekends. I think I can figure out how to work with him on cinnamon rolls." I started walking toward Cottage # 14.

"You're not working with him."

Words coming from a man who came and went as he pleased, who bent the rules as they worked for him, who had his secrets as much as anyone else. We were almost to the cottage when a man sitting in a chair outside of the cottage called out to us, the light on the porch was bright against the dark California night.

"Nice night tonight."

"Hey, Dave," I replied.

Dave and Tina had come to Celestial Way months earlier and literally floated into the community. Dave was tall and lanky. Tina was tiny, busy, and beautiful. The two were inseparable. Dave and Tina had been camping throughout the California valley, trying to find the truth, when they stumbled upon 'the best kept secret in California.' That's what Tina told me.

Dave and Charles had a great conversation on their first day at the vineyard about trying to find themselves in a sea of cults in California. "We've spent time with the Moonies and another group outside of Los Angeles. Bald heads and drugs were starting to take away from the truth, so we're so glad we found the Way."

"We aren't a cult," Charles said to Dave, "We don't allow drugs. Once the drugs are brought into the equation, it is no longer about the truth."

"Right, and so many times," Dave concurred, "the groups start out as 'different' from religions. But ended up just like that. And you know what they say about the difference between a religion and a cult."

"No, what." Charles asked.

"About a hundred years."

The two had laughed, and I could tell that Dave had won Charles over.

We got to the front door of the cottage, moths flying around the light above the door. "The one girl is pretty messed up." Dave offered his take on the girls. "Tina will stay in there with the girls tonight, and I'll be the night watchman this first night. People want to run after they start detoxing. Seen it one too many times."

I knocked as I opened the door to the cottage, Charles right behind me. "How's everyone doing?"

London stood up with a smile like I'd never seen on her. "Everyone's great." She sat down again on one side of Stormy, who looked showered and much better than she had when she'd arrived, with no flowers in her hair and no dirt on her skin. One of London's standard oversized blouses enveloped Stormy as her friend Blaze sat beside her. Blaze was also in a "London" blouse.

"They're just about to settle in for the night," Tina announced. "I've got them in the bedroom. I'm on the couch for the first few nights." Tina's energy, as she flitted around the small living room, kept everyone entertained as the girls sat on the couch and Charles and I stood at the door. "We'll give Stormy and Blaze a tour of the vineyard tomorrow to see all the that awaits them. Right, ladies?"

Blaze smiled. Stormy stared at Tina as she moved from the table to the counter to the window to the couch.

"I've got to clean the Main Office in the morning, Stacie," London told her sister. "I'll meet up with you all in the dining hall at lunch."

"That's sounds wonderful," Blaze answered for both girls, her hand still holding onto Stormy as though she might blow away. Stormy or Stacie said nothing as the room moved around her. With no make-up or other adornments, Stacie and her beauty stood out more than ever. Her hair was pulled back from her face and dark lashes surrounded golden-brown eyes that darted from London to Blaze to Tina.

"Well, we just wanted to welcome you again," I said, as I put the aspirin on the counter. I looked to Charles, who stared at Stormy. I could not place his mood or expression, something in which I always took pride: reading Charles. At that moment, I knew he was thinking as his tongue moved the green Jolly Rancher around in his mouth, the candy clicking against his teeth. But what was he thinking? He was mesmerized by

Stormy and had zeroed in on her and said nothing since we had entered the cottage.

"Charles, this is Stormy," I said. "London's sister. And this is Blaze. The girls came to the Way this afternoon."

Charles said nothing.

Tina kept the energy going. "Y'all are lucky that you even get a chance to meet the very busy leader of Celestial Way. We don't see him much here since he's always traveling and keeping all the balls in the air. Right, Doctor?" Tina looked at Charles.

"Charles?" I said.

"Yes, balls in the air."

I moved toward Tina and hugged her. "Thank you for taking care of the ladies tonight."

"Charles?"

He followed me out.

"Who is she?" Charles asked.

"Goodnight, y'all. Sleep tight," Dave called to us as we walked past him.

"We will," I called back. "Thanks for keeping watch." I looked at Charles, who was already heading toward the Mother House.

"London's sister." I called to him. "I told you that. What's wrong?" We walked toward the Mother House.

"Nothing, I just wondered who she was."

"Maureen's probably asleep," I said, catching my breath as I stopped. I felt weak and strange.

Charles walked on until he realized I had stopped. He turned back. "What happened?"

I couldn't stand up. I felt myself drop to the ground. Charles ran back to me. "Katherine, are you alright?"

I took a breath. I was glad that another cottage blocked us from Dave's view. No one was outside the Mother House to see us either.

"What's wrong?" Charles leaned down on his knee and put his arms around me.

We were alone for the first time in a long time, and I allowed the single thought that I had denied for several weeks to surface on my lips, a thought that had taunted me for days, something about which I was both thrilled and scared to death.

"I'm pregnant."

9

Esther

Day Five 1976

A round, shiny head was the first thing I saw when I woke up Monday morning. Stav was sitting at the small table in in front of the shaded window of our motel room, reading a newspaper and drinking a cup of coffee. A stream of light was sneaking through the opening and glowing on the top of his bald head like a flicker from a cigarette lighter.

"Where's Alice?" Frankie sat up in his bed, squinted, and looked at Stav. He realized we were alone with Stav for the first time. "Where's Tess?"

"They both needed to leave. I'm here for now." Stav's voice was soft and low, his mouth barely seemed to move under his mustache. Olivia ran to my bed and leaned into me.

"When will Alice be back?" Frankie persisted.

"Not sure."

I looked at the alarm clock on the stand between the beds. "10:30?" The Junior Mints and I were always up early with Momma and Daddy. We had never slept in past 7:30 a.m. "We slept in so late."

What sounded like a gurgling murmur came deep from Stav's chest as his body shook, and he chuckled at my comment. "That was the plan."

"What plan?" Frankie asked.

"We needed you three to lay low in the day, so we asked Alice to keep you up late, so you could rest in the day. It's hot out there, and we can't take you out where people might see you."

From the man who barely spoke came a string of words.

I didn't find any humor in the plan that included, once again, the Duvall children being alone with people we hadn't known seventy-two hours prior to this moment. After Frankie and Olivia finished their bowls of Lucky Charms, I rinsed the bowls and spoons and set them on the small counter to dry. We'd have soup for a later afternoon lunch. Olivia took the box of paper dolls that she and I had made together the day before. I'd drawn the people; Olivia had colored the people—usually in one color each—and I'd cut the people out. The running total was 22 people—three families and three dogs. Olivia laid the paper dolls one-by-one out on the carpet of the small hotel room as Frankie turned on the TV.

We kept the TV on Channel Twelve. Frankie liked *The Electric Company*. Olivia hummed as she moved her imaginary families around. Stav was no longer in the room drinking coffee. He stood outside of our motel door, stirring his coffee. I walked out of the motel room. The warmth of the sun made me sad. Momma would've taken us on a Kiss-the-summer-goodbye adventure to a park or to the zoo. We would have packed our lunches, eaten outside, and talked about what we were looking forward to in the coming school year.

"Coffee spoons." Stav looked off at the main entrance to the Shamrock Motel as he moved the spoon around the inside of his coffee cup.

"Spoons?" I asked.

"*Measure out my life in coffee spoons.* It's a line from a poem."

"A poem about spoons?"

"A very long poem in which a man is talking to himself about feeling isolated. He's struggling with making decisions in life."

I was waiting for the punch line, which hopefully had something to do with coffee spoons.

"He wasn't very good with love. Lots of regret," Stav continued.

What a strange scene: a man with a tattoo of a naked woman wrapped on his arm muscles, quoting poetry about spoons.

"Did anyone really read this poem? Sounds kind of like a pity party."

Stav set the coffee cup on the ledge of the window and pulled out a Winston cigarette. He smiled as he lit it, squinting his eyes. "An interesting concept, don't you think…"

"Pity parties?"

"Measuring your life with coffee spoons."

"I guess so." I was just being polite.

"A coffee spoon is much smaller than a tablespoon or a ladle." Again, so many words from the quiet man. "When all is said and done, it's the little moments—good and bad— that make up our lives."

I looked out toward the pool. If that was the case, I was looking forward to a few more good spoons full of sugar.

"Did you know I'm a mind reader?" Stav must have caught on to the fact that I'd heard enough about spoon poetry.

"Nope." I looked at the tattoo on Stav's other arm, the one without the naked woman.

There were numbers that looked like a date. Stav and I both sat in silence for a while. The stillness of the humid air felt heavy with the threat of more oppression as the day progressed. I looked past the long line of doors to motel rooms to the area where the pool was hidden. Had we really been in the pool the night before, under the glow of the moon?

"I can read your mind." Stav looked at me. "If you want."

"OK." I knew he couldn't read my mind. I had no plans for the day.

Stav took a deep breath and closed his eyes. "Let's see. You had the cleanest desk of anyone in your class last year."

Good guess. While there was never a clean desk contest held, I'm pretty sure that I couldn't get my desk any cleaner.

"Wait. There's more. You think most of the adults in your world don't know what they're doing."

I couldn't be the only one who thought the investigation or whatever was going on was like the crazy chocolate factory episode on *I Love Lucy*.

"And... it's a little blurry, but there it is: you hate stupid questions."

I raised my eyebrow and said nothing.

"You know, like, *ask a stupid question, get a stupid answer.*"

I tried to hide my smirk.

"What?" Stav asked.

I shrugged.

"Like, why is Greenland called green when it is covered in ice? And why is Iceland called Iceland, when it's covered with green land? Or, why did the chicken cross the road? You don't really expect an answer to a stupid question. But if there is one, it better be good." Stav paused and looked at me. "If the professor on *Gilligan's Island* can make a radio out of a coconut, why can't he fix a hole in a boat?"

I laughed.

"What if the hokey pokey's really what it's all about? Got any stupid questions?"

"Nope. Just a real one: what are those numbers on your arm for?" I looked at the numbers 8 09 69. "A code? A date?"

"My birthdate."

"That would make you younger than me."

"This date is my first day of freedom."

"Were you a prisoner or something?"

"Prisoner to the Korean War, and then, to a con game. This date is after both. When I was free."

"What's a con game?"

"A trick. You're told one thing. And you find out it was all a hoax." Stav threw his cigarette down in the dirt by his feet. He took his foot and stepped on it. "I don't want to sugarcoat it to you, Esther. Things are going to get ugly before they get better."

An airplane flew over us, and we both looked up.

"Will they get better?" It was good to finally call out the situation.

"That's the goal. You need to keep strong like you've been. We have the truth on our side, Esther. It's just that people have a way of twisting the truth and making the good guys look bad and the bad guys look good."

I couldn't believe I ever saw Stav as the quiet type. "I don't understand any of it," I said.

"Believe me, enjoy the ignorance while you can. You're going to hear some pretty bad things about your parents."

I already had.

"Mostly, I'm praying for a miracle. I've seen many of them since I started this gig. You might want to have a talk with your higher power, too, Esther. Prayers of children are most powerful." I said nothing and kicked a rock. "You going to be okay?"

"I worry more about Olivia than anything. And Frankie... well, he just knows how to push my buttons. It's what he does when he's tired and scared. Almost like he needs to see if he can get me upset just to make sure I'm still there."

Olivia opened the door, came out, and stood by me. She grabbed my hand and pulled.

Stav smiled at Olivia and spoke to us both. "If you all could lay low until the sun goes down, I'm going to take you..."

"Don't say adventure or a surprise. Don't sugarcoat it." I now felt I could be direct with Stav.

"Got it. I'm going to take you over to a small town in Iowa. Red Oak. After the sun goes down. It's a place where I spent a few summers. My aunt and uncle are sometimes-angels with the group. We'll go to the county fair there. Something to do late at night. Away from Omaha. No sugarcoating. Just another late night. We'll come back here after."

I squeezed Olivia's hand. "Liv, why don't you go in and pick a few of your paper dolls for me. We can play with them and even make a few more." Olivia let go of my hand and ran into the room. I looked back at Stav. After our little poetry/mind-reading session, I felt safe to be bold. "What's going on today? Be honest."

Stav pulled out another cigarette and lit it. He took a puff and exhaled. "Well, there have been about half a dozen 'Duvall Children Sightings' called in to the police station in the past two days. Reports have had you three at the Henry Doorly Zoo, the Ak-Sar-Ben Racetrack, and even a skating place somewhere. Keeping the Omaha police pretty busy. Duvall Mania."

I frowned.

"OK, Tess called that lady… Ramona. Tess gave her the license number your friend gave you. The police are running it through the system." I liked how Stav wasn't talking down to me. "I'm pretty sure I know what they'll find."

"The truth?"

The phone rang in our motel room, and I ran in to grab it before Frankie did. We wrestled, and I nudged him away as I picked up the receiver. "Hello?"

"Esther?" Marty's voice. I took a breath and sat on the side of the bed.

"Where are you?" Had I not been in such a unique and dangerous situation, I would never have been talking to a boy. A cute boy.

"The question should be: where have I been? And the answer: all over. You'll never believe what just happened."

"Is it Momma?" Frankie asked. "Alice?"

I waved him back and shook my head no.

"Your man in the hat is probably being arrested as we speak."

"You mean Jacob?" I asked. Stav pushed the door open and leaned against the frame of the door and looked at me.

"If that's his real name."

"How do you know for sure?"

"I've been casing the joint." Marty laughed at his own serious voice. "You know, like on your detective shows. Your friend Tess called me and asked me to ride my bike by your house and check things out. The police were doing the same thing, even as I rode by." Tess must have taken the piece of paper with both Marty's number and the license number he gave us.

"I've been checking on your house in between blocks of delivering papers. Hiding in plain sight. The police that are protecting your house in regular people cars don't know that I know they are police and don't know that I'm not just a paper boy. I was on Hillside Drive, the block behind your house, when I saw the same brown car that I saw outside of my dad's office the morning the reporters were interviewing Betsy behind her bakery. Same license plate and everything. Same missing taillight. No one was in the car, but I looked over in your backyard and saw your man looking in your back windows."

"You're sure it was him?"

"It was the same guy for sure, from the back of the bakery, but when I moved closer, as close as I could get without him seeing me, I saw the second guy too."

"Two guys?"

"Just like I was shooting fish in a barrel. Imagine that, in the big old city of Omaha, I found your bad guys. Do I get credit for that?"

"Sure. But they didn't see you?"

"No, but I could see them as clear as day. And the big guy, he had something in his hands."

"Something they took from our house?"

"It was hard to tell. It was a box, but I couldn't see it from where I was watching. I rode to Tess's house. I knocked on her front door and have never been happier to see an old lady in my entire life."

"Who is it, Esther?" Frankie whined.

I put my hand over the receiver and spoke to Frankie. "It's Marty. Everything's okay."

"Tess just called the police and told them that a strange man was peeking in the Duvall house."

"Wow."

"The police contacted the plainclothes cops out front who rushed to the backyard. They'll have them both on trespassing. They're going to get your man in the hat."

"Wow."

"You already said that. Say it backwards."

"Wow," I said slowly.

"Say it upside down."

I thought about it for a minute. "Mom." I laughed out loud.

"I've got to get going, but I wanted to let you know that Tess visited your dad today."

"My dad?" I asked.

Frankie heard me say both Mom and Dad and leaned in to listen to the receiver. "He's really sad and worried about you. Tess told him you were in good hands. Are you?"

I looked up at Stav, who was guarding me even as I talked on the phone. "Yep, we're very safe."

The hours of the day dragged on and on as Frankie complained and Olivia fussed. Frankie was so wound up that he ran around the room several times, knocking things over and being silly. I made up a game where I'd hide Frankie's yoyo around the room as the Junior Mints closed their eyes. I'd say green light when they were close to the hidden toy and red light when they were moving away. Three rounds of the hot/cold rebooted game and the fussing began again. Stav didn't leave us once. He sat outside our room most of the day, smoking and guarding.

Dinner was cereal again around 5:00, but Stav promised good food and cotton candy when the sun went down. I'd never had cotton candy, so the idea of eating a pink or blue cloud created a warm feeling of anticipation. Stav joined us as we watched a re-run of *Little House on the Prairie*, my eyes constantly eyeing the light coming from the cracks around the curtain, hoping more than ever for darkness. I thought about the two men who had been snooping around our house. If they were looking for a stolen baby, why would they go looking in a house that was empty of people? Were they looking for something that Momma had hidden? I thought about her little secrets around the house. Had I missed something important? Something that other people wanted and that she needed to hide from the world? Was something hidden behind the hidden M&Ms? Did she have the coveted item that the men were looking for with her right now?

"Maude makes me grumpy," Frankie said as the closing music to the television sit-com *Maude* played, names rolling over the screen.

"Me too," Stav said, his mustache hiding his grin. "Looks like the sun is sleeping and the moon is out to play."

Frankie stood up. "Are we going to that fair now? With cotton candy?"

"We are indeed. You all need to use the bathroom before we go. We've got about an hour's drive before we get there."

The ride to Red Oak, Iowa was uneventful and much needed. I didn't know the term stir-crazy at the time, but I'm pretty sure that we were all feeling the need to get out and stretch our souls. We just needed to get out.

Bonnie and Kenny Becker lived on a road off the interstate. You couldn't see the interstate from their farm, but you could hear it late at night. That's what Stav told us on the ride from Omaha. "I spent a few summers de-tassling corn in Red Oak as a kid. My brother and I slept out on the porch every night. We'd listen to the whiz of the big trucks moving on the highway late into the night."

"You were a boy?" Frankie asked.

Stav laughed. "I think so. Might have been a dream."

Bonnie and Kenny were standing on the porch of a big, light-yellow farmhouse as we drove up the long drive. They were waving to our car with warm smiles and looking exactly like the grandparents I'd never had but always wanted. Kenny was in work pants and a clean white buttoned shirt, and Bonnie wore a faded blue house dress, a white apron covering the front of it. The sound of the tires of Stav's car moving along the gravel of the driveway slowed to silence, and Stav spoke out of the rolled-down window. "Looking for a nice place to stop for dinner. Any place out here like that?"

"You've come to the right place," Kenny yelled back. "Bonnie makes the best fried chicken in Iowa."

We poured out of the car, and Frankie ran to a nearby fence. "Cows? Real cows? Look at their big fat heads." Four cows stared at us from a distance, chewing their cud and moving their eyes toward Frankie, glaring in the wake of his offensive comment. Olivia grabbed my hand.

"These are city kids, Uncle Kenny," Stav told the couple moving down the steps from the porch. "Cows are a big deal." Frankie turned and grabbed Stav's hand without even a thought. Stav's tattoos and bald hair seemed out of place, and I squinted and struggled to imagine Stav as a boy on a farm in his childhood summers.

"Kenny and Bonnie, these are my new friends Frankie, and Miss Olivia, and Esther."

I guess we weren't going to mention that we were also the kids that everyone in Omaha was on the lookout for. Not a word about our jailed father and our missing mother. It didn't take me long to realize that Stav had filled his aunt and uncle in on our secrets, and that they were more than happy to help us pretend that we were just some silly city kids making a visit to the country on a warm end-of-summer night.

"Please, call us Kenny and Bonnie, kids. We can take a tour of the farm after dinner."

Stav directed us to wash our hands in the bathroom off the kitchen. Frankie was so impressed with the little Dixie cups that he filled three cups of water until I gave him the stink-eye.

"Wow, this house is so big," Frankie said, as we moved back into the dining room. "Where are all your kids?"

"Bonnie and I are old. Our kids are all grown. It's just the two of us in this big old house."

Even though we had eaten our cereal only two hours earlier, we ate like we hadn't eaten in days. Bonnie had her dining room table set with beautiful china, and I salivate even today when I think of a meal that could make a sad, almost-ten-year-old forget about the events of some bad days. Fried chicken like I had never had and have never had since in my life. The rolls, homemade. The mashed potatoes, full of butter. The Duvall children had never experienced corn on the cob, and the task of buttering a piece of bread and rolling the cob in the bread was almost more fun than eating it. When we thought we could eat no more, Bonnie walked out of the kitchen with a homemade apple pie. We learned the words al a mode that night and will never forget the meal at the Becker farm.

"Esther, I hear you have a birthday coming up," Bonnie said as she put a candle in my piece of pie. I'd never told Stav about my birthday, so I assumed Tess had told him. Kenny didn't miss a beat when he saw the big eyes of Frankie and Olivia and put candles in their slices as well.

"Make some good wishes," Kenny said, as he stood back after lighting all our candles.

"I wish for as much cotton candy as I can eat tonight!" Frankie said, before blowing out his candle.

"Candy," Olivia said.

I wasn't about to waste a wish on something as silly as cotton candy. I said nothing as I blew out my candle. I wanted so badly for my parents to be in the same room eating corn on the cob and pie a la mode. And that years from now, we could laugh about the fun night on the farm with the Beckers and their cows.

"Well, I'm doing the dishes tonight since I pulled the short straw," Bonnie said as she took my empty pie plate.

"I can help," I said as I stood up and grabbed Olivia's plate and silverware.

"I do believe there is a county fair waiting for you all, after a quick tour of the farm. I've got this covered, but thank you for the offer, Esther. You kids have fun, and make sure that Kenny and Stav behave."

As Frankie got up and ran to the front door to be the first one on the tour, Olivia and I took our time. I stepped into the living room, Olivia right behind me, and I peered at the pictures on the wall. Scattered across the collage were the faces of a boy and girl, close in age, at different times in their lives. In the center was a large portrait of the grown girl and another portrait of the grown boy.

"Pretty," Olivia said.

We were both looking at the woman with long dark hair in a pink sweater looking up and to the right and smiling as if she knew exactly where she would be going in her life.

"Ladies," Stav called from the front door. "Tour's starting!"

Olivia and I moved toward the door, and I called to Bonnie. "Thanks again for a wonderful dinner, Mrs. Becker."

"Enjoy yourselves now!" She called as the screen door slammed.

After the tour, fireflies flickered out beyond the fence where the cows had been before dinner. The sparkles were calming as a coolness covered the humid air from the day. The smells from the Becker farm were so different from the city I thought I could get lost out here and be happy forever.

Olivia's whimpers interrupted my peace as we followed Stav and Kenny out to a truck. "No, no..."

"What's wrong 'Liv? We're heading to the fair. It's going to be fun."

"No." Olivia walked toward Stav's car and stood. With all the excitement, Olivia had gone without her music box for the past several hours. I think it must have occurred to her as we walked by the car. "I'll get it. Don't worry."

I opened the car door and pulled the bag out of the back seat. Stav looked back at us. Kenny was already in the driver's seat of a red pick-up truck, and Frankie in the back bed waving to us. "We're riding in a truck, Olivia!" Stav stood by the truck waiting for us. He lifted Olivia up and placed her in the back. I crawled in on my own.

Frankie may have liked riding in the back of a truck, but Olivia was terrorized by the experience. Halfway down the road out of the farm, Kenny stopped, and Stav brought her in the cab with him. We got to the fairgrounds within fifteen minutes. The lights and sounds were similar to Peony Park, but the smells were of animals and a sweetness I couldn't name. Stav and Kenny flanked the three of us, and the innocence of the outing along with the pure good souls in Red Oak distracted me from this little fact.

Couples were walking hand in hand. Men were standing near a game and laughing loudly. I took in the fair but kept an eye on both Frankie and Olivia. We went on a few underwhelming rides; I didn't complain, but I wasn't entertained. We ate big puffs of blue clouds that melted in our mouths, so Frankie was happy. Olivia was not a fan of the texture of the mysterious treat, so I grabbed some napkins to wipe her hands. As I grabbed the napkins, I saw two small children sitting behind a trash barrel: a boy not much older than Frankie and a girl, smaller than Olivia. They were dirty, their clothes and skin covered in filth. They were sharing what looked like a paper bowl of french fries seemingly taken from the trash or handed over to them from a generous vendor. My heart dropped. Stav saw me and helped pull more napkins from the container.

"Kids of the fair workers, I'm guessing," he said as we walked back to Kenny and the Junior Mints. "Carnival urchins." Twenty-five hours earlier, Stav had said barely a word to me. We had talked so much in the day that I felt like he knew me. "Don't be sad for them. They know nothing else."

I put my head down.

"They probably have loving parents."

Their parents worked the fairs, they traveled across the country, maybe even didn't go to school. Are the carnival urchins as lost as we are?

"I think the kids might want to see the Mutton Bustin'. What do you say?" Stav's attempt to divert attention wasn't working for me.

"What's that?" Frankie asked.

"You get to take a ride on a lamb, kind of like the men who ride bulls in the rodeo. Would you like to do that?"

"Yes!" Frankie screamed.

As we moved away from the carnival urchins—and the new reality of life for me—toward the arena with the mutton busters, I saw to my right a woman in a booth, sitting alone. She wore a long, dark blue dress, with a dark blue covering on her head. She was old but beautiful, which seemed strange to me. A paradox. The woman sat beneath a sign with the outline of a large hand. The writing above the hand read *Palm Reader - $1*. The writing below the hand: *Past, Present and Future*.

The past was perfect.

The present was uncomfortable, to say the least.

The future? I'm not sure I wanted to know what would be happening even tomorrow. Would I want to know my future? The answer was easy: Only if the future is back to perfect. I knew the Duvall children, after all that had happened in the past days, could never go back to the past as it was.

Never.

"Want to go check it out?" Stav asked me. "Everything's been about the Junior Mints. We have a little time before the next round of Mutton Bustin'. Here's a dollar. Check it out for fun."

The woman motioned for me to come to her. "Come." Her voice matched her looks. Old and beautiful.

"We'll wait right here." Stav held both Liv's and Frankie's hands.

I wondered if there was no line by the booth because it was so late or because people didn't care to hear about the future. The woman moved a curtain and directed me into the booth.

"Sit." She motioned to a beautiful, plush ruby-red chair, identical to the one on the other side of a table where she moved to sit. As I sat down, I looked back to see if Stav and Kenny were still standing where they'd said they would be. They were. Stav nodded to me. Kenny waved. The empty table between the woman and me was covered with a black tablecloth. A strange-smelling candle on the table was the only light in the small dark booth.

"Your hand?" The woman held out her hand as she spoke. I guessed we were skipping introductions.

I held out my hand.

"Ah, the left hand? Is that the hand that you write with?"

"Yes."

The woman took my hand, held it with her warm hands, and looked at me. "Are you open to the truth, young one?" Her voice was thick and throaty.

I nodded, only to be polite. The nod was also a lie. I didn't want any more truth today. Also, I didn't believe that this woman could tell me anything about me or my life. She was sitting alone late at night in a booth at a county fair in Iowa.

"The hand does the best at reflecting ourselves. Your whole life can be found in the lines in the palm of your hand." The woman then looked down at my hand, paused, and tilted her head.

"You have an interesting palm for such a young soul."

The woman traced a line on my palm several times. "This, this is your heart line. Simple and pure still. You have a good handle on your emotions."

I've got that going for me.

"And this line, deep and long. This is your head line. You are clear and focused."

True.

"The break in this line—your life line—is very interesting. You are so young to be prone to big changes in your life."

I looked at the woman's eyes as she read my palm.

"This last line here. Why, only some people have it."

I heard Frankie fussing out by Stav.

"It is your fate line."

I caught my breath. I really didn't believe this woman, but she knew about the big changes, and I knew what big changes felt like. What if she really could tell me my fate? What if she could tell me what was going to happen to my parents, Frankie and Olivia?

"And *your* fate line runs through your lifeline."

Is that bad? Is that good?

"It is so very hard to read a young person's hand, but the intersection of the two lines does not lie. It usually means that you are self-made. But that makes no sense. You are so young." The woman furrowed her brows. "It says that you have developed aspirations early on." The woman kept staring at my hand but said nothing for several seconds.

"Are we done?" I whispered.

"Yes." The woman looked at me and smiled a forced, sad smile. I pulled the dollar from my pocket and placed it on the table.

"No charge for you, young one with an old soul." The woman moved the dollar back to me. "Good luck in your life."

Was it even legal to be a palm reader and wish someone good luck? Isn't there some statute of some kind that says that would be redundant or ironic, depending.

"Thank you, ma'am." I picked up the dollar and walked back to Stav, Kenny, and the Junior Mints.

"Well," Stav said with a grin. "Learn anything interesting?"

"Did that lady tell you that you were going to be a princess when you grow up?" Frankie asked. Olivia giggled. Stav had filled him in on the woman's job while I had been in the booth.

"Nah, just silly things." I pulled out the crumpled dollar and handed it to Stav. "No charge."

"Looks like they're starting," Kenny said. "I'll go get Frankie in the line-up."

Frankie ran to keep up with Kenny.

"You okay?" Stav asked me, Olivia by his side.

"Sure."

We got to the fence of the Mutton Bustin' Rodeo. Frankie and Kenny were on the other side of the fence; Kenny was putting a cowboy hat on Frankie and helped him get on to the lamb.

"So, this is for real?" Stav said. "Wish they had had this at the fairs when I was a kid."

Frankie waved to us from the little gate that would open into the small arena, and I hoped, someday, that Frankie would have this memory and not any of the bad moments from this past week. "Giddy up!" Frankie yelled, and once the gate opened, he was sitting on a small lamb that ran out into the arena. Frankie hooted and hollered and laughed, and as he darted around the arena on the lamb, the crowd cheered and laughed at the adorable, animated boy with the dark curly hair and the big blue eyes. Olivia smiled but leaned into Stav for protection and reassurance.

"He's alright, Miss Olivia. He can't get too hurt falling off a little critter like that," Stav said just as Frankie fell. There was a pause, and Frankie got up and cheered.

"Again?" he yelled to Kenny.

Adults in the crowd roared with laughter. Everyone looked to Kenny. I looked where Kenny was looking and saw a woman whispering to the woman next to her as she pointed to Frankie. "We're done, buddy. Come on out." Kenny motioned to Frankie to come near him. Frankie pouted as he left the arena and attention.

"We're heading out." Stav was serious as he rushed me and Olivia toward the exit from the county fairgrounds. Kenny walked with Frankie a good ten feet behind us, and we all got into the truck to head back to the farm.

"Do you think they recognized him?" Kenny asked as he put Olivia in the cab. Frankie and I jumped into the back of the truck.

"Not sure," Stav mumbled.

Once we got back to the farm, Bonnie walked out to the truck and helped Stav and Kenny get us back to Stav's car. The adults talked outside the car. Stav pulled the styrofoam smiley face off his antennae and hugged his aunt and uncle. Kenny and Bonnie waved goodbye to us. On the ride back to the Shamrock Motel, I sat in the backseat with the Junior Mints; Frankie and Olivia both fell asleep against me as soon as we left the farm, one on my left and one on my right, both smelling sticky-sweet and entertained. The radio played softly in the front seat: *Moonlight Feels Right*. I knew we were back in Omaha when I saw a big screen from a drive-in theater. I recognized the girl on the screen as the same young actress in *The Bad News Bears*. The movie was playing again, only this time on a gigantic outdoor screen. I still have never seen the *The Bad News Bears* and never plan to. It had been the backdrop to one of the worst times of my life.

"Stav, will you answer another question... again, no sugarcoating?"

"Sure. Shoot."

"If Mom and Dad kidnapped a baby, why are the police after us?"

Stav was quiet for a long time.

"Well, the police are after you to use you as leverage with your parents. They think your dad will talk if he knows the police have you. They don't understand that we are keeping you safer from the other people."

"Other people."

"The bad guys from your mother's past. If they can get to you, they can get to her. They know that."

I gnawed on that thought for a while. Too many indefinite pronoun references. The girl in the picture on the wall at the Becker house suddenly popped into my head. "Stav?"

"Hmmm."

"Who's the woman in the pictures on the wall of Kenny's and Bonnie's living room?" Stav was quiet again.

"She had a pink sweater on. Had really dark, pretty hair."

"My cousin Cheryl."

"Where does she live?"

"No one knows. She lives somewhere with a terrible husband. I call him Butch the Bully. I can't remember his real name."

"Why is he terrible?"

"He won't let Cheryl talk to any of her family. He hurts her."

"Hurts her?"

"He calls her mean things... and I suspect that he's hit her... Why?"

"That's the dumbest thing I've ever heard."

"That he hurts her?"

"That she doesn't leave him. She has the nicest parents in the world, and she lets him bully her? She could leave. That's just dumb."

"Cheryl's probably one of the smartest people I know."

"Then how could she be so dumb?"

"You'd be surprised how easy it is for people to control other people."

Frankie struggled to get comfortable. His sleepy voice called to Stav in the front seat, "Hey Stav?"

"Yes, sir." Stav said.

"Why is the lady on your arm naked?"

Stav paused and answered. "Because she couldn't find her clothes."

The answer must have sufficed as Frankie settled down.

I whispered to Stav, "Ask a stupid question."

I couldn't see, but I knew Stav was smiling.

10

Katherine

1968

Like a blanket of promised but erroneous protection, the overcast skies of the December morning cast a foggy hue over the entire hill of vines in the view from my office window.

Bold colors of October and November foliage were absent, but the remaining vines held the assurance of the next strong crop. Two men headed to the top of the hill of endless rows; I recognized them as Dale and Richard, the two men in charge of irrigation, frost protection, and monitoring of grape quality. We called them the Wine Whisperers. They were getting a head start to the day, lifting foliage wires to support the growing canes.

"Someone was ready to start the day." Maureen stood in the doorway of my office holding Luna, my sleepy two-year-old with big, blue eyes. I named my second daughter after the moon, the only stable fixture in my life at the time. Every night, above the rows and rows of vines, the moon showed up. My constant. I knew that same moon would be in my new world, wherever that might be. Luna reached out to me, her messy hair proof of a good night's sleep. "Dah."

"Sorry, Mom. I tried to keep her in our room as long as I could." Merlot was nudging Luna with his nose. Both Maureen and Luna were still in their nightgowns. Maureen, a thirteen-year-old who had just recently passed me up in height, was beautiful. If someone didn't know her, they might pass her off as someone much older; her maturity reinforced that thought, setting her apart from most of the young people at Celestial Way.

"No problem." I reached out to Luna. "I needed to take a break. Hello, little angel." Luna put her head on my shoulder as I hugged her.

"I think I'm going to pass on the meeting this morning. I'm not feeling that great." A pattern.

I was picking up on the fact that Maureen was avoiding the Selection Committee, with excuses of being too busy, too tired, too sick. She went to her daily lessons for schooling, participating less and less in activities with other young people. I knew that I needed to confront Maureen one day on what had been going on since the early fall—not attending meetings that were about meant to prepare her for a leadership role at Celestial Way some day.

"OK, I'll let Margarite know." Today was not the day. "Eugene and I are heading out to the cemetery today. It'll be a long walk, but you're welcome to join us. That is, if you're just taking a day off."

Sadly, Captain, the only grandfather figure my daughters had ever known, had passed away three months earlier. We knew he was fading, but the loss was great, and he joined eighteen other Celestial Way family members who had passed away since I'd been at the Way. Paradise Fields, the Celestial Way cemetery, was right before the Big Barn. The area was called The Beyond. After that was an area that children were always told not to wander: Beyond the Beyond. Close to the roughest area of the terrain and about half a mile beyond the furthest cottage, Paradise Fields first housed Miss Rosalie, the schoolteacher who had come here for her retirement back in 1959, and the first Way member buried in Paradise Fields.

"I'd love to, but I really don't feel that great." Maureen looked pale and sad, more than anything. I'd had suspicions that her attraction to Levi and the reality that she could never be with him, were starting to wear on her. A *Romeo and Juliet* story in the California valley; the Celestial Way family versus the world. "Please put fresh flowers on his grave for me."

"MoMo." Luna called out to Maureen and reached for her. Luna could walk but she loved to be held. The continual back-and-forth game was exhausting yet adorable. Merlot followed Luna each time she was passed on to another. Luna called Maureen MoMo and me Dah. I have no idea why. There was no word for Charles. He was hardly around. When he did come near her, Luna would squeal and reach for Maureen or me.

"We will. I think London is joining us. Can I get you anything?"

"No, just don't be mad at me, Mom. I'm sorry I keep missing meetings."

"Don't worry. I'm here for you. You know that, right?"

The sound of a truck outside interrupted the moment. I knew that truck. Maureen knew that truck. Cars and trucks came and went, most driving past my office window, but this one in particular, was Mick's truck, bringing supplies and sunshine at least once a week. Merlot barked at the sound of the truck. Luna giggled.

"I'll go change Luna and get her ready for your trip to Paradise Fields."

Again, avoiding.

I wasn't expecting Mick that day in December. He'd been by two days earlier with the community medical supplies. He wasn't due for another week. I looked out the window. Mick got out of the truck and headed to the back. Levi stayed in the passenger's seat, not jumping out and running in as he had in past years. Levi, now sixteen, had dropped out of school and was working full time with Mick. He was taller than Mick, and a younger, slimmer version of my tether to the world. I left my office and went out to the loading dock near the kitchen.

"Couldn't stay away?" I yelled. Mick still made our nocturnal drives, but only when Charles was out of town. During the day, we kept up the façade that we were just business partners. Charles was in Chicago, but Levi was in the front seat in the morning. "What brings you back, Mick?"

"A big order, Kat." Mick looked at me with furrowed brows. "Didn't you know you had a big order coming today?"

"No. We're good for the week." I looked in the back of the truck and saw two large boxes. Merlot jumped up into the back of Mick's truck and started smelling the boxes.

"Hey, buddy." Mick rubbed Merlot's ear. "It looks like these boxes are from Sun Valley Supplies, a place in southern California. I've got a list of what's in the boxes here." Mick pulled a clipboard from the front seat of his car.

"Hey, Levi," I said.

"Hi, Miss Katherine," Levi replied and looked forward. No mention of Maureen, no eye contact.

"It says here," Mick moved to the back of the truck again as he spoke, "that we have some new-fangled cork inserter, and what looks like a pretty expensive wine label maker, several stainless-steel fermenters, and a wine-rack. Where do you want them?"

"Who made this order, Mick?" I oversaw all orders, and I'd never placed this order.

Mick looked to the top of his form. "Charles Armstrong is the name on the top of the order form. Looks like he made this order last week. I'll have Levi move these boxes for you. Are you thinking back in the winery?"

"Sure, the winery." I was floored. Charles had made so many changes since the death of Captain. The Main Office was now locked at all times. The Direction Team, comprised of all men, most who traveled with Charles now, met twice a week. Rocco was training the younger men who had been selected to the elite squad how to drive so that more of them could join the business trips. Everything had to go through him, and now he was pushing me aside from the business.

"Levi!" Mick called. "I need a hand."

Levi got out of the front seat and jumped up in the back of the truck. Merlot, the now full-grown dog, jumped up on him and brought out the first smile I'd seen on the teen.

"Just sign here, ma'am." Mick winked as he handed me the pen.

I signed the form as Mick grabbed another box and went toward the hallway to the winery. Beyond the truck up on the hill, a few more workers had joined the Wine Whisperers, as the fog had begun to lift. Row after row, lines of rows creating long visual bars. Rows that used to represent order to me now looked like the bars of a jail cell; I was in a prison, and I suddenly felt like I couldn't breathe. I had felt sucker punched the day that Charles nixed all visits to Celestial Way, the weekend stays from our wealthy customers. Deep down, I knew he wanted control. He was cutting off time with one of my dearest friends, Bernie Cutler. Bernie could still order all the wine he wanted; he just couldn't come and stay here anymore. Control.

Charles did allow one last weekend for the Cutlers in October, after much persistence from me. I planned on bringing a special bottle of wine to the Cutlers on the first night of their last weekend stay and spending some time with them. They too were not happy about the "changes in management" as Bernie called the situation. I pulled one of our best Cabernets from the wine cellar and walked out to their cottage at the base of the hills with the best view in the whole vineyard.

"Knock, knock." I held the bottle and the wine opener as I called from the porch of the cottage.

"Door's open! Come on in, Katherine." Bernie's wife Franny was one of the loveliest people I'd met in my life. "We were hoping you'd come by."

"Right here, my love." Bernie was right behind me as I walked in. "I was taking one last walk through the vines. I have been up and down the Sonoma and Napa valleys. I have been to vineyards in France and Italy. I have never fallen in love with a place like Celestial Way, with its beauty and simplistic values. I feel like I'm going back in time whenever I'm here. I still can't believe it's the last time we'll come here." Bernie hugged me. "I hope you're planning on sharing that bottle with us."

"Absolutely." I caught the emotion in my throat as I tried not to cry.

"Let's sit out on the porch as the sun goes down," Franny said as she grabbed three glasses.

Bernie opened the bottle of wine and set the bottle opener and the bottle out on a table on the porch. "We'll let this one breathe a bit."

We all sat down. The silence lasted for a few minutes. Maybe Bernie and Franny were taking in the view; I was thinking of what to say.

"What's going on, Katherine?" Bernie asked.

"Well, the new crop's bringing in more than the last. That's what we always hope for." Bernie looked at me and paused.

"Changes. I guess," I said.

"Are you going to be alright?"

"Of course. I'm just going to miss you two so much." One tear raced down my cheek.

"You know," Bernie said as he stood up and picked up the bottle of wine I'd brought. "A person is a lot like a bottle of wine."

"How so?" I asked, relieved that we were talking about wine and not the current state of Celestial Way affairs.

"Well, just think about the descriptions from the experts." Bernie poured Franny the first glass of wine.

"Bernie is the expert on wines," Franny said.

"I do know my wines, Fran. Take this bottle of Cabernet. One of my favorite wines from Celestial Way, by the way. As a wine, this Cabernet is the king of the red wines, full-bodied with a robust tannin presence, a strong backing of fruit—black currant, plum, raspberry —and perhaps some leather or oak, with a slower wood-aging than most reds. The final punch: this Cabernet is a rocky fist in a velvet glove."

Franny said, "Bernie all around, the rocky fist in a velvet glove."

"Why thank you, my love," Bernie said as he poured me a glass of the Cabernet. "I was leading the witness, Katherine."

Bernie winked at me and poured himself a glass of the Cabernet, set down the bottle, and sat down.

"We've had the conversation before," Franny said under her breath. I laughed out loud, and the laughter felt beautiful with the sunset and a good wine.

"My Franny here is a good California Chardonnay, pure, refined, but with a little citrus kick. And our dear Captain." Bernie held up his class.

"To Captain," Franny said as she and I both held up our glasses to toast the departed leader.

"Captain, much like a good bottle of Pinot Noir from France, was solid. My best bottle of Pinot Noir, after a sufficient sip, of course, would be described as generous, plush, and delicate, with just a hint of licorice."

"Amen," Franny mumbled.

"And you, my dear Katherine, you are a New Zealand Pinot Noir, elegant, fresh, and harmonious, vibrant with smooth tones."

"Why thank you, Bernie." I took a drink.

"Wait, I'm almost done. Let's see. Eugene. What an anomaly. Though he'd never drink a German Riesling, he is truly a mature, soft, and zingy Riesling with a hint of apricot. And Charles."

Tension filled the moment as Bernie paused.

"Charles is an Australian Shiraz." Bernie dragged out the word Shiraz.

From far off, a hawk yelled out. We sat for a moment.

"Dark, seductive, firm, concentrated, with a strong cut."

No one drank as we sat in silence.

A warning in a code of fermented grapes, a language Bernie knew I would understand. Warning: I'm in a bad marriage to a controlling man who is never around.

Fact: I signed up for it.

I had two daughters who needed stability so I could figure out how to deal with my misery. My husband was taking over my role for fifteen years, controlling me. There was a very good chance that he had slept with other women as I knew two children at the Way who looked very much like him. I could handle the situation if my daughters had structure and security. I heard the warning loud and clear. I'd be fine.

"To Celestial Way," Franny said as she held up her glass.

Bernie and I held up our glasses to the sunset and toasted our destiny.

Mick and Levi came back to the truck. "All boxes delivered to the winery," Mick said. "I'll be back next week, Kat. Oh, I almost forgot to tell you. We're heading to the moon."

"What?" I asked.

"The United States is racing to get the first man on the moon this coming summer. What I wouldn't give to catch a ride on that truck."

"Hard to even imagine."

"Everyone's talking about it. Oh, and John Lennon just said that the Beatles are bigger than Jesus," Mick said as he got into the cab of his truck. "People aren't really happy about that."

"Who's John Lennon?"

Mick's head went back as he howled a laugh so loud that it echoed throughout the dining hall and all the hallways. "I'm obviously not doing a great job of keeping you updated. You do remember Jesus, though, right?"

I smiled.

Mick stopped. I knew he wanted to hug me, to comfort me. "You know, Kat, a dead body comes floating to the surface, eventually."

"What?"

"The truth, ugly as it may be, will always show itself in time, always."

"What if I don't want to know the truth?" We had just scratched the surface of the man that I'd married.

"You don't always have that luxury. It's going to be alright though, Kat. I promise."

As Mick drove out of the Celestial Way loading dock, I believed him.

"Are you still going to Paradise Fields?" London had an uncanny habit of sneaking up on me.

"I just have a few more things to do in my office. Eugene said he'd push the stroller if we bring Luna. It's a perfect day for a long walk."

"Would you mind stopping by Stormy's cottage on our way?" London had eventually begun to call her sister Stormy after she got here. "She's still having a hard time."

Stormy was having a hard time, but it wasn't with drugs anymore. Stormy was having a hard time with Celestial Way. The lifestyle of the community was not something that Stormy would've ever signed up for. Pruning vines, tending to children, making food, being selfless. Not one thing on that list engaged the wanderlust nature of London's sister. At one point, she'd told London that she felt like she had been forced here.

Stormy's response was a source of contention for me. On the one hand, I felt that Stormy had been saved by the Way. We had taken her in, tended to her as she had gone through withdrawal, fed her, and gotten her off a very wayward path. On the other hand, I understood her state. Stormy did not fit the mold. Stormy's sidekick Blaze had transitioned well; she was loved by everyone in the community as she brought a new energy and joy to any job she did or any group she worked with. Stormy, on the other hand, was starting to live up to her name as she was continually getting in arguments with other members of the community.

"And what are we going to do when we stop by to see Stormy?" I really didn't have anything to offer Stormy.

"Maybe you could convince her to stay. You could show her that she just needs to find her place here. Like you did with me."

London's remarks brought me back to the early years. In my first years at Celestial Way, I was head over heels in love. My purpose every day was to get up and spend time with a man I adored. I also thrived in my role as mother and business director. I had my own office, and I felt great purpose in what I could do for the community. London did not feel that purpose. When London seemed sad or lost, I was there for her. I was the one who convinced Captain to have London clean his office. I had observed London in the kitchen. She was obsessive about cleaning. Captain gave her a trial week and hired her after her first time cleaning.

"This one knows how to bring order to the universe," Captain told me in his thick accent. "I like her drive."

London loved the honor of keeping order for the leader of the community. She dusted and polished the big, rich furniture. She cleaned the wood floors until they shined. She even brought order to his files and redesigned the layout of the room. London worked for Captain daily, so she knew of his little problem with whiskey. Even though the word codependent was not a common term at that time, we all knew that was exactly what she was. Captain was dependent on drinking and therefore needed London.

And London needed Captain to need her.

No easy way to put it: Captain's death had derailed London. The hole in the Way after his passing impacted her the most. Charles was nothing like Captain in his leadership approach, and to a certain degree, Charles found London in the way. She was still allowed to clean the office but only when Charles was not in it.

"Katherine, could you help Stormy find a job here at Celestial Way? Could you find her something to do that will keep her here?"

Keep her here?

Stormy could not leave Celestial Way. Charles would never allow it.

"Hey, you two." Eugene stood in the doorway. He too was lost without Captain. He also needed Captain to need him. The dysfunction of it all somehow had felt functional at the time. Everything changed after Captain died. Charles still had plenty for Eugene to do as he proved to be the biggest muscle in the community, but Eugene still looked like a cart missing a wheel. He was a bit lost without the man he had protected for so many years. "Did I miss some sad news? You both look too serious for such a beautiful day."

"Let's go get Luna and head out to enjoy the day. Eugene, we're making a stop at Stormy's cottage on the way, if that's alright with you."

Eugene looked at me and raised one eyebrow. We were all leery of the Stormy Factor. "Everyone needs a jacket," London said as she pulled on a big, bulky brown sweater.

"It's pretty chilly out there." I grabbed an extra blanket for the stroller even though Luna was bundled up plenty. Eugene wanted stroller duty so he could spend more time with Luna, who adored Eugene. London had grabbed a basket of food from Lottie. When I had gone to get Luna, Maureen was reading to Luna in her bed. Maybe she really was sick.

"Just a quick stop to see Stormy," London promised.

"We do need to get to the cemetery and back before dinner." I knew we'd be fine with time, but I really didn't want to stop by and visit Stormy. I racked my brain for an idea of a job for Stormy. Unfortunately, I couldn't think of anything at Celestial Way that would mix with her Storm Factor. We got to Stormy's cottage, and London ran up to the door and knocked. No one answered. The look on London's face was clearly one of great panic. She opened the door and called out to Stormy.

"Storm?" London moved into the main room of the cottage and called again. "Stormy?"

Eugene held Luna as he and I walked into the cottage. Merlot sat down on the front porch as Stormy sauntered out from a bedroom. She looked as though she had just woken up, but I had discovered— several months after Stormy had arrived—that she always looked like that. Bedroom Eyes. That's what a guy I dated in college called them. Sleepy-looking eyes on attractive girls. Their enticing eyes appear smoky and never fully open. "It makes them look like they want to go to bed if you know what I mean." I knew that I never connected with the girls with Bedroom Eyes. They always seemed to focus those sleepy eyes on the good-looking boys in the room.

"Stormy, are you okay?" London ran to her sister. In a brief second, my brain took in the strange juxtaposition of the two sisters, evidently from the same parents but apparently from two different worlds.

London and Stormy, standing next to each other. Eye to eye.

Stormy, with her striking yet sharp beauty, demanded the attention of any room she was in, even as she sat silent. Her clothes always grabbed at her angular, fit curves, pulling in stares from all in the room. Stormy's unique eyes glowed as they moved slowly across every person in the room.

London and Stormy were polar opposites, in their strange juxtaposition.

London was the *down* to Stormy's *up*, the *brown* to her *pink*, the *gloom* to her *vavoom*.

London kept her mousy hair short and choppy, her dark, oversized glasses constantly moving down her nose. Her choice of clothes was boring and predictable; oversized blouses and long skirts above men's sandals cried out: Don't look at me. I had once told London that there were many men at Celestial Way with whom it would be fun to spend time. Her response had been curt and simple, "The odds are good, but the goods are odd." I laughed so loudly as I realized she was right. The men at Celestial, aside from the Direction Team, were big men, little men, old men, gay men, most of the rest of them fell into the odd-men basket.

"Do you want to come with us to the cemetery?" London asked her sleepy-eyed sister.

"Why would I want to do that?"

"Just something to do. Where's Blaze?"

"Somewhere out there." Stormy pointed out the front door to the hill. "I'm not really sure."

"We need to get you out of your rut," London said as she moved beyond Stormy into her bedroom. "For starters, let's open up your curtains." London pulled both bedroom curtains open, and shouted, "Look at that! You've got the most beautiful view in the world right here." Eugene held Luna as he and I stood in the doorway to the bedroom watching London's engaging production.

Stormy wasn't amused.

"I'm going crazy here, you know that," Stormy said as she sat on the bed.

"You just haven't found your purpose," London persisted.

"My purpose is to get out of this place."

As Stormy spoke, something on the bedside table, near the lamp, caught my attention.

The light from the lamp glowed on several crumpled cellophane wrappers: Jolly Ranchers, sour green apple.

Dead body.

The dead body came up to the surface to float, just as Mick had said it would. London wasn't the only one at Celestial Way encouraging Stormy to stay. Because London and Stormy were looking at each other as they talked, they didn't see me look at the nightstand. Eugene did though. He looked where I looked. He looked at me. I looked away.

"Time to head to Paradise Fields," Eugene said as I darted through the living room and out the front door, Eugene with Luna right behind me.

"Dah," Luna called as her arms moved toward me.

"Sorry, Katherine," Eugene said as he passed Luna to me.

"No need." I pulled Luna into me and kissed her. "It's not like we didn't guess that he's been busy around here. He's a very busy man."

Eugene looked down as London came out to the porch where we were waiting for her. "Well, that went well, don't you think?" London didn't want to lose her sister again.

"Yep." Eugene moved the stroller toward me as I put Luna in.

"She'll come around," London said. "She always took a little more time to get things. You know, like in school and life."

"Yep," Eugene said again as he pushed the stroller toward the end of the cottages. Most of the cottages were empty, as the people who lived in them were all working or at least looking for a purpose. We had about seven more cottages to pass before the walk to the cemetery.

Charles and Stormy.

My mind wandered as the three of us walked along a dirty path to the cemetery. I was upset, of course, but not because I was jealous. I was way beyond jealousy. I had looked forward to the trips that Mr. Charles Armstrong took since I had a better rhythm with the girls without him. His attention to other things and women was not a problem for me.

Charles and Stormy.

Of course, Charles would look at the younger women, the beautiful women. I never asked. He never told. We got along fine.

I was upset, though.

I was upset because he knew he could do whatever he wanted. He felt entitled. He was above the laws that he enforced. He controlled everything.

A dead body had risen to the surface, but we already knew that the body was dead.

Luna started to fuss just as the Big Barn and Paradise Fields were in our vision. I knew she was hungry. Eugene made funny noises and bounced the stroller as we moved more quickly. I pulled a bottle out of my bag and handed it to her in her buggy. She grabbed the sides and calmed down as she drank. "We're almost there, Luna. Hang in there." I hoped that she could nap on the ride home.

"Do we want to eat first or head to see Captain's grave?" London looked at me. I looked at Eugene.

"What do you think?" I asked.

"I'm with Luna," Eugene answered. "Let's eat."

We picked a spot under a big tree, or at least the biggest in the area which would provide shade. Actually, Merlot picked it out as he ran to the tree and sat. About a hundred yards behind the tree was the large barn that was built the year I first came to Celestial Way. We no longer had horses, so the men used the barn as a place to congregate socially. I pulled out a bowl and poured water from a bottle for Merlot; London pulled out the plates, sandwiches, and cookies. It would be good to eat. I was looking forward to the picnic, not so much hanging out in a cemetery.

Truth: I was never much of a cemetery person.

The dead were not in this cemetery. The evidence of their physical existence on this earth was buried within the fences in Paradise Fields, and it was all a little creepy that we thought this spot made us closer to the dead. A dead body floating to the top of a lake is not the person who walked the earth but a shell of what had once been.

Truth: My marriage was dead.

My dead marriage was floating in my head as I struggled to swallow a bite of the sandwich that Lottie had made that morning. The shell of what had once been a promising union was crumpled up on the side table of a bed, and I was okay with it.

"Captain would be happy that we all came together," London said. "He'd be *thrilled beyond measure*." London mimicked Captain's accent on the last three words.

"He would have loved watching the girls grow up," Eugene added.

Luna sat in my lap and cooed at Merlot. She held up crackers to feed him, and he slobbered on her hands, making her giggle. "At least I have the girls." I realized after the words were spoken that I had said them aloud.

"What?" London asked.

"She means," Eugene said, "that we're lucky to watch the girls grow up, and that Captain is still watching them, though only in spirit."

London looked perplexed as she tried to keep up. We finished our lunch, put away food and plates, and packed up the blanket. London pulled out a bouquet of flowers from her bag; I was relieved as I had forgotten to get some, per Maureen's request. We left the picnic basket and stroller under the tree and began walking to the gate of the cemetery. Eugene carried Luna, and I followed behind London and Eugene.

Death surrounded us.

Small headstones graced the graves of the many people who had passed away since my stay that had begun fourteen years earlier. In the center of the cemetery was a much bigger headstone where Captain had been buried. London moved toward the headstone in a hurry. She placed the flowers at the base of the headstone. I think she found comfort here. I was anything but comfortable.

Etched on Captain's stone in big letters:

Captain Walter Victor Schubert

August 9th, 1900 - November 5th, 1968

If I should go before the rest of you

Break not a flower nor inscribe a stone,

Nor when I'm gone speak in a Sunday voice

But be the usual selves that I have known.

Weep if you must, Parting is hell,

But Life goes on, So sing as well.

-Joyce Grenfell

I remained a few feet back with Eugene. After London placed the flowers, she sat and appeared to pray. Maybe somewhere in her past, she had gone to church. Not likely. Maybe somewhere in her psyche, London's spiritual quest made prayer a natural, unlearned gesture. The wind blew against us, and I sensed a cool front moving in.

Merlot broke the silence with loud barking.

Normally a well-behaved dog, Merlot took off running and barking toward a large shed at the end of the cemetery. I was sure this was where Raymond kept equipment for the upkeep of the grounds. The door to the shed was ajar, and Merlot forced the door open and moved into the shed. The quiet, reverent moment was gone; Luna was crying. I was calling out to Merlot, and after Eugene handed Luna to me, he ran to the shed to see what had upset the dog.

Eugene moved into the shed and called to the dog. "Merlot. What do you see, little buddy?"

When I got to the shed, I handed Luna to London and followed Eugene inside. "Come on, Merlot. We have a treat for you." I had nothing, but I'd lure him out and give him a treat back at the tree. The barking had stopped. I could still hear Luna crying, and neither Eugene nor I could see the dog in the darkness of the cool shed. My eyes began to adjust, and London pulled the door all the way open so that the light from the day would help us find our dog. I could hear rustling in the far end of the shed, and Merlot started to bark again. He was looking behind an old barrel. His low, deep growl was not familiar to me.

"It's a mouse or some creature," Eugene whispered. "The poor thing's cornered. We just need to get Merlot out of here."

"Come on now, Merlot," I cooed. "We're heading home… treat!"

My eyes adjusted to the dimly lit shed. At the opposite corner of the shed from where Merlot was growling was a table that seemed out of place. I moved in that direction as I still called out. "It's okay, Merlot."

When I got to the corner with the table, I saw many large figures against the left wall. The figures were covered with blankets or tarps. I moved toward the figures first as I heard Eugene wrestling with Merlot. I pulled one of the tarps off and looked at and felt the stone object at the same time.

"What are those?" London called from the doorway. Luna had calmed down and was babbling, almost echoing what London said.

"I don't know. This one looks like a statue." I blinked my eyes and could see what looked like a statue of Mary with Jesus. The traditional Madonna. I moved the tarp off another statue. I didn't recognize the figure but recognized the statue as religious. There was another statue that had fallen on its side. It, too, had a tarp covering it. These had to be the statues from the abbey chapel before the monks had moved north. But contrary to what Charles had told me, the statues had never moved on with the monks. They had been moved and hidden. They were not to be a threat to the new idols planted for Celestial Way.

"I've got him," Eugene said as he grabbed Merlot's collar and wooed him to the front door. "Come on, big guy. We've got a treat out there somewhere for you. Right, London?"

"Right," London said as she moved toward the tree, still holding Luna and looking for a treat to entice the overly upset dog.

I moved to the table in the corner of the shed and found two boxes. One had a brown two-pocket folder. I couldn't see what was in the pockets, but my ire and the hair on my arms were up, and I knew I could not look at these items in the dark shed. I couldn't take the boxes, but I grabbed the folder and tucked it into my jacket.

"What are you all doing in here?" Raymond, the caretaker, stood in the doorway of the shed. His silhouette, solid and stern.

"Hey, Raymond," I said. "We came here to visit Captain's grave, and my dog chased a mouse into the shed. So sorry."

"Oh, Miss Katherine, I'm sorry. I didn't know it was you." Raymond's smile revealed crooked teeth behind his big lips.

"I think Merlot may have knocked over a few things," I said as I moved the statue on the ground upright. "Sorry about that. Hope we didn't mess up your system in here."

"No worries at all, Miss Katherine." Raymond said as he held the door open for me. "Can I give you all a ride back to the Mother House?"

"No need. We enjoy the walk." I walked out of the shed into the bright sun, my eyes adjusting to the light.

"Well, then, enjoy your walk, Miss Katherine." Raymond shut the door to the shed and put a lock on it. He walked back to his truck, parked just beyond the Beyond. Raymond stood outside the truck as we packed our things, and he watched us move back toward the Celestial Way campus.

"What was that all about?" Eugene whispered. Luna had fallen asleep in the stroller.

"I'm not sure." I adjusted the folder under my jacket.

We all walked the mile and a half back to the Way in silence, mostly because Luna was sleeping, but also quiet with thoughts of what had just happened. I lagged behind and pulled out the folder at one point. I looked over the top sheet in the left pocket.

RD Schedule

Below that was a list of men from Celestial Way, alongside dates and places.

RD?

I remembered hearing that term from the Direction Team. On the bottom of the page, in bold letters: Recruitment Duty. We had never needed to recruit since people seemed to find us. Or at least stumbled upon us.

Recruitment?

Unless others didn't find Celestial Way. Maybe Celestial Way found others.

I looked at the list again. Names, dates, and places. The list of places for RD included Happy Hollow Park and Zoo, San Jose International Airport, and San Jose Museum of Art.

Airport.

Had I been recruited to come here? Was it not a beautiful accident, as Charles always called it?

How strange that I'd be at the airport when you were. What a beautiful accident.

Changed my life forever.

How convenient had it been that Charles had been at an airport at that time when tired and vulnerable college kids were on their way for the semester break, after finals? I shut the folder and tucked it neatly back into my jacket. As I adjusted the folder, a piece of paper fell out. I looked down to pick up the small, shiny white piece of paper and realized as I picked it up that it was a photograph, a Polaroid photograph.

As my eyes focused on the picture, I could see a woman lying on a bed, a sheet covering part of her body. A young woman—a naked woman—Therese Maltese. In black letters, on the bottom white ribbon of the photo were the words: Sexy and willing.

My heart stopped.

Therese was one year older than Maureen and had also been born on the vineyard. Her mother, Joanie Maltese, still worked in the fields. We never knew the father as Joanie had come to Celestial Way pregnant and, I was now assuming, recruited. Young Therese was in a bed in what appeared to be one of the cottages. Therese's body was beautiful. Therese's eyes held fear and sadness.

Therese was clearly naked.

I quickly put the Polaroid picture in the folder and saw more pictures in the folder. I tucked the folder under my jacket. I suddenly didn't want to see any more dead bodies float to the surface.

"The princess is awake!" Eugene called back to me. I heard Luna fuss.

Eugene pulled Luna from the stroller as Merlot ran up and smelled Luna's diaper. London took over empty-stroller duty as I caught up to the group. "Find anything interesting?" Eugene must have seen me take the folder from the shed.

"Not good," I said. Eugene raised an eyebrow, seemingly not surprised.

We were almost five cottages into the area when a small figure yelled to us, waving her arms. I recognized Tina. She yelled out to us, "Hurry!" Her arms motioned for us to move faster.

"Maureen," she yelled.

Eugene handed Luna to London as he and I raced to Tina. "What about Maureen?" Eugene yelled.

"She's—she's not good." Tiny Tina turned around and ran toward the Mother House.

Time stopped as I ran. I could hear the blood pulsing in my head as I moved in what felt like slow motion. I could see Tina reach the front doors to the Mother House, Eugene not far behind. I could not move any faster. I knew London would take care of Luna; I needed to get to Maureen. I was clutching the folder, no longer under my jacket but still close to my body. I would not lose the evidence.

Lottie appeared in the doorway. She was crying. I couldn't hear anything as I got closer to the archway in the entry to the Mother House. The world was quiet, deathly quiet. Her mouth moved, but I heard nothing.

Suddenly sound.

"I'm so sorry, Katherine." Lottie came up to me and hugged me. She sobbed as she spoke. "We didn't know. We had no idea."

I ran into the Mother House and moved to the hallway that led down to the living quarters. Eugene and Tina were moving into our living quarters; Lottie was running behind me. When I got to the door, I braced myself. I lived through my daughters. I needed my daughters. I, too, was codependent. I needed them to need me. I needed to be there for Maureen and Luna. I heard crying in the room. Loud wails. I knew that cry: Maureen.

Maureen was alive!

Her cry echoed in the room, out the door, and down the hall. It was the happiest and saddest sound I'd ever heard. I remember taking my jacket and the folder and throwing them on the floor, the folder underneath my jacket. Merlot barged in before me and ran up to the bed. I looked again at Maureen and saw that she was holding something.

A baby.

The tiny baby in her arms was blue.

"Momma," Maureen cried.

"Maureen," I said. "I'm so sorry."

On the opposite side of the bed, I saw Tina and another person. Blaze was standing right by the head of the bed, her hand on Maureen's head. The surreal moment was made euphoric by the fact that Maureen was alive. I still could not get my head around the baby in my daughter's arms.

"Rocco."

That was all Maureen had to say.

Rocco—Charles' right-hand man who oversaw the Youth Committee. In the early years, Maureen had enjoyed being a part of the group. She had felt honored. It was only in the past year that her comments to me on the group had been limited to not at all. Rocco, a man thirty years older than Maureen, was never mentioned. And now she was naming him as the father of the lifeless child in her arms. I wanted to scream. Someone had hurt my daughter and taken advantage of her, and all the while, I thought she'd been safe. I thought I was protecting her, even in my unhappy marriage.

How in the world can we put a man on the moon, and I can't even protect my own child?

I leaned into Maureen, hugging her and touching the baby. "I am taking you from this place. I promise no one will hurt you again."

11

Esther

DAY SIX 1976

"Do I have to wear socks?" Frankie was tired, and I was tired of him whining.

"Nope."

It was close to noon, and again, the Duvall children had slept in later than ever. Stav told me that we were heading into Omaha, so I was helping the Junior Mints get dressed. We had all slept in our clothes, but I took a warm washcloth to wipe down their bodies and helped them change into another set of clothes that Tess had dropped off.

"'Cause I don't want to wear them."

My buttons.

Pushed.

Frankie continued, "I hate socks."

Frankie could wear his underwear on his head. What did I care what anybody thought about the Duvall children? We were all tired and ragged. So, judge us. I'm not sure why it was suddenly alright to go out in the city during daylight. Adults

always seemed to change the rules every time I turned around, and Frankie wasn't the only one bugging me anymore.

The morning news weatherman had just finished the weather report when Sherry O'Hara, with a flashy name and a flashy smile, stood in her flashy fuchsia suit on our neighbor's front lawn. "The explosion, which took place late yesterday afternoon at the home of the Duvall family, started a fire that destroyed most of the house until firefighters were able to put it out. Chief Thorfinsen of the Omaha Fire Department said that it was a good thing that no one was in the house. Presently, Clark Duvall is being held at the Douglas County Jail. Tara Duvall and her three children are still at large."

"Large." Olivia was putting all her paper dolls into the sack that Tess had delivered them in.

"We're large?" Frankie asked Stav.

"Looks like it." Stav stared at the blaze on the television. He didn't even try to change the channel.

"Our house blew up?" I asked.

Add it to our list of strange tragedies: blown-up houses.

"Or someone blew it up."

Sherry O'Hara stood on Mr. George's front lawn, our crispy house behind her, and I knew that Mr. George was either not around at the moment, or mad as hell that she might mess up his perfect grass. "We still don't know what started the fire, but firefighters believe the explosion began in the kitchen."

Behind the flashy reporter was our little house. Our beautiful little white house on Parker Street was burnt to a crisp. What had once been a nice house with a pretty front lawn and flowerpots on each side of the door was now a burnt box—a box that had once seemed like the safest place in the world to me. Had the fire destroyed that part of my life, or had the fire revealed the home for what it really was: a box, four sides to the box, nothing more? Had the past several weeks destroyed my family? Or had the dog days of the past month simply revealed the truth of what my family was: not the family I'd thought I had?

Black replaced the white. Fear replaced the comfort. Bad replaced the good.

Olivia began to whimper as Frankie yelled, "What about my baseball? What about my rock collection?" His words ended with tears.

I hugged Olivia and calmed Frankie. "Good thing Tess grabbed our favorites. How did she know what to grab? We've got your GI Joe and Olivia's paper dolls."

"You've got the music box and the MGM book I gave Tara," Stav added. I didn't know that Momma had received the MGM book as a gift from Stav. "I think we can go back to the house later, and I'll bet we will find a few things you can brush off and use."

The phone rang and Stav grabbed the receiver from the cradle on the first ring. "Shop's open. Yep, saw it. They're here staring at me as I speak… okay… park in the back… the north side… got it."

A commercial replaced our burning home. "One, two, three. Three licks to get to the center of a Tootsie Pop." A smart but silly owl confirmed the million-dollar question.

"How soon can you all be ready? Tess wants us to meet her."

"We're ready now." You get what you get. Frankie wasn't wearing socks, and I wasn't brushing anyone's hair.

Olivia sniffled and grabbed the bag with her paper dolls and the music box, which was starting to show the wear-and-tear of our strange days. The upper right-hand corner of the glittered rainbow background had pulled away from the small frame of the box. I wondered if we could find glue or tape where we were going. Frankie ran out the door to the white Rambler that no longer had a smiley face on the antennae. The sky was completely covered with dark, gloomy clouds, and I was just fine with that. I helped the Junior Mints settle into the backseat before I moved to the front seat. Stav drove out of the lot of the Shamrock Motel. We all looked out the window of Stav's car and watched the world whiz by. Trees and buildings. People and cars. Stav played the radio on the ride to the police station. ABBA's *Momma Mia* blared from his staticky radio. Nobody sang.

"This really doesn't make sense," I said as Stav parked his car behind a big old building.

"Life or this parking spot?"

"The police station? I can read. You've been hiding us for days and now you're bringing us right to the people you were hiding us from? It doesn't make any sense at all."

"Quid pro quo."

"Quo," Olivia said. Her head was looking deep into her bag. The bag and its contents were her constant, her security.

"Why are we here?"

"Tess struck a deal with your friend Ramona. Ramona needs you to identify the man who may have taken you. Ramona promised that the newspaper and television folks wouldn't know about it. A contract."

I said nothing.

"You know, you scratch our back, we scratch your back."

Olivia whimpered.

"You help us out, we'll help you out. Quid pro quo."

"Got it, a new word. It looks like Ramona gets the better end of this quo deal. Tess helped them out by giving them the license plate number of the brown car and having Marty turn the bad guys in. They keep the reporters away. That's it? What are we really getting in your pro quo? It looks to me like you're walking us right into a trap. These are the people who have Daddy. The people who say Momma's bad."

"You're still hiding. Kind of like hiding in plain sight."

"Like fish in a barrel."

"I swear, Esther, there's a grumpy old man inside of your ten-year-old body."

"She's not ten yet," Frankie argued, "Hey, look! Tess." He pointed to a door under a fire escape. Tess waved at us and smiled. Today she wore a purple dress and dress shoes. She looked funny dressed up. We got out of the car and walked toward her. "Over here! You all look great."

We looked like carnival urchins.

"Frankie and Olivia, we have some snacks for you while Esther visits with Ramona. Sound good?"

"Snacks are good," Frankie said as he allowed Tess to hold his hand. Olivia walked with me, Stav behind us, down a long, dark corridor. The sounds of our footsteps bounced off the walls and high ceiling of the corridor, clouding the hall with a haunting rhythm.

"Stav?" Olivia asked.

"Yes," Tess said as she smiled. "Stav will stay with you two."

"We're going to take an elevator to the top floor. Would you like to push the button, Olivia?" Tess asked. Olivia looked down as she walked. She didn't want to push the button.

"I will," Frankie said. "I like pushing buttons."

I looked back at Stav, who raised one eyebrow.

The elevator ride took longer than it should have, and when we stopped at the third floor, I thought I'd throw up. I didn't want to see the man in the hat. And yet, part of me thought I'd be sad if he wasn't there. That would mean he was still out there looking for us. The elevator doors opened, and three people stood waiting for us: Ramona, my-best-friend Kemper, and a very tall older black man in uniform.

"Greetings! Have I missed you three or what?" Ramona had on a maroon suit, her dark hair down, swaying as she moved toward us. She hugged Frankie and smiled at Olivia. Beautiful citrus embraced us in her hug. "And Miss Esther, I'm so happy you agreed to come."

I had a choice?

"Esther, Frankie, and Olivia, I want you to meet Chief Caswell. He's here to help you through the process of identifying the man who took you from Dr. Vaughn's office."

Chief Caswell was the tallest man I'd ever met at that point in my life. He had a slow but kind smile as he moved to shake my hand. "Esther, I've heard a lot about you. Thank you for coming." Chief Caswell's white teeth against his black skin glowed.

I shook his hand and felt better.

"You and I will go a little farther down this hallway to a room. I'll be with you the entire time."

I turned back to the Junior Mints. "I'll be back soon." Olivia looked like she might cry.

"Save me some snacks." I forced a smiled.

I walked with Chief Caswell to the end of the long corridor. The pounding of the rain outside hit the roof above us as we entered a small dark room with a big window covering most of one wall. "In a few minutes, several men will walk into the room beside our room. They won't be able to see us. We have a window, but the side in their room is a mirror." I'd seen an episode of Candid Camera with a similar window. If I hadn't been so scared, I would have found the whole experience captivating.

The door to our little room opened and Ramona and another officer entered. Ramona squeezed my arm.

"Does the man in the hat know that I'm here?" I asked.

"All the men," Chief Caswell said, "know that people are on the other side of the mirror. They just don't know if the inspection is for their case or for one of the other men in the room. They have no idea who's on the other side of that mirror. They're handcuffed and will be taken back to their cells after they leave. You're safe with us."

The light in the other room went on, and Office Kemper opened the door and held it as six men walked in the room, each man looking down as the six formed a line against the far wall. The men walked in like zombie soldiers. The second to the last man to walk in was the man in the hat, without a hat. I knew it the moment I saw his profile.

Six men stood before us, each holding a number, facing our room.

Six little monkeys jumping on the bed.

One through six. Officer Kemper's voice came through a speaker in our room. "Turn to your right." All six men turned to their right.

One fell off and bumped his head.

"Turn to the front again."

Momma called the doctor, and the doctor said...

"Number one, move forward."

No more monkeys jumping on the bed.

"Number two, please move forward."

"That's him." My throat burned as I forced my words out.

Number two was the bad monkey. The second man was the man in the hat.

"You're sure now?" Chief Caswell's voice was as quiet as mine. The rain came down hard as we all looked toward the monkeys.

"Yes, sir."

I had never been more certain of anything. The Junior Mints and I had spent no more than an hour with the man, but I knew it was the alleged Jacob. Without his hat and oversized coat, Jacob looked like a tall, thin boy. He looked young. He looked scared.

Chief Caswell asked me, "Could you take one more look at each man, Esther? Please."

I did as he asked. My eyes still landed on the second monkey.

Chief Caswell looked at me. I told him without hesitation, "The man holding the card with the number two took us from Dr. Vaughn's office. Sir?"

"Yes, Esther."

"Would it be alright if Frankie and Olivia didn't have to do this? I'm a hundred percent sure."

Chief Caswell moved toward me and shook my hand. "I think that's a good idea. The second man is also the man we picked up from your house. The young boy, Marty Westerholt, also identified him and another man. I think we can be done." He moved toward the wall and pushed a button. "Thank you, Kemper."

Kemper looked toward the mirror, confused.

"We're done here, Kemper. You can take them all back."

Kemper, with the help of another man who had waited in the hall, moved the men out of the room and back to their cells.

"What will happen to them?" I asked.

"Them?"

"Those men."

"Well, Esther, every one of those men is in here for one crime or another. They will be charged, and most will spend some time in jail."

"That's sad."

"It is, but we don't want them out doing bad things like taking children or blowing up houses."

Ramona took my hand. "Esther, I can take you to the room where Tess and the kids are."

"Thank you, Esther." Chief Caswell stood tall. "I've got some paperwork to do with your case, but I appreciate you helping us out."

"Sure." I almost added: any time. I didn't. I never wanted to be in a police station again. Ramona walked me down to the other end of the corridor. The rain competed with our footsteps to drown out any other noises or thoughts.

Frankie and Olivia were not in the room. I panicked as I looked beyond the room to a small office. "Where are the Junior Mints?"

Tess walked out of the back office and turned to me. "Esther!"

"Where are Frankie and Olivia?"

"They took a walk down to the cafeteria. I guess there's an ice cream machine there. I promise you they're fine."

The door opened, and Frankie exploded into the room first. "They had three kinds of soft ice cream, Esther. It was amazing."

"Olivia pointed to the strawberry for you, so we brought you back a strawberry cone."

Tess handed me a cone. "Hope that works for you." The voice of Tess and her expression did not match. Her voice was high pitched, but her face was tense.

Something had happened.

"Strawberry's great. Thanks for picking it, Liv."

"Olivia had vanilla," Frankie said as he did a little jig, which I suspected meant he needed to use the bathroom. "And I had a swirl. Did you know you could swirl ice cream?" Stav was in the doorway. He wouldn't look at me.

"A swirl?" I asked Frankie.

"Yah, like a vanilla and chocolate swizzled together in one... I have to go to the bathroom." Frankie ran to the back office which had a bathroom. I held my cone and looked at the adults in the room.

"You might want to lick your cone, Esther. It's starting to melt." Ramona pointed to my cone.

"I'm not hungry."

Tess took my cone and walked out of the room. We all heard her heels click as she moved to a trash can to throw out my cone. She clicked back to the room. As she entered, Frankie came out of the bathroom.

"Can we leave now?" He looked at Tess. "Are we heading back to the motel?"

"Let's get everything we had when we came," Tess said. "Olivia has her bag…" Tess was walking out of the room as she spoke. We all followed: Ramona, Stav, Olivia, Frankie, and I, like compliant soldiers heading into a line-up. Frankie pushed the button, and we all fit into one elevator. I wondered if everyone was coming to the Shamrock Motel for a party or if they were just coming to send us off in the back alley. Once the elevator doors opened, Frankie ran out into the corridor and down to the door where we had entered.

"Hold up, big guy." Stav's voice was stern.

Through the door window, I could see that the sun was starting to shine. I hoped that the rain had cleaned up the bad feeling of the morning. Stav pulled the heavy door open, and we all moved out toward the daylight. Surrounding the stoop from the back door were men and women with cameras and microphones. I saw Sherry O'Hara in the front of the crowd of cameras and reporters with microphones, her pink suit screaming for the center of attention.

I looked at Stav. I didn't need to look at which direction his eyes looked.

"You lied."

12

Katherine

1969

Timing was everything.

Planning was crucial. Discretion was vital.

I knew, probably more than any other member of our community, that choosing to leave Celestial Way could very well be the last decision I'd make in my life. Others who had spoken aloud their desire to 'move on' from the community were often gone the next day without as much as a goodbye, mysteriously so. I knew it wouldn't be easy for me, especially since I was married to the leader of the community.

I had no idea.

In my anger, the evening of the death of Maureen's baby boy Daniel, I started packing clothes and items to leave. Maureen was healing in her room, and Luna was asleep. Charles would not be home for another two days. Eugene and I had decided to leave in the night before Charles and the Direction Team came back. Eugene wanted out, too. He said that he was tired of the paradox. Helping the *Londons* and lost souls of the world and bringing them into a deceptively protective environment from the evil of the world to then open them up to a sneaky, predatory environment that took advantage of their history and weakness. Knowing that a layer of filth lay beneath what I had thought was a safe place for my daughters, I wanted to take my daughters and go as far as I could, away from Celestial Way, as soon as I could.

Celestial Way had once been such an amazing place of nirvana for me. In my early years at the vineyard, when Maureen was a baby, I felt sorry for the rest of the world. Then slowly, ever so slowly, Celestial Web had become a gigantic spider web, hidden by the beauty of the land and the grapevines. In time the grapes, hanging to the vines, believing in the vines, struggled. Those who struggled to leave would move back and forth to get out, like the fly who is caught in the web, thrashing to escape. And then, it stops. After that, the spider wraps the fly up and eats it.

"What do you think you're doing?" Charles stood in the doorway to our bedroom. His eyes were bloodshot, his clothes wrinkled. He'd been drinking. News of the baby must have gotten to Charles and brought a quick end to his business trip.

"Folding clothes," I whispered, my hands shaking. "The girls are sleeping." I refused to look at him. I could regroup. Eugene and I could change our plan.

"You're not thinking of leaving, are you, Katherine? Because that would be bad. Very bad."

What did he think? The rape of his daughter had been good?

"You never cease to amaze me, Katherine." Charles walked into the room. "You somehow, somewhere through the years, lost your gratefulness for the great gift given to you here. This place saved you, and this is the thanks I get. How in the world do you think you could ever leave here?" Charles moved toward me. I stepped back and looked into his dark grey eyes. "You changed, Katherine. And you will need to make that right. Very soon."

"You lied." My voice was shaking.

"Excuse me. I didn't hear you."

"You lied." My voice was stronger and louder.

Charles laughed a deep, dark laughter I'd never heard before. "I lied? I'm pretty sure you're confused."

"You lied to me the first time I met you. You weren't dropping a friend off at the airport? You were working your Recruitment Duty, and I was your victim that day. You went to an airport looking for exhausted college kids on their way home. I was vulnerable. You used that. You lied."

"Oh, my dear Katherine." Charles sat down on the bed and smiled at me as he took my hand. "You wanted every single lie I told."

"I loved you," I cried.

"Oh. Come on now, Katherine. You can't be that simple. You were in love with who you were with me. Never in love with me. Call it what it is."

I pulled my hand back. "There are bad things happening here. Now. I want to take the girls away from…"

"From?"

"From Rocco. From your so-called Youth Committee, preying on our children. From all the lies about what you do on your so-called business trips. I found receipts from strip joints and expensive restaurants."

Charles' head snapped at the mention of receipts.

"And pictures, Charles." My voice was shaking. "Pictures of naked young girls. I don't care what you do when you are away. But I don't like what you're doing to all these people making money for you here. You take advantage of everyone around you. And I don't want to be a part of it anymore."

Charles was silent for a good minute. I knew his secrets, and he looked rattled. "How innocent you sound as you throw blame around so effortlessly. You were a willing mark. My beautiful, willing mark, Katherine. Please own your role in the ploy. You've benefited from so many of the things you attack now. Wouldn't you say? You played a role in taking advantage of all these people. I gave you every prospect to grow. And now, what you're doing to destabilize us...." Charles stood up, walked to the window, and looked out. "You with your beautiful office. Your comfortable life. All your 'people' rushing around to please you. Speaking to you with respect. You won't walk away from these good things."

"Everything changed when I saw our daughter holding her dead baby this morning." Tears filled my eyes as my voice shook. "Your daughter, not old enough to drive in the real world, was pregnant by a man old enough to be her father. Do you want to talk about how wonderful Celestial Way is now? How can you not see that?"

"You're not leaving."

I looked down at the clothes on the bed. I'd been so excited to leave.

"People can stay here and live the purpose of a high power with all its goodness in the Rapture. Or people can leave and face a terrible world."

I cringed. His Rapture was a racket. The gig was up.

"You will never leave, Katherine. You made a deal."

"I never made a deal. Never."

"Your father. Your mother. Wouldn't it be so sad for the truth of their world to be announced to the world? Wouldn't it destroy your little Connecticut family's world, Katherine, for your father to go to prison? Also, your mother to know about his precious little Rita. Why, it would destroy that Fallen Family of yours."

"That's how you work?"

"You will stay and play the role that you chose to take on. Your choice is to be here."

"My choice is to leave." I would be the one fly that got away.

"You couldn't make it one day in the world today, Katherine. You don't have it in you. You'll die before you leave."

"Is that a threat?"

"That's the truth."

Charles left the room. I prayed he would stay somewhere else that night. In a cottage with any number of his little followers. I took a deep breath, and the saddest revelation moved me to thinking of my new plan: Charles had never asked how the girls were.

I needed to get my girls away from this place. Far away from Celestial Way. Planning was crucial.

Discretion vital.

Timing was everything.

During the eight months following the cryptic threat from Charles to me, the silent plan unfolded. Notes passed from me to Eugene to Mick to me and over again, passed under doors, in the back of Mick's truck, under flowerpots. No words spoken aloud. Too many eager ears around the Way.

The plan unfolded.

Like a long spiral staircase.

In an unusual, interesting order, with clear direction, in a slow, quiet ascension.

Eugene—August is a good time to leave. The Direction Team will be in Washington, D.C. for two weeks. Will probably be spies here.

Mick—I have a man who works with the Cult Exiting Commission. Will help find identities for you all after the escape. Working on it now. Assimilation.

Katherine—I want to be with girls at all times as we move to safety.

Eight months. The waiting was terrible. Charles moved into Captain's old quarters, still pretending that we were a strong couple while he was leading the Celestial Way community and Gatherings and in the dining hall. By May, it became apparent that London's sister Stormy was also pregnant. In early June, Stormy's baby was born, and her tiny baby lived. Stormy appeared, for a short time, content in staying at Celestial Way. Stormy named the baby Dawn. I really liked the name. I hoped the intent had more to do with a new day ahead than a hippy nod, but we will never know.

In late June, Stormy left. The baby was in the crib when Blaze got up, but Stormy had seemingly left in the night. Her restless spirit could not be stopped. London took over the duty of caring for Dawn, the premature baby girl, in hopes that the baby would be enough reason for Stormy to return someday. The remaining days of the summer of 1969 were hotter than most, and while most of the people at Celestial Way were worried about that year's crop of grapes, I was worried about the grapes of wrath and the safety of my daughters until I could pull them away from the place.

In July, America cheered as the country witnessed the first man on the moon. Most of the people at Celestial Way had no idea of the monumental event; the rest of the country smiled as astronaut Buzz Aldrin played *Fly Me to the Moon,* sung by Frank Sinatra. Not far from Celestial Way, another controlling man named Charles was leading his followers to a Helter Skelter murder for his mission.

As we moved closer to August, I felt a beautiful peace in the hidden knowledge of our escape plan: The Great Escape. Several times, I found myself daydreaming about being a part of a world I had been away from for close to two decades. I could catch up on all the lost years. I could go to movies. I could drive a car. I could take my girls to all sorts of wonderful places around the world. I'd seen the movie *The Wizard of Oz* in the theater as a young girl back in Connecticut, and I will never forget the scene where Dorothy opened the door from her black-and-white world to the colorful world of Oz.

At one time, Celestial Way was my colorful world, and, over time—through the years, through the hours— the colors dimmed, and a shadow overtook the vineyard.

I looked forward to the colorful world, even with all its bad things.

By August 1st, the heat was unbearable for workers outside and those of us inside, and my excitement about the escape was hard to hide. Charles and the Direction Team were due to leave for their wine convention on August 6th and to return on the 15th. The Great Escape was scheduled for August 9th, with every detail planned by the three of us mapped out in our written correspondence.

Katherine—The truck must be quiet as it rolls into Celestial Way. Most people are in cottages far enough not to hear, but we can't take any chances.

Eugene— Personal items should be packed in Mick's truck the week before. We need only to get in the back of the truck and leave. Put them in on his delivery day. Make it look like you are helping him load his truck.

Mick—New identities are set up for Katherine and Eugene. The girls' identities can be set up once we get you all settled in the final place.

Eugene and I had to sign a few forms for the lawyer friend whom he and Mick had met during their time in the Korean War. Dean Foltstein, with the Cult Exiting Commission, was more than happy to guide us through the appropriate yet discreet methods of creating our new identities. The paperwork included lines that asked for our names on our birth certificates. Our legal names. I had not used my birth-given name in years. For the past fifteen years, I had been Katherine.

Katherine.

Miss Katherine.

The wife of Charles Armstrong.

The head of the business office.

Mom.

Kat.

Movie Star.

I was still legally Katherine Marie Wayman. I hadn't been Katherine Marie Wayman, daughter of Jan and Donald

Wayman, sister of Howard Wayman, for such a long time that I had to look at the words as the ink dried. We would take on new names out in the world. Who would we be?

If I chose a different name for myself, would I not still be me?

"If it makes you feel any better, I feel the same way," Eugene said as we filled out the paperwork. "I haven't been Eugene Michael Stavinski since the war."

"And in Korea, you were always Stav. Just Stav," Mick said as we quietly loaded the truck the week before we left. "You've never really looked like a Eugene to me..."

Several weeks before our Day of Freedom, I found several stapled papers folded over under the flowerpot near the loading dock.

Important Info, Kat. Give it to Eugene after you read it.

Mick's handwriting gave me great security each time I read a note from him. The packet was helpful. Mick's friend, Dean from the Cult Exiting Commission, had put together whatever helpful information he could pass on to us to help us prepare for the transition out of Celestial Way and into the world without leaving breadcrumbs for Charles to find us. Eugene and I were different from other people Dean had worked with. In most cases, Dean's most challenging work was convincing people that they were in an abusive situation, one with inappropriate control from others. It was a slippery slope helping those people, since what he was doing could also be seen as brainwashing, though that was not the intention. There was no need to convince us that we were in a toxic environment. Eugene and I knew that Maureen and Luna needed to be away from not only the control but the abuse that would only get worse.

The stapled pages in the packet from Dean had a title on the first page:

Starting Your New Life

I could have a second chance with my life. I could reinvent myself, again. This time with caution. I took a deep breath and read.

Creating a new identity can be an exciting and stressful process. Most people look to either the excitement or the security of a new identity as a positive start on life, or they wouldn't be making such a significant change in their lives. However, creating a new, clean identity must be taken seriously so as to ensure your new life is untraceable.

Important documents must be created by reliable sources.

My heart began to beat, with both fear and excitement.

Important Guidelines for Your New Life

-Stop all communication of any kind with people in the previous life.

-Remember not to talk about your previous life at all with people in your new life. Be confident in the new story of your history. Write down the created history of your new identity and reread it on a regular basis.

-Do not tell anyone in your new life any of your secrets or past, even if you trust them.

-Keep a low profile. Do not take on any jobs or leadership roles that would call attention to yourself.

-Rent a storage locker and place a very good lock on it. Place all the materials from your previous life in the lockbox. Get two keys for the box. Keep one and give the other to a trusted individual who will always have the key with him or her.

-Do not put your money in a bank.

-Do not register to vote.

-Remember that details are more important in your life than in that of a person with a real identity.

-Remember, failing to plan is planning to fail.

A few words jumped out at me: a person with a real identity. What was I getting my daughters into with this move? Don't hesitate. The option to stay is not an option.

Failure in this escape was also not an option.

On August 7th, the day after Charles and his team left, I could barely keep my feet on the ground. Neither Maureen nor Luna knew of any part of the plan. I was going to wake them in the night. My goal was someday to get the truth of Celestial Way to the right people and put an end to the evil agenda. For now, I wanted to get my girls as far away as possible from their father and the people around him.

Eugene—I'll be outside, waiting for the truck. Bring the girls to the back of the truck. 2:13 a.m. Once packed up, Mick and I will push the truck while Katherine sits in the driver's seat with the car in neutral down to the end of the dirt road. That's the plan.

Katherine—I love the plan. I have never been happier! 2:13.

Mick—Keeping quiet is the most important part of this day. Fly me to the moon! 2:13.

2:13 a.m.

We were to leave in the middle of the night. When the night owls finally settled down, and when the early birds were still not up.

"Do you have a minute?" London stood in the doorway, looking exhausted and sad.

My one concern had always been leaving London behind. London was special, and I knew for a fact that taking care of Baby Dawn had been overwhelming for her. The sleepless nights, along with her concern for Stormy, had been weighing on her. The day that she came to me in my office, I knew she needed me.

"Always. Where's little Baby Dawn?"

"Blaze is with her for a while. I just finished cleaning the Main Office."

"I'm sure you could use a break, if even to clean an office. Babies are a lot of work. But the good news is that Dawn's really starting to put on a little weight."

"I'm scared." London's lower lip trembled.

"London, I'm here for you."

London moved into the room and sat down. "I don't know what to do."

For a moment, I was worried that London had tapped into our secret plan. Hadn't we been discreet enough?

"About what, London?"

"About everything. Dawn cries every hour she's awake. How will I ever find Stormy again? It was a miracle that we found her the first time. What should I do? Dawn needs her mother. I need ..."

When I found out that Stormy was pregnant, I knew who the father was. The pain in my heart was not for me, a woman scorned by her husband in plain sight. The pain was for my daughters, who were related to Dawn, and probably several other children that they didn't know about. I got up and moved from behind my desk. I shut the door. I sat down next to London. "Dawn will be fine," I said as I put my hand on London's arm.

"I'm not sleeping at all. I worry about Dawn, growing up here, with, you know..."

"Would you ever consider leaving?"

"Leaving? Never." London sniffled as she pushed her glasses back up the bridge of her nose.

"Why not?"

"For one, bad things happen to people who leave Celestial Way."

"You mean out in the world?"

"And I'm pretty sure the Direction Team would never allow it. I don't think people ever even make it outside of Celestial Way. If they even suspect you're thinking about it... I've just heard things."

"What things?"

"Bad things. Being invisible and cleaning the Main Office means that sometimes, I hear things."

"Like?"

"Like, I'm pretty sure Dorian was killed by someone on the team." The larger-than-life Dorian, with a punch-to-the-pinot attitude on life, had left Celestial Way right before Dawn was born.

"Dorian? Didn't he go back to help with his family farm in Iowa? His mother was sick or something."

"Is that what Charles told you?"

"I don't remember all the details."

"A lie."

"How do you know?"

"I overheard Rocco and Vince talking about it. They came into the Main Office on a night when I was cleaning. A few years ago. I was in the back office. They didn't know I was there."

In the spacious Main Office was a side room, which was probably a closet but was big enough to be another office. London cleaned the main room with the huge desk; many dark wood bookcases wrapped around the large room, important looking books gracing their shelves. A large dark wood table was just to the left of the desk where the Direction Team held their meetings. The back office, which London was talking about, was off to the right as you entered the large room. Without windows, the dark little room had a small table in the center of the room with no chairs around it. A low shelf about twelve inches out from the wall was on all three corners of the room, but not on the wall with the doorway. London called it the Dump Office. This was the room where extra items were dumped and where the food and drink for meetings were stored. It was also the room where Captain's whiskey was kept and where Captain had spent many a day drinking.

"Charles was out of town, and it was late at night. I was cleaning then because I knew I could play with the gadgets, the cameras, and the recorder after I cleaned. When Rocco and Vince came in the Main Office, they were very loud. I knew they'd been drinking. From my life with two parents who drank, I knew that the truth comes out when you drink. My brother called alcohol the Truth Serum. I moved behind the door to the Dump Room and held my breath. Rocco said that Dorian and

Charles had had a big argument the week before, back in the winery after the wine-making team was gone for the day."

"London, why didn't you tell me this?"

"There's more. Rocco said that Charles was mad."

"About what?"

"Charles knew that Dorian was on to him."

"On to him?"

"Rocco told Vince that Dorian knew something he wasn't supposed to know. He was slurring his words as he said that Charles couldn't afford to have him around anymore. And he said…" London stopped. She looked so tired.

"Said what, London? What did Rocco say?"

London swallowed. Her eyes looked strange, like she wasn't in the room with me but back in the Dump Office several years earlier. "Something like, a good friend will help you move, but a best friend will help you move the body."

"What does that even mean?"

"They talked about the 'second graveyard' and how nobody else better piss Charles off. They killed Dorian, Katherine."

"You're sure?" I didn't want it to be true. Dorian had done so much to make Celestial Way successful.

"Yes. They'd kill someone if they thought that a person knew whatever Dorian knew. No, I'd never leave Celestial Way."

"2:13 a.m. Saturday night. Sunday morning."

"What?"

"If you're interested in leaving."

London stared at me through her large glasses.

"By the dock."

"You're leaving?" London's eyes teared up. She took off her glasses and rubbed her eyes.

"Come with us."

"I can't."

"Bring Dawn, and we'll go as far as we can from this place."

"There's more. Charles..."

"Charles," I said with clipped words, "is not the king of the world."

"He is," London replied, "if he knows about your past."

"Your past?"

"I told them. Him."

"Him?"

"Charles. At The Revealing. Years ago. When I first came here. I told Captain, Charles, and Rocco that I killed my mother."

"But..."

"I did. I killed my mother. I shot her."

"You..."

"By the time the police got to our house—they saw my drunk father. They saw my dead mother. They saw the gun on the floor. They saw me holding onto my little sister. We were so young, and the cops who came to our house that night had been there so many times before. My brother was out with friends that night. Probably a good thing. He would have defended my dad. The cops assumed my dad had killed my mom. They looked as relieved as I felt when they handcuffed my old man. Never even tested the gun for fingerprints."

"I had no idea." Poor London. If she didn't have bad luck, London wouldn't have any luck at all.

"And nobody else did. Until I 'revealed' it. Charles knows. He would use that against me."

"Wow."

"He would. You know that. And my prison is real prison. Without Dawn. Or the possibility of finding Stormy again." The strange collateral that Captain and Charles had stolen from us in the form of our darkest secrets would be a guarantee for them, if we did not go along with his agenda.

I leaned into London and hugged her. "I love you, London." London sobbed as she clung to me. I wondered if anyone had ever told her those words. I would never see quirky, wonderful London again. I cried too. I would miss London, but my daughters' lives were worth the gamble.

"2:13, London." I said nothing more.

Two nights later.

August 9th.

2:09 a.m.

The Mother House was empty since Charles was out of town, and Captain's old apartment where he'd been staying was empty. I had stayed up after the girls had gone to bed, just waiting. I looked around the apartment in which I had lived for the past fifteen years. I would miss nothing. My window was ajar, and the cool night air smelled good, but no wheels on the gravel not far from my window could be heard. I went to Maureen's room first.

I bent down and whispered close to her ear, "We're leaving."

Maureen sat up and rubbed her eyes as I put my finger to my lips. Hand motions only, after that. I picked up a sleeping two-year-old and wrapped Luna in a blanket as Maureen put on her shoes and a big sweater that I'd set out for her. We moved quietly out of the apartment and down the long hall to the dock area.

I saw movement outside of the window by the large doors to the loading dock. Mick's truck was there. I was elated. Even I had not heard the truck drive into Celestial Way. Two silhouettes of men's bodies stood near the truck: Mick and Stav. I handed Luna to Maureen, and rather than open the large dock doors which were open most days all day long, I opened the regular door with the window to the right of the doors, slowly, so slowly. As I motioned Maureen out the door, I saw a third body moving around by the back of the truck: Levi. The silhouette of Levi with the full moon glowing behind him. Movement near Stav's legs: Merlot. Hadn't even barked once.

Good boy.

Mick moved toward me and smiled. His fingers formed the universal signal for OK, the thumb and pointer finger forming an "O," and the remaining three fingers waving comfort as he moved to hug me. Mick smelled like heaven. We were really doing this. A surreal feeling encouraged by a strong jolt of adrenaline moved me toward the back of the truck. Eugene and Levi helped Maureen up into the back of the truck, Luna still firmly held close to her. Levi hugged Maureen in such a loving embrace. Mick picked up Merlot and set him up into the back of the truck. His toenails made a clicking noise until they reached a blanket. I looked out toward the cottages. One last look. A silent good-bye to a place that I'd once loved. Cottage after cottage, lost soul after lost soul, aimlessly grasping at hope in a place that was hopelessly using every one of them.

Motion.

My heart skipped a beat.

From the closest cottage, I saw a dark figure moving toward us quickly, probably fifty feet from the back of the truck. A second figure appeared. Practically chasing the closer figure. I looked at Mick, who looked back at me and mouthed what I could see from the light of the moon: "London."

London was carrying the tiny baby Dawn close under her jacket. Blaze was keeping up with her as they got to the back of the truck. Mick gave me a look that showed not blame, only concern. I put up the universal OK signal. We would be OK. Truth be told, I was glad London and Blaze had come. We would work out the glitches later. I wanted to save them all: Lottie, Dylan, the Wine Whisperers, Dale, and Richard, and so many more poor souls. I wanted to take them all away from Celestial Way. I would save them all.

I motioned toward London and Blaze with a finger to the lips and a motion to the back of the truck. London handed Dawn to Blaze. Blaze turned to Eugene who helped her up into the back of the truck. London pulled something out of her pocket. In the moonlight, I could see it was a photograph, taken with the Main Office Polaroid. She pointed to Maureen and waved the picture toward her. Eugene grabbed the picture and handed it to Maureen. I knew the picture because I had been there when it was taken. It was the first and last picture taken of baby Daniel. It was London's idea. Before the burial of the baby,

London smuggled the camera into the room where we had swaddled the stillborn child until decisions were made about the burial. London had taken the picture as a gift to Maureen for when the time was right. Maureen was deep in grief for so long that London had held back until the time was right.

The time was right.

London put her hand to her heart and waved to everyone in the truck. She hugged me and ran back into the darkness near the cottages. The image of London running was the last thing I remembered before the pandemonium.

Off in the distance, a coyote howled at the moon, a long, sad howl that took over the night. Merlot growled a low growl in response. Dawn began to cry. We had not once considered the coyotes, who had grown in numbers in recent months. We'd thought we had everything covered.

We were wrong.

From inside the dark Mother House, Mick and I could hear the sound of the bell, though muted. It was the bell over the door in the Gathering Room. I had not been alone in the Mother House. Mick motioned for Eugene to close the back of the truck. Merlot jumped out of the truck and ran to me before Eugene complied as Mick darted toward the cab to get in and drive the truck. He looked back at me and motioned for me to head to the front passenger side.

My feet froze as I saw a figure in the window moving toward the dock door. Then, there were two figures moving toward the door. Merlot barked at the figures and ran to my side. The hall light flicked on, and I could see Dylan and Cubby, a twelve-year-old boy who had grown up at Celestial Way. Dylan made eye contact with me as he waved something in his hand.

A gun.

"Go," I yelled to Mick. "He's got a gun!" No need to be quiet now.

"No!" Mick yelled.

"Go!" I screamed.

The truck started and moved out with a roaring engine.

Dylan opened the door so quickly that it slammed against the wall. I stared at the once bratty red-headed kid who had grown to be a pudgy, power-hungry teenager who wanted to be accepted into The Chosen so badly that he'd use a gun on a woman.

"Your mom will be very upset with you, Dylan. What will she say when she hears you have a gun?" I was stalling. Where would he have gotten a gun? There were no guns at Celestial Way. The truck was almost to the bottom of the hill, coming out of the long driveway. I didn't want Dylan to shoot at the truck. I was scared to death, but I used a calm tone to demean Dylan.

"Wait, stop!" Dylan yelled at the truck and started shooting in its direction, but it was now far enough down the hill that his bullets couldn't hit it.

"Charles put you and a boy in charge when he was away? What was he thinking? He left boys to do a man's job?" A surge of confidence filled me. I had saved my daughters. Even if I died tonight, I'd saved my girls.

Dylan ran back at me and my insult and pointed the gun at my face.

"Don't shoot her!" Cubby's high-pitched voice, almost ready to change, sounded like a girl. "The Doctor said not to shoot her."

"Go ahead, Dylan," I said. "Shoot me. You know you want to." I could see the whites of Dylan's eyes as he breathed heavy with a growing rage. "Come on, aren't you one of The Chosen now? You need to protect Celestial Way, don't you?"

"Don't do it, Dylan" Cubby cried. "The Doctor wants her alive. Remember?"

"I'm guessing," I taunted, "that your job was to stop anybody from leaving this place. Am I right?"

Dylan moved closer to me, his gun now aimed at my eyes.

"You didn't do a very good job of doing that, Dylan. Several people just left on the truck. Charles will be mad."

Neither boy said anything.

"That's why you two were hiding out in the Gathering Hall. Am I right?"

No answer.

"Am I right, Cubby? You two were supposed to stop us from leaving while the real men were away? Cubby?"

"Yes, ma'am. We were supposed to keep you all from leaving, but the Doctor said very sp-specifically," Cubby stuttered, "that you were to be kept alive."

"You mean Charles said that?" I said.

"Yes, the Doctor, Miss Katherine. He said that."

"You do know, Cubby, that Charles isn't a doctor? He just wants you to call him that. He's not a doctor. He's a liar."

Dylan's arm, holding the gun, slowly moved down to his side.

"He tells you things to keep you here, following him, doing things for him." I felt empowered as I spoke. "While he goes out and does whatever he wants."

"He keeps us s-safe," Cubby stammered.

"At least you think so. Why won't you kill me, Dylan? It would be so easy. Why did Charles tell you to keep me alive?"

Dylan glared at me as he spoke. "Because he wants you to suffer."

I will never know what Dylan and Cubby heard that night that alerted them to the dock.

The coyote howling at the full moon? Could I blame Merlot's low growl? The fussing baby Dawn?

The truck would be turning onto the main highway off the long road from Celestial Way by now.

Without me.

I needed to own my role in the plan that I'd never be a part of. I chose not to blame myself. I would be miserable enough with the sentence with which I had to live. I chose otherwise.

I blamed it on the moon.

The Rapture

True courage is in facing danger when you are afraid.

The Wizard of Oz

13

Esther

Day Seven 1976

"You lied."

Tears swelled in my eyes, and my throat burned. I was looking at Stav, but I was talking to all the adults behind me. Stav. Tess. Ramona. "You all lied."

No one responded as the reporters below started shouting questions at us.

"Where have the children been for these past several days?"

"Who do you believe caused the explosion?"

"Have you found Tara Duvall yet?"

"What is the pending date for Clark Duvall's trial?"

"Who found the children?"

The last question came from Sherry O'Hara. She was still in the pink suit that she'd worn during the morning news broadcast from our house. Big day for the local media. Banner day for the Duvall family. Miss O'Hara stepped forward and looked at Ramona. "While people are relieved to hear that the Duvall children are alive and safe, I'm sure our viewers would want to know where these children have been since the city of Omaha has been worried about their welfare for days."

Ramona stepped forward as she put her arms around Frankie and moved him back toward her. "The children are safe, but we will not be answering any questions at this time."

The crowd of reporters, cameramen, and a few stray, curious people stared at the three of us, standing in the back-parking lot of the Omaha police station. We were in the spotlight. Three children who looked like carnival urchins. The onlookers' eyes were full of pity, maybe also sadness or sympathy, but clearly pity. The same eyes that look at a car accident as they slowly drive past an accident. Eyes that say, I want to see your suffering, but I don't want to be near you.

"Where will the children be staying tonight?" Sherry O'Hara yelled out, her camera man following her every move. I thought of Kathy Krisko in her pink clothes. Would she grow up to be a Channel Seven reporter? Suddenly, I was not as big a fan of Sherry O'Hara.

"Thank you." Ramona took my hand and Frankie's hand and turned back to the door. Olivia held my hand.

Sherry O'Hara's voice lingered as we moved into the corridor. "You heard it here. The story that just gets stranger by the minute. The Duvall children have been found and are safe. Omaha deserves to know where these children have been for the past week. Channel Seven live."

Ramona led the group to the far end of the corridor and opened a door that took us down a staircase.

"That was the lady from TV, right Stav?" Frankie asked.

"Yes." Stav held Olivia's hand as she moved one step at time down the stairs.

"Will we be on TV?" Frankie asked.

"TV," Olivia said as we entered the small room.

"You guys will be on TV tonight," Ramona said. "Maybe we can watch it together."

"Where?"

My voice boomed off all four corners of the stairwell.

"Where're you taking us tonight? The zoo? The fire station? Maybe a carnival in a small town in Iowa?" I wanted to cry so much but didn't. My head and throat ached.

"Esther..." Stav said.

"What? We need to know what's going on."

Not one adult spoke.

I continued my rage rampage. "You've been hiding us for days. Protecting us. And suddenly, you bring us here. What happened? Who called the TV people?"

Tess looked at Stav.

Stav whispered, "Tara did."

"My mom?" I asked.

"Is she here?" Frankie asked.

"Momma," Olivia said.

"First," Tess said, "I'm sorry if you feel hurt, Esther. I can understand. What you all need to know is that Tara's safe." Tess opened a door to a different floor, and we all followed behind her.

"And Daddy?" Frankie asked. I could hear his voice quiver.

"Your father's fine too." This time Ramona spoke. I was sick of her saying that it was good that my dad was in jail. What's so great about that?

Tess motioned us into a room and sat down on an old couch and patted the spot next to her. "Why don't you all take a seat?" I sat down on the couch. Frankie sat close to Ramona. Olivia sat on the rug on the floor, and Stav, his big body in an awkward pose, sat down next to her. Tess continued. "The plan's changed fifteen times in this day alone. The explosion at your house really changed the plans from what we all hoped would be best. That's why you were at the motel. We're missing one key piece, though."

"Key," Olivia repeated.

"The men who made your house explode and who took you from Dr. Vaughn's office are from a place in California where Tara used to live."

Ramona cleared her throat. "Your mother has something that those men want. It's something they don't want the authorities to see or hear. They think they burned the tape in your house. The leader of the group in California thinks that the fire took care of things. Now, he ..."

I cleared my throat. I spoke. "Now he wants the Duvall children. And Momma wants the people in California to know that we're protected by the chief of police in Omaha."

"That's right, Esther."

"So, the policeman guys," Frankie asked, "aren't the bad guys after us."

"No, Frankie. We just need to get that tape." Tess said, almost to herself. "We need the key."

"What's on the tape?" I asked, my arms still crossed.

"Proof." The word came from Stav.

Buying time.

That was fancy adult talk, for *we don't know what to do next, so just entertain yourselves while we wait for a clue.*

Time moved slowly as we waited for news from Ramona. Olivia pointed to the MGM books that Stav had brought with us to the police station. I picked up the large book, and the three of us sat on the uncomfortable couch in the cold room. We opened to the most-viewed page: the middle spread of a full-color photo from the *The Wizard of Oz*. Olivia pulled out her music box as Frankie joined us on the couch. Stav sat on a chair reading the newspaper.

"There he is!" Frankie said as he pointed to Toto. Olivia wound her music box.

"Yep," I said. "There's the dog we're going to get someday." These are the words my mother always said when we sat with her and the MGM book. "And there," I said after I turned the page, "is Frank Sinatra and Gene Kelly dancing at sea." I pointed to the scene from *Anchors Away*.

"Sea," Olivia said as the beloved music played. "Key."

"Where's the swimming pool page?" Frankie asked.

"Way back here." I turned the pages to a scene where a beautiful woman was diving into a pool. The colors of the water and the woman's swimsuit were so bright, they almost didn't look real.

"Lady." Olivia pointed to the picture.

"The lady was…" I stopped and read the name of the woman in the picture. I realized our mother had never read her name. "Esther Williams."

"Hey, that's just like your name. You're the lady in the pool, Esther."

"Horses," Olivia requested.

I turned to the picture with the horses at the beginning of the book that showed the set of *Gone with the Wind*. Women dressed in beautiful hoop-skirt dresses and men in clothes from the era faced the camera for a mug shot while several horses stood off in the background near a big mansion. The title of the picture: *Gone with the Wind* Set—Tara and Twelve Oaks.

Tara.

Missing pieces to the puzzle.

I'd never read the script below the picture until that day at the police station. *Clark Gable, Vivien Leigh, Leslie Howard, Olivia de Havilland, and extras on the set take a moment to pose for a casual picture.*

Frank.

Clark.

Olivia.

Esther.

"Turn the page, Esther," Frankie demanded.

Tara.

"Esther!" Frankie moved toward the book and turned the page.

"Key," I said to myself.

Olivia pulled back the corner of the glittered material on the music box that had the sparkly rainbow on it. The past several days had taken its toll on the small music box. *Somewhere Over the Rainbow* had played so many times since

Momma had left that the music was coming out slow and marbled, and the small plastic ballerina was sluggish in her rotation. The colorful glitter was falling off, and I wondered how Olivia would cope if the darn thing croaked. Olivia pulled at the tattered upper right corner of material, right behind the ballerina. Olivia pulled a small yellow envelope that had been tucked behind the glittery rainbow and opened it. She pulled out a small key and a piece of paper. She gave me the paper.

I read the scribbled print on the paper, in our mother's handwriting: *Box 708, Omaha Postal Office, Downtown.*

"Let me see that, Liv." Frankie grabbed the key from Olivia, and Olivia whimpered as the door to our room opened. Ramona had no expression on her usually animated face.

"Sorry, guys. No word."

"Look, Ramona, we found a key," Frankie said as he ran to Ramona with the newly found treasure.

"The key!" Ramona shouted and grabbed it.

14

Katherine

1976

*T**hree may keep a secret if two of them are dead.*
- Ben Franklin

Charles knew how sick I was. He knew how weak I was.

He just didn't know how powerful I was.

I lay in the bed in my room, looking out my window to the hills that once had comforted me. Now, they only reminded me that I was here, and my daughters were out in the world. The pain in my heart was greater than the pain in the center of my abdomen.

"Knock, knock." London moved the door open with her hip and came into my bedroom with a tray of food. "Need to keep your strength up, lady." London set the tray down on the bedside table. "You can't leave me, Katherine. You're all I've got. The stew isn't as good as Lottie's, back in the day. It's pretty good though."

We'd lost Lottie shortly after the Great Escape seven years ago. Most believed she had died of a heart attack; no one ever knew the prognosis of people or their conditions at Celestial Way. The blind theories were just that: grabbing-at-straws autopsies. I personally believed Lottie had died of a broken heart. After hearing what her son had done and how he stood in alliance with Charles in his redirected mission, Lottie was beside herself. Everything she had thought she was protecting her son from he eventually had become.

"Eat! We need to get you stronger." London helped me sit up on my bed.

We both knew I'd never get stronger. The pain in my abdomen and the demise of my health 'looked like cancer' to Clarence, our Celestial Way doctor, who'd come to the winery years ago. He had been a family doctor in his previous life, and while we trusted him, his wisdom was a bit antiquated at best.

"Why are you so chipper today?"

"I've got good news." London handed me a spoon and napkin and moved to shut the door to my bedroom. "We're going to take this place down. Are you with me?"

How many times had I wanted just to get up and leave, walk right out the door and never return? Too many to count. Charles had squelched that dream after the night of the Great Escape. Dylan and Cubby, who now liked to be called by his real name Jacob, had locked me in the back room in the Main Office until Charles had returned. Charles had unlocked the door to the back room and stood in the doorway. I was sitting in the corner on the floor.

"You think you've won. But," Charles said, "you will never win. I'll make damn sure you don't. And just as a little sign of how serious I am. I just shot your damn dog."

I took a breath. I could not cry in front of Charles.

I had won.

No one had ever escaped from Celestial Way. Charles knew I'd won.

But he still chose to push my buttons.

"If you ever, ever try to leave this place, exposing your Fallen Family is no longer your greatest fear." Charles moved into the small room. "Stand up." He grabbed me and pulled me up. He moved close to my face, so close he could kiss me. I could smell his sour-apple Jolly Rancher breath. The breath of a man I had once adored. The breath of a man I had made love to through the years. I hated this man. "If you ever leave, I will hunt down your daughters and kill them both. That I promise you, my dear wife."

My parents and brother.

Button pushed.

My dog.

Button pushed.

Charles knew all my buttons to push.

He had put them there.

I remember thinking that night as he walked out of the back room of the Main Office: *You can spend the rest of my life pushing my buttons, but you know I still won.*

London's smile broke my mind away from the memory of the threat of Charles. She was giddy with whatever plan she had in mind. I was curious but doubtful.

"You and me, and what army?" I laughed but was stopped by the pain in my abdomen.

"Expose him. Shout to the world what's been going on here. Have him pay legally for what he's done for years. End it all."

"Don't you still worry about what Charles and the others on the team know about your past?"

"If you die, I'll have nothing here, Katherine. Dawn's safe. Stormy's never coming back. I'd rather take the risk now. I feel really good about this."

"London, I love your enthusiasm. But I don't have the energy to even sit up and eat the stew you brought me. How could we ever take on Charles and his Direction Team?"

"With this." London pulled out an object from her pocket. It was a box. She opened the box and showed me a black round object. "This tape."

"My brain's foggy. You're telling me that thing will bring this place down?"

"This tape and the picture and files you found a few years ago in the cemetery. You gave them to me to hide in my cottage. Who would ever think to look for anything like that in my cottage. Charles and his men don't even acknowledge me when I walk by them. Do remember the file?"

"Yes. I'd almost forgotten about finding the pictures and file."

"This tape has a conversation that, if we can get to the right people, will be evidence of the bad secrets here. We have to look at this differently than as the victims we've allowed ourselves to become. We have nothing to lose."

I said nothing as I moved the stew around with my spoon. I knew that we had no way of communicating with the outside world. Mick was long gone. Charles had made sure that he no longer worked for us. I grieved the loss of Mick almost as much as my daughters.

"I have on this tape the discussion of selling drugs, lots of drugs. Rocco also mentioned killing one of the girls here last week. Murder."

"How'd you tape them?"

"The key. I still have the key that the Captain gave me to clean the Main Office. Charles doesn't know that. I can go into the Main Office any time I want. I know how to use all the gadgets that Charles gets, so I started taping the sessions of Charles and his Direction Team. I would turn on the recorder in the Dump Room and replay it later."

Voices of workers on the hill echoed outside my window.

"Katherine, this tape in my hands is gold. I taped them last night. I went in and listened early this morning when no one was in the office. The voices of Charles, Cliff, Rocco, and Tiller are all identifiable. They use each other's names as they talk about… the awful things they're doing. They made plans on this tape. Specific plans. I've taped so many discussions where the conversation is hard to hear, or they talked about the wine business, but this, this is the most valuable thing I've ever had.'"

"I still don't understand how we get this out?"

"I've got it all covered. Just trust me."

"Where do we begin?"

"With a letter."

"A letter?"

"What's in the last note that Mick left for you? Under the flowerpot. Before Charles fired him?"

"It was a note with a person's name. The one who helped everyone get new identities: Theresa something. Just a name and an address. No phone number."

"You still have that."

I did. Under my mattress. "But the note said it would be dangerous if Charles found out who that person was. He said not to contact her."

"But he gave you the name."

"He did."

"We won't contact her. We'll have someone else contact her."

"OK."

"So, we have the name and address of the contact."

"Yes."

"And I have this tape and a plan."

15
Esther
1976

We had a sleepover—that's what Tess told Frankie—in one of the offices of the Douglas County Jail building in downtown Omaha. Stav saw a few reporters camping outside, so we decided to wait inside.

I'd woken up in the middle of the night and sat up for a while. Everyone around me was fast asleep. Frankie, Olivia, and I were all sleeping on cots that a nice man had brought after Ramona left. The itchy-scratchy dark green army blankets covering us smelled musty as I looked around the room. I could see the shape of Tess on the couch and Stav in a chair. I wondered how he could sleep sitting up. I had a feeling that Stav didn't sleep much at all.

The luster of new adventures at every turn was starting to take its toll on Frankie and Olivia, and I could tell that Tess had been trying her hardest to find fun distractions for the odd reality of the past week. Before we'd gone to sleep, Tess had Stav find a small, outdated TV, which had most likely been sitting on a shelf in the same closet where our itchy blankets had been tucked away for the past century. They had set the TV on a small table near our cots and plugged it in.

"It's almost ten, and I thought you might want to see yourselves on the news."

Two weeks earlier, my parents would never have let the Junior Mints stay up this late, and a few days earlier, the adults had been turning off the news to protect us from the truth. Here we were, still in our clothes, getting excited about seeing ourselves on the news. The familiar music for the opening of the news came on the grainy black and white television, and Tess shushed us.

"Our top story tonight brings good news to our viewers who have been worried about the three children of Clark and Tara Duvall." The screen showed footage of our run-in with the media that day from the opposite perspective than we had from the back steps we had stood on with Ramona. The camera honed in on Frankie, Olivia, and me and pulled back to show that we were outside the back door of the jail.

"An anonymous call to all three Omaha news stations sent reporters and cameramen to the back side of the downtown police station. The call came from a phone booth in the midtown area of Omaha. The three children looked safe and healthy with Officer Ramona Ramirez."

We aren't making a statement at this time.

Ramona spoke to the group of reporters on TV, just as she had earlier that day. It was strange to see the moment outside the back of the jailhouse, a moment we had already lived. The footage was a reminder that this was not some bad dream. In addition to the television reminder was the picture of the Junior Mints and me, standing in front of Ramona. I will never know which camera out in the crowd took the picture, but every news outlet, all the way up to the Associated Press, used the shot that captured me behind Frankie and Olivia. The adults had, of course, been cropped out of the picture, and the focus was on the three young children. I had worn denim shorts and an ugly green shirt for two days. Frankie's hair was dark, curly and unruly, but his blue eyes were sharp. Olivia's long, dark blonde hair was lighter than I remember against her dark blue shirt. It was Olivia's eyes I remember the most. Her brown eyes were framed with dark lashes and a deep fear. We looked like lambs to slaughter. I didn't remember feeling that way since Tess, Stav, and Ramona had been right behind us at the time of the picture as they had been for days. I do remember feeling angry that we'd been on a wild ride with no end in sight, but plenty of lies.

"So, for now, we're just here waiting?" I had asked as Tess tucked us in.

"That's right, honey."

"Waiting for what?"

"For Ramona to bring us news." The dark circles under the eyes of my nosy neighbor lady kept me from asking any more questions.

"Good night, Esther. Sleep tight, Junior Mints."

Like the players in a game of Capture the Flag, we lay in hiding. Waiting. When the game was over, when the flag was captured, one kid would wave the flag and shout, "Olly, olly oxen free." And the other kids would know that the game was done, and that it was safe to come out. In our long game, longer than a game of *Chutes and Ladders* with Frankie, we were waiting. The game was called Days of Lies, and we were praying for someone to shout that it was safe to come out. Safe to see our parents. Safe to quit running and hiding. I wanted so badly for someone to shout, "Olly, olly, oxen free."

I tossed and turned for a while. The man in the hat and his partner in crime were in the big building where we were having our sleepover. That thought creeped me out. At least they were no longer after us. They were behind bars. I opened my mind to a thought that I had been thinking since we entered the building that morning: was my dad in this building? The reporters kept saying that he was waiting, too. Waiting for a trial. I didn't ask since I wasn't sure I wanted to see my dad in this bad place. I wanted to see him free. At least we had something in common for the moment. We were both waiting.

I was finally able to get to sleep.

The next morning, in the seven days of lies, Ramona was still not back after lunch. Looked like more waiting. Stav took Frankie and Olivia on a tour of the facility, trying to fill the hours of our waiting game. Tess told me to stay with her.

"Dr. Vaughn wants to talk to you." Tess folded one of the itchy blankets.

"Why?"

"I'm not sure." She picked up another blanket to fold. "She just asked to meet with you."

"OK."

Ten minutes later, Dr. Vaughn was at the door. "A better day today, Esther?" Dr. Vaughn had her hair pulled up. The deep brown of her hair made her green eyes flash.

"Yes," I lied.

"I'm heading down the hall for a while." Tess smoothed her hair. "I'll be back in a bit."

"Thank you, Tess. Esther, why don't we sit down on the couch? Are you alright with me talking to you?"

"Sure." No fish, no seven-up. Hopefully, no three-wishes talk.

"You're quite an amazing girl. With all that's been going on."

I didn't know how to respond, so I didn't.

"I called your school this week." Dr Vaughn cleared her throat.

"My school?" Would I even be going to school? Now I could be the even more strange girl. Everyone would know what had happened to me.

"I met with your principal and school counselor."

"Why?"

"Because we talked about how I can help you and your brother and sister get through this coming school year."

"I think we'll be fine. We just want my mom and dad with us. Will they be?"

"Lots of good things are about to happen. We think. We should have a better idea of what's going to happen after Ramona gets back. Whatever happens, you'll benefit from a little help from people who... can help. Esther, you're a smart girl who..."

"I'm not that smart. Sorry to interrupt, Dr. Vaughn, but I don't understand any of this."

"This?"

"What the adults keep saying. How my mom used to live in a bad place. With bad people. The people who are after us right now. I don't get it."

Dr. Vaughn sat silent as I continued. No pop, no fish, no games.

"Why would anyone stay in a place that was bad? With bad people? Why wouldn't you just leave? Guess I'm not that smart."

"The best way I can explain what happened in California is to tell you about boiling frogs."

Another one of Dr. Vaughn's tricks? Just don't break out any frog puppets.

"Did you know that if you put a frog in boiling water, it will jump right out? But live frogs will stay in lukewarm water as the water starts to boil, slowly, ever so slowly. They just stay, unable to perceive danger or the threat; they will stay until they die."

"So, you're saying people in the California place didn't know the place was bad?"

"At first. People actually thought they were part of something good. It's the same in any relationship, too. It can start out seemingly good. And then, abuse and threats. People who are in charge can abuse power, or a person in a relationship can start to take advantage of their partner. They'll say strange things like, *You need me. No one will be better. Here is good. There is bad.*"

"Then how did my mom know it was bad? That she was in boiling water?"

"Her mother. Tara's mother pulled a curtain, so to speak, and found some bad things. I really don't know too much."

"Do you know anything about a baby named Daniel?"

"No, sorry, Esther. I do know that a man named Charles Armstrong wants to come here. That would not be good. But Kemper's been helping you."

"Kemper?" *Not-my-favorite-person Kemper?* I wrinkled my nose.

"Yes, Charles Armstrong called the Omaha police shortly after your mother disappeared to say that your mom and dad were guilty of kidnapping a baby from their community. That's when your dad was arrested."

"How did he know we were in Omaha?"

"I don't know, but I do know that Kemper told him several lies."

"Does this Charles know the guys he sent are in custody?"

"The whole country knows. That was in the news. Your house exploding was on national television."

"So, what were the lies? That Kemper told him." In those days of lies, these were the first lies that hadn't been told to the naïve Duvall children.

"He told Armstrong that they have Tara in jail too. He said that the media doesn't know that. The news thinks your mom is still in hiding. Like she is. And," Dr. Vaughn continued, "he said they were flying with the kidnapped child to California. To the compound. That made Armstrong happy. We needed to hold off until…"

"The key," I said.

"Right, the key. Tara called the police yesterday morning, after she called the television stations. She told them to find a key. The two men who blew up your house thought the key was in the house. They wanted it or what the key opened not to be found by anyone. We don't know for sure, but we think whatever that key opens is going to bring us all the answers. I almost forgot—the main reason I wanted to talk to you was about this." Dr. Vaughn picked up the envelope that she had set on the side table.

My name was on the envelope in cursive with a blue pen. The envelope was similar to the one that had been on our counter for the last few weeks.

"Apparently," Dr. Vaughn said, "the school's been trying to contact your mother for a while. They've called and sent something through the mail."

"What did they want from her?" I asked.

"The principal didn't want anything from her. He wanted to meet with you and your mom and the counselor about the results of your test."

"Did I fail?"

Dr. Vaughn laughed and answered. "No, Esther, you didn't fail. In fact, you did very well, better than most kids your age and better than most adults. You had a very high score on your IQ test. Do you know what that means?"

"That I'm precocious?"

Dr. Vaughn's laughter was louder and longer this time. She threw her head back and got herself together. "Esther, you're so funny."

I wasn't trying to be funny.

"I mean, you're a very smart and humble young lady. You're unique."

"I don't want to be weird though. Any weirder than I am. I have a strange name. Now I have this." I threw my arms up and looked around the room. "I have what happened to my dad and mom and… I don't want to be smart. I don't want to be different. I don't want my principal to put me in the grade ahead. I want to disappear." I couldn't hold the tears back any more.

"It's alright, Esther. The principal just wanted your mom to know how well you did. They wanted to share some summer programs and camps for boys and girls just like you. They wanted to congratulate you."

"OK." I sniffed and took a deep breath. "I don't think I'm too excited to grow up in this world if so many people want power over other people. How can you tell who the good guys and bad guys are? How do I know if my teachers are good people?" Suddenly, Kathy Krisko's mom popped into my head. What if she was trying to control me through the Daisy Troop? That could be my out.

"Good question. It isn't easy. Sometimes, children are told to obey and follow rules from adults so often, and they don't realize when a situation is bad. I guess I would say that if something doesn't feel right, listen to that feeling. I had a blind client once who was finally able to get a dog that had been trained to help her in her daily activities. Julie knew her dog had been trained. She just didn't know how. One day, she was walking with her dog, and they were standing at a crosswalk. She was ready to walk and signaled that to the dog. The dog then pulled her back. But her signal to the dog had been to move forward. The dog disobeyed. He saved her life."

"Why?"

"Because the dog had been trained to disobey when his owner was in danger. Intelligent disobedience. That's what they call it."

"Intelligent disobedience." I tasted the words. Sounded a lot like stranger danger.

"The dog was trained to obey the owner until the situation was not right."

"Esther!" Frankie exploded into the room. "We went down a secret staircase and got potato chips from a big machine. Only they weren't potato chips. What were they, Stav?"

"Fritos," Stav said with a grin.

"Fritos!" Frankie said. "Ay, ay, ay, ay! I am dee Frito Bandito!"

Olivia smiled as she stood close to Stav. Tess and Ramona walked in behind them. "Greetings!" Ramona stood in the doorway in jeans and a sweatshirt. On the front of the sweatshirt was a football and the words Nebraska Cornhuskers National Champions. Her hair was pulled back in a ponytail, and she still looked radiant. "I come bearing good news."

"Everyone, take a seat." Tess scurried us to sit down.

"It's been a crazy twenty-four hours, but since Miss Olivia found our key, so much has happened." Ramona smiled at Olivia, who leaned into Stav and grinned. "What we found in the lockbox at the post office was enough evidence for the FBI to send men to make an arrest of Charles Armstrong and the men who were part of his mission."

"Praise God," Tess said as her eyes teared up.

"A team of FBI investigators moved the community members to an old hotel in San Jose while other investigators scoured the compound. The FBI's been waiting for some strong evidence to take this guy down for a long time. I'm sure it will be on the national news tonight, but I don't have any details. Just general good news."

"And what about our mom and dad?" Frankie asked.

"The most important news, Frankie. Because of the information uncovered, the charges of kidnapping have been dropped. Since Tara and Clark were really helping to take the baby to safety, and they played a role in getting evidence, the FBI is dropping the charges."

"What does that mean?" Frankie asked.

"It means you get to see your parents soon."

The entire room cheered. More tears from Tess and a few from Stav.

"We'll know more with each passing hour," Ramona said as she hugged Frankie.

"Hey!" Frankie pulled back from the hug. "What was our surprise?"

"Surprise?"

"The day in the doctor's office. Where were we going to go? If we hadn't gone with that man in the hat?"

"You have a good memory, Frankie. I was going to take you to the library and then for ice cream. I think you ended up having quite the adventure instead."

"Where's that heart necklace you always wear?"

"Oh," Ramona said as she inadvertently touched the area around her neck that no longer had her necklace. "We, uh, are no longer... we broke up."

"I'm sorry, Ramona," I said. I really was.

"I'm not," Ramona said. "That man was never going to marry me, Esther. He lied for years. And to be honest, I don't know if I wanted to be married to him. What I think now is that my head is clear to think about what I really want. Maybe I'll be like Nancy Drew, Esther. And we don't really care if Nancy's married or not, as long as she has a new mystery to solve, right?"

"Right."

"I feel free now," Ramona said. "I guess I was kind of a prisoner."

"Ramona," Frankie said. "Was your old boyfriend a Waterloo?"

"Waterloo?"

"You know like the guy in the song," Frankie answered.

Ramona looked at me for translation.

"It's a long story," I said.

"Well, maybe you can tell me the story on the drive to Tess's house. You're all free to go. It's safe to go out now."

Olly, olly oxen free, I thought to myself and smiled as we picked up our things to leave.

Game over.

16

Two Worlds Collide

August 1976

The game was over.

But there were still so many questions.

Two worlds collided at the exact moment that Ramona put the key from Olivia's music box in the lock box at the main post office in downtown Omaha, two FBI agents standing behind her.

The agents, who had just flown in from California, were just as anxious as Ramona to see what was in the box for both professional and personal reasons. Agents Michaels and Lori Fenway had been working on the Celestial Way case for years. They'd even spent a year undercover at the vineyard as *Dave and Tina*, a wayward couple trying to find nirvana in California. Charles had trusted them and was never aware that he had two FBI agents under his nose, but after a year—though the agents sensed the cult was doing more than just helping souls transcend this wicked world—they were never able to find solid evidence of any illegal activity.

Curtis and Lori suspected that Charles Armstrong and his men were abusing younger girls on the compound. They also suspected criminal activity with the so-called wine sales. Lots of innuendos, flags flying everywhere. They left in the middle of the night in the summer of 1969. Because they were part of the "trusted" team, they had never been considered a flight risk and were, therefore, never monitored. After they left, they moved on to work on the Charles Manson case following the monstrous murders the evil man orchestrated.

In the late summer of 1976, Curtis and Lori had been following the news about a young couple in Omaha who had kidnapped a baby. They learned that the person who filed the claim against the young couple was Charles Armstrong from a small winery near San Jose. From where their case had left off years earlier when they had left the Californian winery, the story was now picking up again. And it all started with a letter.

August 2nd, 1976

The day Tess received the letter from Bernie Cutler, she had planned on getting her hair done.

She never did get her hair done.

She barely moved as she read the words on the paper, coming from a man she'd never met. It was clear. It was specific. Exciting and terrifying at the same time.

Dear Theresa,

I was made aware that you are an important person or link to my friend Katherine's children. Sadly, my dear friend Katherine is dying. That is the main reason she is asking for her daughter. She knows this could be the last time to see her. She wanted me to contact you with information about the place where the girls used to live and criminal evidence that she'd like to pass on to the oldest daughter to get to the right people.

Since communication is a delicate thing, it will not be easy to keep in touch. If Charles Armstrong ever finds out that she is planning what she is planning, he will kill not only Katherine but the girls as well. She contacted me secretly. She'd like your response to me to be discreet as well, as Charles knows of my friendship with her, and we would not put it past him that he might be tapping my phones.

On August 15th, Katherine is planning on calling 911 during a window of safety time. She has been very sick and has not received any medical attention for her condition. Her call will be valid. I will be on the road outside Celestial Way as this happens. Later, I will be outside the hospital when her oldest daughter comes to see her. Katherine would like her daughter to be greatly disguised. Wigs, glasses, whatever to make sure that no one could identify her as Katherine's daughter.

We would like her to come to San Jose's Good Samaritan Hospital on Monday, August 16th, at 9:00 a.m., right when visiting hours begin. She will sign in as the alias, Doreen Whitfield. This is just a made-up name. Katherine will let nurses know that "Doreen Whitfield" is an approved guest. This is a random name. I will be the backup if she chooses not to come. She will go into the room Katherine's in, and Katherine will have something to give her, along with a written note to authorities.

I am not sure what transportation she will take to get to California, but I will pick her up at the airport. I will take her to the hospital and wait for her in the parking lot while she visits her mother. I will get her back to the airport for her return flight.

I promise I will protect her.

If her daughter chooses to come to California, please call the number below on August 9th at 10:00 a.m. Let the phone ring once, then hang up.

If her daughter chooses not to come, call at 11:00 a.m., let the phone ring twice, and hang up. I live in Houston, Texas, so the time here is Central time.

Katherine made it clear that her daughter doesn't have to come. We have a Plan B if she chooses not to come. She just thought she could see her one last time.

Regards,

Bernie Cutler

August 9th, 1976

Two days after Tess called Bernie in response to his letter—actually seven years to the day of the anniversary of the Great Escape—Tara was at the store with Frankie.

Frankie was having a meltdown over a package of gum he saw on the check-out stand as Tara was trying to pay for her groceries. She had fifteen minutes to get back and pick up the girls from Henderson Elementary School. The girls were with two different counselors, taking two different tests. She caved in and bought the indulgent yellow package of Juicy Fruit gum. Frankie held onto the cart as she moved the cart outside, a skip in his step and a smile on his face for his small but remarkable victory. A tall, large, bald man entered the store. His black leather vest and tattoo-covered arms were noticeable amongst the young and old women pushing carts with purpose around the Hinky Dinky grocery store. He smiled at Tara.

Tara smiled at the man, tears in her eyes. "Eugene." The man moved toward her and hugged her.

"You can call me Stav. Long time no see. I guess it's no longer Maureen."

"Tara. I've been Tara long enough that it sticks. And this, Stav, this is Frankie." Frankie had been born a year after she and Levi landed in Omaha.

"Hi," Frankie said, clutching his juicy, fruity treasure. "Does your mustache itch?"

Stav grinned.

"He looks just like his granddad. Mick would be proud."

"We're about to go and pick up Esther and Olivia...Luna and Dawn. I'm so glad you're here."

"I'm here, and my job is to get you there. I'm here with the update." Stav looked around. "Thursday night. Midnight. A car will be waiting in front of your house." Stav smiled again at the little boy with the curly dark hair and bright blue Irish eyes. "I'm here."

Then he was gone.

In her small kitchen, Tess dialed Bernie's number at 10:00 a.m.

One ring.

She then put the phone on the cradle. The answer was yes.

August 12th, 1976

Tara took her children over to Tess's house after lunch on the afternoon before she was to leave for California. Esther and the Junior Mints played out in the backyard as she sat with Tess at her kitchen table.

"I'm feeling so many things right now," Tara said, tears in her eyes. Sadness for her mother's pending death. Excitement to see her. Anxiety about being away from her children and Clark. "I'm scared."

Tess reached across the table and held Tara's hand. "It'll all work out, hon. The angels will be with you every step of the way."

Tara knew the angels. They had rescued her from Celestial Way seven summers before. And while establishing her new identity and home in Omaha, the angels had taken the five who had escaped from Celestial Way to a small motel on the outskirts of Omaha for several weeks, where Tara had taken care of the fussy baby girl Dawn. She, Blaze, and Luna had watched a lot of television. It had been something new to the two girls who had never seen a television, and watching the anomaly was something to do while Eugene and Levi worked with the angels to set everything up. With no geography lessons ever—why would Charles want his young members to know anything about the world—Tara had had no idea where Omaha was. She had just trusted the angels.

In the hotel room, Tara and Blaze had watched a channel that showed non-stop MGM movies. Some black and white. Some in color. All fascinating to the almost fifteen-year-old girl who, when the time came to pick a new name, chose Tara—the name of the beautiful land in *Gone with the Wind*.

The first time Tara saw *The Wizard of Oz* was during those weeks. Baby Dawn had finally fallen asleep; Luna was long asleep next to her in the same bed. The volume was down, but Maureen/Tara was mesmerized. She was feeling sleepy but stayed awake to the end. The hot air balloon that comes down to save Dorothy said *State Fair Omaha* on it. Tara saw that as a sign. She was glad the angels had chosen Omaha for her new home, even if they couldn't bring her in a hot air balloon.

Tess knew the angels, too.

She was one of them. That's how she had met "Tara" and "Clark" and their three children in the fall of 1969 when they had come to Omaha. Tess, short for Theresa, had first joined the Angels in 1962 after her youngest son had died of a drug overdose in the Bay Area of California. Some tough years led to that day in San Francisco.

Years earlier, in the late fifties, Tess's husband, a successful banker in Omaha, had a sudden heart attack when their two sons were in high school, and the grief impacted each family member differently. Tess volunteered relentlessly. That's how she handled her grief. Her husband had left her with a surprising and enormous inheritance, which allowed her to send her boys to the best of schools. She could have easily bought a bigger and more ostentatious house, but with her boys getting ready to leave the nest, she stayed. She chose to stay where she had raised her boys and instead invested in four of the houses in the neighborhood, renting them out and getting to know her tenants well.

The oldest son, John Ryan, went on a scholarship to college. The second son, Jeffrey, took a tour of California. After spending years in a commune called The Peoples Temple, Jeffrey died of a drug overdose. The day Jeffrey died was the day that Tess began her research and eventually joined the mission to help people safely escape a world of control. That was the day Tess became an angel.

After gathering Esther and the Junior Mints from the backyard into the house, Tara hugged Tess and asked her to pray. Though she was not a religious person, Tara thought that there was no better time than that day to ask for an angel to pray for you on your dangerous journey ahead.

Tara walked across the street with the gang and started making dinner.

"You all can watch some TV now."

"Really?" Esther looked shocked.

"Yep! I'll call you all into the kitchen when Dad gets home and dinner's ready."

Esther and the Junior Mints complied and turned on the TV just as the opening song to *Gilligan's Island* began. Tara walked out to the garage, moved a bag of gravel in, and pulled a Folgers Coffee can toward her. She put her hands in the can and pulled out an envelope of money. How long had she and Clark been saving in that can for a vacation, for the kids' future, for a new kitchen table? For anything other than a trip across the country to say goodbye to a dying mother and expose the illegal activity of a cult that once had been her family.

After dinner with Clark and the kids and an hour out in the backyard, Tara read to her three children on the couch. She read several books and ended with their favorite: *Are You My Mother*? Esther was already reading at a college level, though she didn't know it, but that didn't mean she didn't like sitting with her mother as she read a story. Tara's voice was animated as she read about the baby bird hatching when his mother is gone and heading out to find his mother. Olivia held tightly to her mother's arm as she worried about the baby bird.

A kitten, a hen, a dog, a cow, none the baby bird's mother.

Frankie sat at the edge of the couch, watching his mother. He could not sit still throughout the search.

A boat, a plane, and the gigantic power shovel. They, too, were not his mother. The exhausted baby screams for his mother; he wants his mother!

Finally, the mother.

As the two reunited, Olivia relaxed. Frankie cheered. Esther smiled.

"Are you my mother?" Frankie mimicked his mother's high-pitched voice of the baby bird.

"I am. And it's about time for the baby birds to rest in their nests."

"First," Frankie stalled, "I want to hear about the Ohio story."

"OK, Mr. Staller. A long, long time ago, the beautiful Princess Esther was born in—"

"Ohio!" Frankie shouted.

"O," Olivia whispered.

"That's right. She was born in Cincinnati, Ohio," Tara lied. Olivia grinned, her eyes bright with excitement.

"And, even though our grandparents died..." Frankie continued with the story, a recording that we all knew so well.

"We weren't sad. Since we knew that they loved us, oh, so much," Tara continued. Esther no longer took part in the routine.

"And you moved to Omaha, and then boom!" Frankie said.

"Boom," Tara continued, with such conviction, it almost felt true, "the twins took over the world."

"And then?" Frankie wanted more.

"And then, it was time for my angels to turn off the day."

"Aww," Frankie grumbled. "No fair."

Tara marched all three Duvall children to bed. Once the children were all asleep, Clark helped Tara pack a small duffel bag. "You won't need much," Clark said.

"Right."

"Since you won't be gone long," Clark added.

"Right," Tara said as she put the bag down and hugged Clark. "I'm going to miss you."

Both sat on the couch and held each other until midnight. Clark carried the duffel as Tara and he looked out the front door. Stav stood against his white car, a yellow smiley face on his antenna, and waved.

When the two men met, Stav held out his hand with a grin. "I don't believe we've met."

"Clark. I'm Clark Duvall. And you?"

"Just call me Stav." Stav winked. "You look good, Levi."

"Thanks, Eugene. Stav, take care of my girl."

"Will do, sir."

Stav drove west on interstate I-80 with Tara for several hours.

Somewhere in a California winery, a man named Charles was having drinks and cigars with his Direction Team in the Big Barn. He had no idea the direction his life was about to take.

August 13th, 1976

On the day that Esther's mother disappeared from their world, Tara Duvall was having breakfast at a café in a Little America Hotel just outside of Cheyenne, Wyoming.

She moved her food around her plate with her fork as Stav told Troy Starr his role in helping get Tara to San Jose. Stav and Tara had driven through the night, and while he encouraged Tara to sleep, she couldn't shut off the day. Troy was an old truck driver who had lost his daughter to a cult; he wasn't sure if his daughter was alive or not, but she was lost. That was for sure. "Looks like you two connect with Keith and Wendy Putnam at the Nevada Winds Truck Stop, just outside of Black

Rock City," Stav said as he put a piece of paper on the table. "This is their contact information. Tess lined this one up, so we know they're solid. The drive from here to there will be about seven hours or so. Directions from Tess to Wendy were, and I quote, *Feed the girl and make her sleep*."

"I feel honored to be a part of this whole thing," Troy said. "I'm your whole ride on the backend. I'll meet Bernard Cutler at the start of the drive back."

"The Putnams plan on making the seven-hour drive on Sunday to San Jose. Bernie Cutler will take it from there. He's flying in from Houston and renting a car for you two. Sunday is the day that London and Katherine make the call. This is really happening. You all right with all this? Katherine said you can back out at any time."

Tara put her fork down. "I'm good."

"I promise I'll get you to the next leg of your journey, Miss Tara."

Tara smiled. She missed her babies.

August 14th, 1976

On the morning that Tara slept in late at the Putnam home, London checked under her mattress for the sixth time that morning.

She and Katherine agreed that London should have the box with her in the event that Charles searched Katherine's apartment while she was sleeping. He was suspicious for sure, but for what, he didn't know. She had surprised him once before. Never again. He just didn't trust Katherine, even as she lay dying. Charles was counting down the days until his pretend wife was no longer a concern. She couldn't die soon enough.

The box under London's mattress was a large cigar box that protected the audio tape of Charles, Rocco, and Dylan, the Polaroid pictures of countless girls in sexual poses that read like Tarot cards, and the folded Recruitment Duty papers with handwritten notes that suggested grooming activity. While most of the items were blurry pieces of evidence, the tape was the most clear and important piece of illegal activity. The box was everything to London. The box was her ticket to see Dawn again. It was her freedom. The box meant that Charles Armstrong would no longer control the lives of so many.

The box was her redemption.

Her Rapture.

August 15th, 1976

On the morning that Keith and Wendy Putnam were starting the seven-hour drive with Tara Duvall to the San Jose airport, London was beside herself in anticipation of the 911 call.

Neither Keith nor Wendy had lost any child or sibling to a cult. Not all stories of the angels were about loss. They themselves had escaped a cult. Like Tara, they had their own story: one of survival. The two had followed a man named David Brandt Berg, who called himself Moses David or Father David. Keith and Wendy were close followers in the founding years of Children of God and wholeheartedly supported Father David's prophecies—founded on a theology from apocalyptic Adventist tradition—of comets and Armageddon and the second coming of Christ. Tara sat in the backseat of a burnt orange Toyota Corona mesmerized by the stories of their following and unfollowing of the extremely unstable Children of God leader.

Tara realized that her unique childhood and Great Escape were not as unbelievable as she had suspected. She and Clark thought that no one would ever believe the strange existence at Celestial Way. New excitement for the unveiling of Celestial Way overcame her anxiety, and Tara felt that the huge curtain—painted with a perfect picture of people coming together to make wine in an idyllic setting—she was about to pull down would finally reveal the place thirty minutes from San Jose for what it really was. All at once, Tara couldn't get to San Jose fast enough.

As Tara listened to stories on her road trip, back in the Mother House of Celestial Way, London checked on Katherine. Katherine looked worse than ever, and London wondered what she would do if Katherine died before she called 911.

"Today's the day," London whispered as she brought a fresh pitcher of water into Katherine's bedroom. She looked behind her shoulder after she spoke. She always looked over her shoulder.

"Yes," Katherine whispered back.

"The men will be heading out to the Big Barn after dinner. They never get back before midnight. I've been watching the past several Sunday nights. Believe me, Sunday nights have become a big drunken night for Charles and his men, and we picked the perfect night to do this."

"Maureen?" Katherine's voice was barely audible, but London read her lips.

"Maureen's on her way. I haven't heard otherwise." London was now doing invoices for the restaurant purchases of wine, and Bernie had written *All is as planned* on the back of his most recent check. "Just rest until the sun goes down. You need to save your energy for the second time you save people from this place."

Katherine closed her eyes, and London looked at the woman who had been a mother and sister to her for almost twenty years. What would she do without her? London couldn't believe that it had been seven years since Stormy had left her. It'd been seven years since she'd seen Maureen, Luna, and Dawn. She wondered where Eugene and Blaze had ended up. The only truth she knew was that the five former Celestial Way family members were no longer here. London quietly shut the door and went to Katherine's old office, where she now did so many of the tasks that Charles had allowed her to take on since Katherine had become too weak. She sat in the chair by the desk and waited.

Two hours later, a group of men, loud and obnoxious, walked from the Main Office past her door. Rocco, Dylan, and others. Though she was visible from the hallway through the doorway, not one man, including Charles, acknowledged her.

It was good to be invisible. London waited.

As the sun went down, London waited. Her fingers strummed the desk over and over again. The gesture calmed her as she took deep breaths and waited.

At 9:00 p.m., London pulled the key to the Main Office from her pocket, the key that Captain had given her so many years ago. She walked down the long hallway and stood at the door. She put the key in the lock, her hands shaking with both fear and excitement. The smell of men overtook her as she moved to Charles' big desk. London hadn't made a phone call in years. The old rotary phones were all she knew, but she had watched Charles make calls from the one phone on the grounds. She had seen him push the buttons on the new phone he had exchanged for the old only within the past year. And she knew the numbers to push.

At 9:30, London pushed the buttons. She moved the receiver to her ear. No more waiting.

"911, what is your emergency?" The woman's voice on the other end of the line was serious and nasally but also calming.

"I need help." London's voice was shaking.

"You'll need to speak louder, ma'am. What is your emergency, and where are you located?"

London had rehearsed this conversation so many times in her head. The words were all muddled as she tried to push them out. "A woman is dying. Can you come soon?"

"Yes, I'll get an ambulance to you, but hon, I need to know where you are."

"Yes, I'm at Celestial Way, just outside of San Jose."

London could hear the woman clicking buttons or something. "Is that the vineyard on Cattle Ranch Road?"

"Yes, yes, that's it." London had been worried that no one knew where Celestial Way was. "Yes, but wait, please tell the ambulance to turn off the siren as they get closer to the place."

"Slow down, ma'am. We can do that. Are you with the woman now? Is she wounded?"

"Wounded?"

"Has she been shot? What are her injuries?

A broken heart. A lost life.

London started crying. "She's dying. Don't you believe me?"

"Yes, ma'am. An ambulance is already en route."

"No sirens. Remember, no sirens."

"We remember. And your name?"

"London."

"London, can you stay on the line?"

"No, I can't. I have to go."

"London, don't hang up yet. Where will the ambulance find you?"

"I'm going to try and get Katherine to the road."

"Katherine?"

"Yes, the dying woman. No sirens, please." London hung up and ran quietly to her room. She grabbed the box from under her mattress and nothing else. She wanted nothing else from this place to go with her into her new life. London put the box in the bottom of a burlap bag and placed the handle of the bag over her shoulder. She ran to Katherine's room.

"Katherine, it's time to go. This time, for real. This time, you and me." Katherine was too weak to sit up. "Lean on me, Katherine. Don't leave me now. You've got to stay with me. Maureen's coming."

"Maureen?"

"Yes, you'll see her soon. And Bernie. Bernie's at the end of the road. He's going to follow us to the hospital."

Katherine leaned into London. London picked up the woman who had always been bigger than life and stronger than most in the room. Now, she was a bag of bones. London moved slowly and silently out of the Mother House and got as far as halfway down the long dirt road to the Cattle Ranch Road when she needed to rest. She pulled Katherine off to the side of the road in front of a tree. London looked up the road and saw the figure of a thin man standing at the top of the road.

"Hey!" the man yelled. It was Jacob, who was technically a man at age 21, but he always seemed like a boy to London. London's heart was beating. "Who's down there?" Jacob yelled. "Get back up here."

The crackling of cars on a rocky dirt road caught both London's and Jacob's attention. The silent ambulance turned onto the long drive. London set Katherine down and ran to the middle of the road and yelled, "Here! She's over here!" London pointed to the tree. The headlights of the ambulance turned on.

"I'm running to the barn, London. I'm going to get Charles."

Three men ran out of the back of the ambulance up the road toward Katherine. They put Katherine on a stretcher and moved her to the ambulance. Bernie Cutler was standing next to his car. He gave London a thumbs-up and motioned for her to get in his car. The ambulance moved slowly down Cattle Ranch Road toward San Jose. Bernie followed.

A few miles later, the ambulance turned on its siren. London smiled as she held tightly to the box in her lap. She'd never been happier.

August 16th, 1976

On the morning that Tara was to visit her mother at the San Jose Hospital, Bernie and she had coffee in the early hours out on the mutual deck of their two hotel rooms.

"You've grown up so much since I last saw you. You're almost like a different person." Bernie took a big sip of his coffee.

"I can tell you're having a hard time saying my now-name." Tara grinned.

Bernie and Tara had connected the evening before at the San Jose Airport, near the bathroom by baggage claim. That was the plan. Tara introduced Keith and Wendy to Bernie. Everyone shared a hopeful yet nervous smile. A fingers-crossed kind of smile. Tara had hugged her new angel friends and walked with Bernie to his car in the same parking lot where Katherine had walked with Charles to his car two days before Christmas, twenty-two years earlier.

"I know. I keep wanting to call you MoMo like Luna always called you. How is little Luna?"

"Luna is now Esther. And Esther turns ten this week."

"Wow."

"She doesn't know."

"Know what?"

"Esther doesn't know that I'm not her mom. She doesn't know that I'm her sister. It wasn't a deliberate decision. She was so little, Bernie. She called me MoMo, and that, over time, turned into Momma. And when Frankie came along so soon, we made choices about our family. We made choices to lie."

"You were protecting her. I know that."

"We were. But now, when this all comes down, either now or as she grows older, she'll find out. I just don't want her to resent me for, you know, hiding the truth. Strange things, after living as her mom for so long and telling the 'stories' from her early years, I started to believe them myself." Tears filled Tara's eyes.

Bernie put his hand on Tara. "You don't have to do this, Tara." He said her new name, her real name. "Both Doreen and Darren Whitfield are the made-up names on the approved visitors list. I'm your backup. Always have been."

"I need to see her. I better go in and put on yet another lie." Tara laughed as she opened the sliding door to her hotel room.

An hour later, in a blonde wig, sunglasses, and trench coat, Tara sat in the parking lot of the hospital with Bernie, waiting for 9:00 a.m. visiting hours.

"You should probably take the sunglasses off after you enter the hospital," Bernie said.

"Oh, right." Nervous laughter from Tara.

"But you have the other glasses?"

"Yes." Tara pulled out the dark-rimmed, large-framed glasses and put them on.

"I wouldn't recognize you. The lady at the Information Desk can tell you what floor and room number."

"Right."

"You can do this."

Tara took a breath and opened the car door.

The woman at the Information Desk smiled. "One moment. Yes, Ms. Wayman's on the fourth floor, room 445. You'll need to sign in at the nursing station."

Tara took the elevator to the fourth floor. She caught a reflection of herself in a mirror in the hallway. At first, she thought it was another woman walking near her. Relief.

"Can I help you?" A cute, young nurse with a pageboy haircut looked up from her paperwork.

"I'm here to visit Katherine Wayman in room 445."

The nurse looked at a security guard who was standing against the wall near a door. Tara saw 445 on the door. "Ms. Wayman has an approved list of visitors. Your name?"

"Doreen Whitfield."

"Doreen?" Again, the nurse looked at the guard. "Yes, you're on the list, Ms. Whitfield. Sign here. I think Katherine's been looking forward to your visit. The doctor asked that visitors stay no more than fifteen minutes. Ms. Wayman needs her rest."

"Thank you." Tara walked up to room 445. The guard smiled at her as he opened the door.

A small body lay in the bed: Tara's mother. Tubes from her nose and in her arms looked like a net holding her to the bed, keeping her from floating away. The woman who had always been in charge as a strong, vibrant, beautiful force in any room looked almost childlike. Tara moved to the bed and caught her breath. No tears. You have only fifteen minutes to say goodbye. No tears. Tara put her hand on her mother's hand.

"Mom."

Katherine woke, her eyes wide with confusion.

Tara took off her glasses. "It's me. Mom, I'm here."

"Maureen?"

"I'm here."

"You're—you're beautiful."

"Well, this is a wig. I—I missed you so much."

"Luna?"

"Luna is good. Has a birthday this week. She'll be ten."

"Ten?" Tears filled Katherine's eyes.

"She's amazing, Mom. Super smart. And Dawn's good. And Levi and I have a son. Frankie. He's spunky like Mick." Tara ran her hand up and down Katherine's arm, gently caressing her. "Everyone's good."

"Safe?"

"Yes, safe."

"The box."

"Box?"

"The guard has a box for you. Get it to the right people." Katherine's words were soft and barely audible.

"Yes."

"Yes." Katherine closed her eyes.

"I love you, Mom." Tara kissed her mother's forehead.

Katherine's eyes opened. "Love you too." Her eyes closed again. Tara sat for a few minutes, and panic and urgency set in. She needed to get the box and go.

Tara kissed Katherine and whispered. "Goodbye, Mom. Thank you for my life." Tara walked out the door and turned to the guard, who nodded his head.

"Follow me." The guard moved to the nursing station. The young nurse opened a drawer, pulled out a box, and handed it to the guard. "Not sure what's in there, but Ms. Wayman was adamant that you get it." The guard handed the box to Tara.

"Thank you." Tara felt a jolt of energy surge through her body as she touched the box. "Thank you."

The ride down to the lobby seemed to take forever. Katherine took her glasses off and put on her sunglasses. She put her head down as she headed to Bernie's car.

Just get to the car.

Bernie was in the driver's seat of his rental car. He, too, had on sunglasses now, and he had pulled the hood of his jacket over his head. Tara opened the door and hurried to sit and shut the car door.

"Are we good?" She showed him the box.

"We are. We need to get out of this parking lot. I'll feel a lot better then." Bernie started the car and looked up. He looked into his rearview mirror to back out of his parking space and froze. Tara looked at him.

"What?"

"Don't move. Don't turn around."

Tara looked into the mirror outside her passenger car.

Charles Armstrong, carrying a bouquet of flowers, pranced behind their car toward the hospital. Tara hadn't seen her father in seven years. Grey streaks through his hair were the only difference from the handsome man who had governed Celestial Way throughout her childhood.

"The gumption," Bernie said under his breath.

"He can't be on the approved visitors list."

"Oh, that man's not on the list, but he will do whatever he wants."

"Why would he visit her?"

"I don't think he'd be coming to apologize. Thank God you got in there and out with the box when you did. I'm pretty sure that he's looking for what's in the box. Let's get out of here."

Charles grinned at the woman behind the nurse's station on the fourth floor of San Jose Hospital. "Don't you look amazing today." Young pageboy nurse had finished her night shift. Grumpy, older, you-can't-mess-with-me, seasoned nurse Hattie had replaced her.

Nurse Hattie looked up. "What can I do for you?"

"I'm here to visit my wife." Charles shook the flowers. "Anything I can do to brighten up her day."

"Who are you here to see?" Hattie could not be snowed.

"I'm here for Katherine Armstrong. My wife. I'm her husband."

"You already said that. Looks like we don't have anyone here under that last name."

"Try Wayman."

"Yes, we have a Katherine Wayman on this floor. Your name?"

"Charles Armstrong."

"I'm not seeing that name on my approved visitor list."

"Strange. They must've just assumed…"

"Nope. Definitely not on my list." Hattie looked at the security guard in front of room 445. A very young guard stood at the door. He had replaced the night guard only moments earlier.

A darkness came over the face of Charles Armstrong, an evil as deep as a dark, seductive, firm, concentrated Australian

Shiraz with a strong cut. "I'm here," Charles said with his teeth gritted together, "to see my wife." Charles walked to the room where the guard stood. "You'll need to step aside as I need to give these flowers to my wife."

The guard hesitated. Charles moved past him and opened the door. He'd stand outside the door and give this arrogant son of a bitch no more than ten minutes with the dying woman inside. Apparently, his wife.

Charles moved swiftly into the room, threw the flowers on a chair, and looked under the bed. He checked under a blanket over Katherine. He wasn't sure what he was looking for, but he wanted to cover every option. Nothing. Charles pulled out a sour apple Jolly Rancher from his pocket and put it in his mouth. He looked at the motionless body on the bed and moved closely to Katherine's face. Maybe she'd already died. Maybe his worries were over. He touched her arm. Katherine's eyes opened, and panic and fear covered her face.

"Oh darn, not dead yet?"

A quiet moan was all Katherine could muster. She tried to scream for the guard. Charles moved even closer to Katherine, close enough for her to smell his sour apple breath.

He smiled.

"No more games from you, woman."

Katherine looked toward the door.

"Whatever you and your idiot little friend are up to, the game's over. We'll find that London; you know we will." The candy clicked against the teeth of her once-upon-a-time dream.

Katherine's face relaxed. Charles had not seen Tara.

"You're not telling a soul—especially the dumb-ass boy scout outside your door— anything that you might have discovered about the Way."

Katherine closed her eyes.

"No one would believe you anyway."

Katherine opened her eyes and looked into the eyes of a con man. That's all Charles ever had been. Just a con. The box was on its way to the right people. Her girls were safe. She had won again. She felt at peace and smiled.

"What are you smiling about?"

Charles panicked as he knew he had just a few minutes.

"Stop smiling."

Charles looked to the door and grabbed a pillow from the window ledge and put it over Katherine's face. "Stop smiling." He held the pillow firmly against her face and counted. She moved only a little and stopped.

"There, no more smiles." Charles pulled the wrapper from a Jolly Rancher and put it on the stand next to Katherine's bed. He left the room and grimaced at the guard as he sauntered past the nursing station.

"Hey," Nurse Hattie yelled.

Charles looked at the woman and stopped.

"You forgot to sign in."

Charles glared at the sorry excuse of a woman.

"You got your visit. Now sign the sheet."

Charles moved toward the station.

"I'll sign in now if it will put a smile on that beautiful face of yours."

No smile from grumpy nurse. She knew his kind. He was the man who used his good looks and charm to get what he wanted. She wasn't buying any of it. Charles picked up the pen on the counter and took the clipboard with a piece of paper on it. He started to sign and saw the name: Doreen Whitfield.

"Who's Doreen Whitfield?"

"I just got here. She must have signed in with the night nurse."

"Katherine doesn't know anyone I don't know." Charles pursed his lips and took a deep breath. "Who's Doreen Whitfield? I need to know who visited my wife. Who is she?"

"How would I know?" Grumpy nurse had had enough of Charles Armstrong, and she looked at the security guard and raised an eyebrow. "At least she was on the approved list."

"Is there a problem, sir?" asked the security guard.

Charles dropped the pen and the clipboard on the counter and moved down the hallway to the stairwell. He needed to find the woman who cleaned his office. Had Doreen Whitfield changed her name to London years ago?

Where the hell was Doreen Whitfield?

August 17th, 1976

On the morning that Bernie drove Tara to California Dreaming Truck Stop, just outside of San Jose, to connect with her ride home, Charles Armstrong threw a tantrum in the Main Office of the Mother House of Celestial Way.

"So, you mean to tell me that no one, not one of you, has any clue where that London girl is from? Where would she go? Who was close with her? Her real name may be Doreen

Whitfield. I need someone to look up every Doreen Whitfield in the country."

Rocco, Dylan, Tex, and Scotty, the main men on the Direction Team, stared at their leader. Charles slammed his fists down on his desk.

"No one?"

"We may not be able to find her, but we could shut her up," Tex said. Everyone looked at the tall, usually quiet member of the team. "What about nabbing the little kids? You know where they are." Tex looked at Charles. "That would keep the adults out there quiet. Until we find London."

"You know where the kids are?" Scotty asked Charles.

Charles said nothing.

"And if we get the kids," Rocco continued, "London would see that on the news and shut her big trap about whatever she knows."

"I like it," Scotty said. "Boss?"

Charles was silent. The room followed his lead. Charles knew where the children were. He had known for years. Following The Great Escape of 1969, Mick had made only one more delivery to Celestial Way. Even though Katherine had insisted that Mick had nothing to do with The Great Escape, Charles fired the delivery man of over twenty years. Whether he had been a part of the escape or not, Charles had seen the way Katherine was when Mick came to the winery. He wanted her to suffer, but he still had his suspicions. Charles suspected Mick was his ticket to finding where the children were. His suspicions had been correct.

Several months after The Great Escape, Charles had Rocco follow Mick every day, from a distance, on his delivery route, and once, not on delivery, when he drove all the way to a little white house in Omaha, Nebraska. When Rocco had called from a nearby restaurant and asked if he should kill the people in the little white house, Charles had said no. Not because he cared but because he had to be strategic. Charles had chosen to hold on to his knowledge of their location until he needed to use that card.

He needed that card now.

"I think it's a good plan," Tex said.

"I need," Charles said so softly that the men in the room weren't sure what they heard. "I need one of you to go to Omaha and get those kids."

"I'll do it." Dylan had been quiet up until now. "I want this."

"You're gonna need to drive straight through the night."

"I'm your man," Dylan said, his voice liquid vengeance.

Smug and a bit overly confident, Charles drank enough wine to keep him asleep for thirteen hours in celebration of the windfall of a victory. His 'wife' was dead, and retribution was about to come down on the heads of those who had embarrassed him seven years earlier.

Ding dong, the witch is dead.

August 18th, 1976

As Troy Starr pulled his rig into the Sapp Brothers Truck Stop in Omaha, the door to a red Pontiac Catalina opened as yet another angel met Tara Duvall.

A woman with long, curly blonde hair exploded out of her car, and she waved as she ran in front of the truck.

"I'm guessing that's your next angel."

Tara and Troy both laughed, and Tara turned to the man who had driven her home from San Jose. "I can't even begin to thank you, Troy."

The woman in front of the car was still waving, her hair flowing against a perfect tan. "No worries, Tara. You'll pay it back. That's how the angels work."

"I will. I better go meet my new angel."

"Good luck with that."

Tara kept the bag with her box close to her. She held the precious cargo like a child within her. She opened the door and jumped to the ground. She then turned to the new angel and froze. She knew this angel: Blaze!

"Damn, Maureen, you look amazing!"

Yep. It was definitely Blaze.

"Blaze!"

As the women hugged, she said, "Well, not so blazey anymore. Alice. The name I was given at birth. The name I'm happy to embrace again."

"Alice. As long as we're re-introducing ourselves—Tara." Tara held her hand out. "Tara Duvall. Nice to meet you. Now let's go home."

"Well, not home, home. Not yet."

"What?"

"We have a little problem. Just a slight detour."

"I can't go home?"

"Stav knows an angel who works at the call center at the police station. Looks like Charles called in a kidnapping charge."

Charles made a decision that would work very well with the kidnapping of the Omaha children: he decided to make a call to the criminal division of the police department in Omaha, Nebraska. A kidnapping charge would make at least the local news. That was for sure. His accusation was true. The day after The Great Escape, his daughter with Stormy was gone. And Dylan and Cubby had said they'd heard the cry of a very young baby the night that five of his people had escaped. They'd kidnapped a baby, and they should pay for that.

"Yes, my name is Charles Armstrong. I own a vineyard just outside of San Jose, and I want to report a child abduction."

He went into great detail about the couple that had kidnapped his baby: Clark and Tara Duvall. He knew their names. Rocco had found their names on an envelope he took from the Duvall mailbox when he had followed Mick back to Omaha.

"Thank you, sir. We're planning on following up on that. We'll be in touch."

With all his confidence, Charles had no idea that his name was on the national radar of official authorities. Years earlier, the FBI had received a phone call from a vineyard in California. Cryptic but also helpful. The deep voice of a fearful man stated very clearly in a recorded call, "There's something going on here."

"Sir? Could you be more specific?"

"Celestial Way. Drugs."

"And you are?"

"Just know that it's bad."

"Your name, sir?"

"No. I'm just…"

"Sir?"

"No more."

Click.

"Sir?"

Dorian Gray, a once-chef in a small restaurant in a town west of Des Moines, Iowa, had experienced a revelation in his life when he visited several wineries in California in the early fifties and called an end to his journey at Celestial Way. Instead of managing a restaurant, he now managed the winery at the Mother House of his new home. He had never looked back.

Until the day he found an extra box in the truck filled with Celestial Way boxes of wine to be sent to Chicago.

Dorian had never checked the trucks since that was Rocco's job. He and his team checked off the inventory on the order forms as they loaded the trucks that went out twice a week. That day Dorian waved the truck driver down and asked if he could take a quick look in the truck before the truck took off. The driver rolled down his window.

"So sorry. I think I left my favorite work gloves in the back of your truck."

The driver was in no hurry for his long trip, so he stopped and got out to open the truck. Dorian climbed inside.

"They're my lucky gloves. I've had them forever. I think they were on one of the first boxes back here," Dorian yelled back to the driver.

Dorian never did find the gloves—they actually had fallen under a worktable where the grapes were—but he did find something else: a large black bag. Dorian peered inside and found what looked like several white bags. He moved one of the bags and found several small boxes and drug bottles. He read only a few labels when he froze: *Heavenly Hash, LSD-Vine, Angel Acid.*

The truck had arrived empty. Dorian had come out to greet the truck driver to inform him that they would have a double order the next week and might need a second truck. He checked the back of the truck and asked the driver how many boxes he thought might fit. He even stepped in and walked to the back of the truck to check out the space. That's when he had set his work gloves down. They had talked about the pending orders as Rocco's team had started loading the truck.

Dorian wanted no role in moving or selling drugs. The beauty of Celestial Way felt tarnished, like the taste of a bad grape. Sour. Rather than call out Rocco or tell Charles, Dorian made a call after the winery room was done for the day. He had thought he was alone. Tex had overheard the call and confronted Dorian mid-call. Tex had taken Dorian to see Charles then and there.

"Sounds like you made a call, Dorian," Charles spoke to Dorian without looking at him; Tex and Rocco were sitting in the same room.

"Make calls every day. You know that."

"But this call."

"I'm not sure what Tex thinks he heard, Doc, but I was calling in a late order."

"A late order?"

"Yes."

"Well then, have a nice night. See you early in the morning, Dorian."

Dorian left the room. Tex shook his head.

"I heard what I heard, Doc."

"If we wait," Rocco said, "we could see if maybe Tex heard wrong."

"If we wait and watch, we might find out that we're just paranoid. Maybe he was calling his mom." Tex agreed.

"If," Charles said as he pounded his fist on his desk.

"Doc?" Rocco asked.

"If your damn *ifs* and *buts* were candy and nuts, we'd all have a merry Christmas."

Rocco and Tex stared at Charles.

"If the queen had balls, she'd be the king. If, if, if! You can sit here and *if and but* all night, but you won't." Charles stood up and pointed to the doorway. "You won't because you two are going to take care of Dorian tonight."

Rocco and Tex looked at each other and then back again to Charles.

"Go!"

Such a shame since Charles had always liked Dorian.

In Omaha, Alice drove Tara back to her apartment instead of to her home with her husband and children.

Back at the little white house on Parker Street, Esther looked in the cupboard behind the old box of oatmeal and found the bag of M&Ms. She looked in her mother's drawer and looked behind the silky slips and found the picture of the baby Daniel.

Esther then checked on the third secret of her mother: the coffee tin in the garage.

It was empty.

August 19th, 1976

On the morning Esther marked the seventh X on the calendar, Jacob drove into the west side of Omaha, Dylan sound asleep in the back seat. Jacob had come along purely to help with the drive.

Across town, Tara handed Alice a box and a key with the number 708 on it. They stood in the living room of the apartment that Alice shared with her husband, Vincent Tremor. Vincent adored Alice. And Alice adored Vincent. He was a man who took out the trash, stood quietly as Alice babbled on to a stranger, and looked at her as though she was the second coming of Christ, a beaded, bedazzled female version. He was strong, quiet, and secure, something that Alice had never once seen in the men in her life: her father, her brothers, the men in her relationships. Because Alice trusted Vincent with her life, she shared her long story. Vincent became an honorary angel, a badge worn by a few who were close enough to those who had been emotionally manipulated by a cult.

Alice hugged Tara as she took the key and put it in her pocket. She took the box and pulled it to her chest.

"I thought that today was going to be a day of celebration and, and now…" Tara stopped and covered her mouth, tears flowing from her eyes, "now, I have to hide."

"We'll get this figured out, girl. I promise. Vincent should be back for lunch. Sit tight."

"Blaze, I mean, Alice, people will think that Clark and I kidnapped a baby."

"It isn't public yet. And you saved that baby."

"We did. We saved her. The worst part is that I miss Clark and my kids so much. I want to see them."

"Let me run your little errand, and then I'll make a call. Maybe you can at least 'see' them."

Alice drove to the main post office in downtown Omaha, the key in her pocket. The box was in a black bag that she hung over her shoulder as she sauntered into the post office lobby, big and busy, and that was all good as far as Alice was concerned. People may have looked at Alice as she walked into the large lobby of the US Post Office. It was hard to look away from the sparkly and colorful Alice. Most looked and then looked away: another hippie, leftover from the sixties, interesting but not noteworthy.

708.

Alice pulled the key from her pocket and walked down the row of lockboxes until she saw the numbers at eye level.

708.

Alice put the key in the lockbox and turned it. She could see, deep inside the box, several papers and a small box, just as Tara had told her there would be. Tara had done just as the list her mother had given her had guided.

Rent a storage locker and place a very good lock on it. Place all the materials from your previous life in the lockbox. Get two keys for the box. Keep one and give the other to a trusted individual who will have the key with him or her at all times.

Alice placed the box into the lockbox, never looking around the room, never calling attention to herself. Tara had wanted the box in a safe place until the news of the kidnapping had blown over since she suspected that Charles might come to

Omaha to find the box before she could get it to the right people. Alice pushed the box in as far as she could and shut the door and turned the key to lockbox 708. She put the key into her pocket and yawned, a fake yawn, a gesture of the mundane as her heart almost beat out of her chest.

Alice then drove to a phone booth near her apartment and called Tess. Angels used phone booths, when possible, to avoid being traced to home lines.

"Hello." Tess sounded like a sweet little old lady. Alice found that so entertaining, as she was a big, bossy leader on a serious mission.

"Is the dress shop open?"

"Yes, the shop is open. What can I do for you?"

"A customer misses her patterns, and she'd like to see them before the dresses are made." Alice found the dress shop banter silly but understood. People's lives were at stake.

"Alrighty, we can set that up," Tess said and hesitated. "Where can she view the patterns?"

"Peony Park. After 8:00 p.m. Again, she doesn't want to buy the patterns. She just wants to view the patterns. Does that make sense?"

"Yes, I will let the owner of the patterns know." Stav had probably told Tess about the kidnapping accusation.

Click.

That night, as Esther wiped spaghetti off plates, her dad sat on the front porch, his head in his hands. Stav had left a note in his mailbox at work that day:

Heads up. Charles has called Omaha to report a 'kidnapping.' Sorry, Man.

"Might feel better if you took Esther and the Junior Mints to Peony Park tonight." Clark looked up. Tess stood in front of him on the lawn.

"She's safe and in town, Clark."

Clark stood up.

"Don't react." Tess looked down the street and back at Clark. "She's in hiding. We don't need both of you…. Go…. She just wants to 'see' you."

Later, as the Ferris wheel stopped with Clark and the Duvall children sitting at the top, Clark looked down. There she was. The love of his life. The mother of his children. Glasses and wig aside, he knew the angle of her face, the small movements of her head. It was Tara.

Tara, too, was happy. Tears of both sadness and joy welled in her heart.

She saw her little angels and her husband. She wanted to go back to the world that had been so perfect only weeks before. As she rushed from the park out to Alice, Tara pulled a tissue from her pocket to wipe her tears. The key in her pocket—the one that Alice had so fervently protected on her trip downtown and back to her apartment, the key that had been with Tara the entire trip—fell out of her pocket and dropped to the ground.

Tara never heard the clink of the key as she rushed out to Alice's car in the parking lot.

August 20th, 1976

The rain was relentless as Esther watched the digital clock, waiting for the 12:05 call time from her dad. She picked up the phone when it rang at the designated time.

"Tara, where are you?" Stav had called the Duvall home just after noon to let them know that the police were heading to arrest Clark that day. He had tried Alice's apartment, but no one had answered. The call to the Duvall home was risky, but he wanted Tara to stay put with her important box until a new plan had been made.

A young girl's voice answered. When he realized that Tara wasn't there, Stav hung up. Several hours later, after the paper boy came by to collect, several men and a few women took over the small white house on Parker Street. A beautiful woman who smelled like oranges took the Duvall children to McDonald's around the same time that Tara realized the key she had protected for so long was missing. She panicked.

"We need to go back to my house for the second key. We need to go now." Tara had been pacing back and forth on the old rug in Alice's apartment.

"You're not going anywhere, hon. We're in hiding, remember?" Tess had left a note on Alice's apartment with the same message Stav had given Clark.

"Tonight. We need to go back there tonight and get the second key. What am I going to do?" Tara broke down in tears. "Clark's going to jail."

Around ten o'clock, Alice finally agreed to drive Tara over to her house to look for the key. As the music to the opening of *MASH* played on the old television in Tess Folten's living room, Tara and Alice moved from room to room throughout the Duvall home with a small flashlight, looking for the music box.

Across town, just off the interstate, Dylan and Jacob walked into the bar of the Howard Johnson Hotel. They had unpacked their bags in their room only ten minutes earlier. Dylan strutted. Jacob followed behind.

"I'm feeling really good about this trip," Dylan said as he pulled out money from his pocket. "We need to go celebrate tonight. Charles will move me up in the ranks of his precious Direction Team. He's gonna realize how much he needs me."

"What are we celebrating? We don't have the kids yet."

Two hours earlier, the two had driven around the Duvall block several times. Dylan had parked the car at the end of the block and sat for a half hour until they'd witnessed the three children walking across the street with a young woman. When they had gotten to the front porch of a beige hose, an old woman had let them all in.

"There they are," Dylan said.

"Are you sure that's them?" Jacob asked. "You don't want to take the wrong kids back to Charles. He'd be so mad."

"That's the house. Those are the kids. We come back here in the morning and follow them. We wait for the perfect time, and then…" Dylan smacked his fist into his hand. "We grab them."

"But we're not going to hurt them. Right?"

"We do whatever we need to do to get them back to the Doctor."

Dylan and Jacob looked for seats in the dark and smoky lounge. The bartender of the Howard Johnson Inn was a woman with teased hair and heavy make-up intended to hide the wear and tear of her life. Mission unaccomplished. She looked up at the two men who had spent most of their lives under a blanket that separated them from the real world and were desperately trying to fit in. Another mission unaccomplished.

"What can I get you two tonight?" The woman's voice was raspy and loud.

"Set us up with something strong," Dylan said. He cocked his head to the side as he sat down on a barstool. Jacob sat down beside him. "Do you have a name?"

"Natasha's the name. I'm not serving the boy without an ID, though." Dylan looked at Jacob. Jacob looked around the bar for a boy.

Natasha looked at Jacob. "You got an ID?"

Jacob shrugged. He thought she asked him if he had an idea. He had neither an idea nor an ID.

"I'll set you up, Red." Natasha set a drink in front of Dylan. "But I ain't serving the boy. That's just how it is."

"I'm heading back to the room," Jacob said to Dylan. He didn't want to drink anyway. He was nervous about the task they had in the morning.

"I'll be here with Natasha," Dylan said as he winked at the woman from the real world.

August 21st, 1976

On the day that Tess made the best French Toast ever, a brown car sat at the end of the street watching her house.

Jacob sat alone in the brown sedan rental car. He didn't take his eye off the beige house that he and Dylan had seen the Duvall children enter the night before. He sat alone as he rolled down his window, his hand shaking. When the hotel wake-up call came at 7:00 a.m., Jacob realized he was alone in the room. Dylan had not come back to the room after Jacob left the bar. Jacob's first thought was to call Charles and ask what he should do. He was only supposed to be a driver on the long journey, after all. Dylan was the man here to get the job done. If he called Charles, Dylan would be in trouble, the kind of trouble that would get you buried in the cemetery beyond the Big Barn.

Jacob sat up in bed and took a deep breath. He could do this. He didn't need Dylan to 'nab' the Duvall children. At least if he was alone, he could make sure that he did it without hurting them. Once Jacob was dressed, he took the suit jacket and hat he'd brought from the back office and put them on. Dylan had laughed at him when he packed the jacket and hat in his suitcase.

"Are you kidding? No one wears hats anymore. You'll look ridiculous."

Jacob had no idea what people wore out in the world. He just knew that he had memories of some of the older men who had come to Celestial Way when he was a child. They looked so grown up and almost intimidating in that style of dress. Jacob looked in the mirror and smiled at his reflection. He looked like a man. The hat and jacket may have both been a little big, but he felt confident as he wrote down the hotel room phone number on a piece of paper. As Jacob closed his suitcase, something red caught his eye from the unzipped suitcase on the floor that Dylan had brought. Jacob opened the suitcase and found four sticks of what looked like the dynamite Tex used to blow up the rocky terrain at Celestial Way. Each stick had a long wick on it. Confusion and terror mixed in Jacob's stomach as he lowered the suitcase top before leaving the hotel room and locking the door.

He was glad that Dylan hadn't made it back.

Jacob turned on the radio as a red car drove up to the curb of the beige house and parked. A woman crooned a goofy song about muskrats in love. Jacob turned off the radio. The beautiful woman who had dropped off the boy and two girls the night before was back. She got out of the car and walked up to the house. Jacob felt his heart pounding in his chest. He waited until the beautiful woman and the old lady from the beige house walked the Duvall kids to the car. The old lady went back to her house, and the red Pinto drove out of the neighborhood. Jacob followed the car for almost a half hour until it parked in the front lot of an office building. Jacob drove around the back, parked, and got out. He stood on the side of the building until the woman and children had walked in the main door of the building. He then ran to the front door and followed behind the group as they walked to an office.

Jacob stood in the hallway and peered through the glass door to the office waiting room. He stood for a long time and processed his new plan, the one in the event that Dylan wasn't in the hotel after he had the children in the car. Would he drive back to California without him? He knew that Charles had a deadline for them to get back, and Dylan would throw that timeline off. A large, older man rushed past him, panting. He didn't even acknowledge Jacob, which made Jacob feel better. Hopefully, no one in the waiting room had seen him standing out in the hall. One more peek into the room, and Jacob saw the older man open an office door and shut it. The three Duvall children were alone in the waiting area. Jacob burst into the room.

"Looks like you're ready."

"For our surprise?" The boy jumped up and ran toward Jacob.

"That's right. A surprise. Let's get going." Jacob opened the hall door again.

"Are we going to Peony Park?" the boy asked as the smaller girl stood up and grabbed a bag.

"Daddy."

"Give that girl a prize. You get to see your father for just a little bit."

Jacob had not counted on all the questions from Esther, the oldest Duvall child, as they moved down the hall and out of the building. Her prodding and pressing rattled the confidence that Jacob had worn back in the hotel room. Once he had the boy and two girls in the car, Jacob took a deep breath. He had done it. Charles would be so proud of him. Jacob pulled out of the parking lot and drove for several blocks. The streets started to look unfamiliar, and Jacob pulled into a large parking lot and pulled out a map.

"What are we doing here?" Esther asked.

Jacob took one more look at the map. "What the…"

"Is Daddy here?" Frankie asked.

Jacob was lost. He needed to find a pay phone. He would call Dylan, and Dylan would direct him back to the hotel. They would drive back to Celestial Way and be heroes. Jacob got out of the car, shut his front door, and opened the back door. "Get out."

"Why are we here?" Esther sat in the car.

"I told you. It's a surprise." Jacob slammed the door and took Frankie's hand. "Let's go."

"But…" Frankie whined.

"But what? You want to see your dad, right? Come on."

Jacob walked fast, and Frankie tried to keep up. Esther got out with Olivia and took her hand. Jacob opened the big door to the mall. "Come on. Hurry up."

The heat of the day was bearing down on Jacob, and he wished he hadn't worn the coat on the humid Nebraska afternoon. The coolness of the mall helped as he moved through crowds with the children. He needed to find a phone. He had watched Dylan make calls on a pay phone several times as they had driven from California to Omaha. He found a small alcove near some bathrooms with three pay phones.

"I need to make a call. Stand right here. Don't move."

The three Duvall children stood still as he fumbled with the pay phone. "Renee should be here to meet us soon."

"Renee?" the oldest girl asked.

"The lady you were talking to."

Lie.

Lie.

Lie.

She may have been nine, but she wasn't stupid. Esther knew that they should get as far away from the man in the hat as they could. The three Duvall children ran as fast as they could through the cool mall, past great Back-to-School sales with great end-of-summer prices, amid grumpy parents and restless kids. Esther pulled the Junior Mints past the line of ticket-holding moviegoers into the theater, yelling back to the frustrated usher about her brother throwing up, and ran into a dark theater at the end of the hallway.

The fact that their paper boy was sitting several rows behind them, watching the three kids he'd seen the day before huddled in a row near the screen, was just one more strange thing to add to many in the past several days. Esther knew no other option, so the three followed Marty Westerholt to his father's accounting office in a long strip mall.

Marty and Esther were sitting on the floor of the front office of his dad's accounting bay as Jacob, who had driven around Omaha all day, sat in the parking lot of a horse racetrack for three hours, worried about Dylan, that he was dead or that he would kill Jacob for letting the Duvall children slip out of his hands. Jacob was worried about Charles, that he would kill both Dylan and Jacob. Charles had been skeptical about having Jacob go to Omaha, but Dylan had refused to drive through the night without a second driver, and Charles needed the others on the Direction Team for a project, so Jacob had been approved as a driver only.

Dylan had taken full advantage of that and slept through the night as Jacob drove most of the trip. Jacob could just drive off out into the strange world and start a new life. He would have to learn how to dress in the real world. He would have to work hard to fit into a place where he now felt so different. He missed his mother and the slow and comfortably safe world of Celestial Way, a world he knew, a world in which he fit just fine. He could get out of this conundrum and run away, or he could go back to what he thought was a safe place. Jacob turned the key in the ignition and started the car. He made it to the Howard Johnson Hotel as the sun was dropping from the line on the horizon in the most beautiful sunset that Jacob had ever seen.

Long after Marty had left Esther and the Junior Mints in the office overnight, Esther thought about her new friend. His kindness. His humor. Marty's persistence in helping Esther and her siblings moved her to tears as the young boy, who was all about solutions, was the best thing that had happened in the past two weeks. After Marty left the office and Frankie and Olivia fell asleep, Esther saw her school picture from the past year in the opening of the ten o'clock news. That was the first time she had heard about the kidnapping. A missing mother and a father in jail was not enough? Esther's beautiful mother and strong father had kidnapped a baby. The ringing of the phone in the office startled Esther. She said nothing after she picked up the phone. She only listened.

"Esther? It's Marty."

"Marty?"

"You're famous. Did you know that your picture was on the ten o'clock news tonight?"

"I just saw it."

"So did my dad."

The plan was that both she and Marty were to 'noodle' on a plan. He would ride his bike over in the morning, and they would take it from there. Marty was positive. He was kind. That didn't save Esther from her restless night's sleep. A terrible dream with a wonderful epiphany ended her night: Tess was safe. Esther woke up at 4:36 a.m. and called the nosy old lady across the street. She believed her mother had guided her to that thought.

Tess, in a car driven by a large, bald, intimidating man, showed up before the sun rose. Sitting in the back seat of the strange man's car driving across town, Esther realized it was Sunday.

She saw her first sunrise without any fanfare.

August 22nd, 1976

37 58T

Marty repeated the license plate number again and again until he was able to get to his dad's office and write it down.

California. Blue plate. Brown car. Two bad guys. 37 58T

Once Marty realized that Esther and her brother and sister had left the office, he went out to get on his ten-speed. His thoughts of heading back to the house on Parker Street were interrupted by a parade of cars parking in the back parking lot of the strip mall. Two cars were police cars. Soon a crowd of cameramen and reporters made a circle around the back door where his friend Betsy stood answering questions. Marty rode his bike back to the street behind the parking lot to get a better look and to hide. That's when he saw the brown car and the two men, not far from him, doing the same thing: watching and hiding.

Tara and Alice sat watching the Breaking News on the little black and white TV set in Alice's small apartment. The reporters shouted out questions about the Duvall children to the stout woman from the bakery. Betsy had seen her babies. Where had her babies gone?

"I want to go back to the way it was. The key will make this all better. The second key is somewhere in our house. I know it is."

Alice sat next to Tara on the couch, placing purple and green beads on a long soon-to-be- necklace. "But if we didn't find it, no one else will find it. Right?" Purple. Green. Purple.

"Maybe the police have gone through the house and taken items to be examined. Why would they take a music box?"

"You don't know if they did. Maybe it's under a bed. Did we check under a bed?"

"Three times. Each bed. Should I call the police and tell them that I lost a key to a lockbox with important information?"

"You could. But what do you say then? I don't know exactly what's on the tape."

"I have the pictures. I looked through them and shuddered. So many young girls taken advantage of…"

"Tess said to sit tight for the time being. I have a job tonight. I need you to stay here and not leave. I mean it, Tara. Vincent is here for your protection...and to make sure you don't do something stupid. They'd put you in jail, just like Clark. It's not safe for your family until we find that darn key."

"When will you be back from your job?"

"I'll be gone through the night. Vince is here for you."

Around the time Alice finished her necklace, Tess allowed Esther to make a call to her new friend Marty. She felt that she owed him the courtesy of telling him that they were safe. Marty gave Esther the number from the license plate of the two men, of which he was sure one was her man in the hat. Esther took a long, much-needed nap that afternoon. She and the Junior Mints awoke to a strange, beautiful woman staring at them with a smile as big as the moon.

"Who are you?" Frankie asked.

"I'm Alice, and I'm here to help y'all have fun. You're just the cutest little patterns I've worked with in a long time."

Right after Crazy Alice and Frankie jumped on the bed, around the time Alice and the Duvall children were enjoying their A&W meals, Jacob parked the brown car in the Howard Johnson parking lot. He had driven around Omaha all afternoon. Dylan, who had passed out the night before in a hotel room with Natasha, still felt seniority over Jacob and berated him about losing the children as he told Jacob the new plan. At the same time, Tara and Alice's husband Vincent watched the ABC movie of the week, *Brian's Song*, Tara suspecting a tear in Vince's eye at the movie's end. He confessed, "It's a guy-cry kind of movie."

The sun disappeared, and the moon took over the sky, offering lighting to the dark pool at the Shamrock Hotel. In her memory, Esther believed they played in that pool for hours, jumping in to impress Alice, singing ABBA songs at the top of their lungs, and working hard to forget that their dad was in jail and their mother was still missing.

Good and tired—that was the plan—Frankie and Olivia fell quickly to sleep under the musty-smelling covers of room number seven of the hotel. Esther's mind would not allow her to sleep. Alice offered her words of comfort and something more.

Esther learned the truth about her sister Olivia that night, the first painful reality in the days of lies.

August 23th, 1976

"Can't you drive any faster?"

Dylan was shotgun per usual, and Jacob was getting tired of the constant criticism, the non-stop bossy comments that he assumed, were to make Dylan feel powerful. Dylan's voice was annoying; his words, antagonizing; his mission, always governing. Jacob did not say a word in response, as he could think only of the cargo in the trunk. Having driven most of the California to Nebraska trip, he had almost thrown up when he realized that their trunk had been loaded with explosive materials all those miles.

"We blow up the house and call the Doctor," Dylan repeated for the fourth time that day.

It was as though he was in his own world, disregarding Jacob on all counts. Charles had been furious when he'd heard the children were not in hand. Dylan had called the Doctor after Jacob got back to the hotel with the news; he had neglected to tell Charles that Jacob had had them and then lost them. No sense in throwing Jacob under the bus when Dylan hadn't even participated in the task at hand. Execute Plan B. Charles directed Dylan to use the explosives. Charles wanted the Duvalls to suffer. Blow up the house and possibly any evidence of what that London girl had taken from Celestial Way. "Faster. Come on. We'll never get there at this speed."

Jacob had had it. He pulled into the massive parking lot of a large building with a sign that shouted *Skateland*, stopped the car, and put the car in park. About six or seven kids tumbled out of a sky-blue station wagon next to them and ran to the front door of the building.

"What the hell? What are you doing?"

"I'm done."

"Done with what? We need to get over to Parker Street. Now!" The veins in Dylan's temple reddened.

"Done with you. I came to help. I came to see the world. You've yelled at me non-stop. If I'm driving, I call the shots."

For the first time in the past seventy-two hours, Dylan was speechless.

"We will get to the house," Jacob said slowly, "when I get us there. You are not going to talk to me on the drive back to Celestial Way. You will take shifts driving. Understand?"

"Jeez, Cubby, you don't have to be such a grump."

"Don't call me Cubby."

"OK."

As Jacob started the car and moved at a snail's pace out of the parking lot, a red and white truck pulled into the same parking lot and stopped. London thanked the old man in the driver's seat, who had a lisp and a bad addiction to chewing tobacco.

"Really appreciate it, Bill. I wish I could pay you."

"You can pay me by not hitch-hiking anymore, young lady. Ever heard of Son of Sam or the Hillside Strangler?"

"No."

"There are monsters out there who would love to give a pretty girl like you a ride and then leave your body in a shallow grave. No more hitch-hiking."

"Got it." London grabbed her duffel bag, holding the only items she owned now, and opened the truck door. If Jacob had sat fifteen more seconds in that parking lot, he and Dylan would have seen the invisible girl from Celestial Way.

"Are you sure I can't take you to your destination? This can't be where you wanted to land."

"I'm still not sure where I'm landing. Thank you, Bill, but no. I've already made you late for your reunion."

"Hell, there'll be plenty of food when I get to Des Moines. I'll just miss out on some family drama." Bill winked as London shut the door to the truck.

The truck drove off, and London stood smiling, still taking in the "pretty girl" comment from the old man. She'd never been called pretty in her life. She thought that, on her first day in Omaha, Nebraska, a place she planned on calling home, the compliment was a sign of good things to come in her new life. The humidity of Nebraska was something she was going to need to adjust to, but for the moment the humid air felt like a great big bear hug. She walked to the door of the large building and went in to find a phone on the wall just inside the door. Both the coolness of the air-conditioned skating rink and the loud music overcame London, and she realized that she had been away from the real world for a really long time. Loud and happy children in funny clothes and shaggy hair moved past her.

She put her hand in her large duffel and reached for change in the bottom of the bag. A dime. She looked at the name on the piece of paper that she kept safely in her pocket: Theresa Folten. The name was in the beautiful handwriting of Katherine, her best friend ever, the mother she'd never had. London bit her lip to keep the tears from coming. She needed to focus. She opened the large directory below the phone and found a page with names of Omaha folks with a last name beginning with an F. *Fezza, Finney, Finnegan, Folten.*

Three Foltens: *Andrew, Michael, and Theresa.*

She put the dime in the phone and dialed. Three rings. A song played loudly above the skating arena. A woman sang to a man, asking him not to break her heart.

"The dress shop is open."

"Theresa?"

"Who, may I say, is calling?"

"London. I'm Katherine's friend." The last time London had seen her friend was when she kissed her good-bye in the hospital.

Tess had heard of London from Tara. She knew that she was the sister of Olivia's birth mother.

"From Celestial Way. Are you the contact?" London was worried that she had the wrong number.

"Yes, dear. Are you safe?"

Safe?

Safe like traveling the past week, catching rides from strangers to get to Omaha? Safe like sleeping with the homeless in the parks at night? Safe like washing her face in gas station bathrooms? Safe like driving with a car full of men from Denver to North Platte? London did not have anyone holding a gun to her head at the moment. So, London replied, "Yes, I'm safe."

"Hold tight, hon. If you tell me where you are, I'll come to pick you up."

"I think I'm on a street with the name Military. I know this is going to sound strange, but on the building, it says *Skateland* in big letters."

Beautiful laughter belted out of the receiver in London's hand. Tess had not laughed in days. "Oh, hon, it could be worse. It could be an accounting office. So, London, is this place where you are just off the interstate?"

"Yes!" London was excited. She liked the old woman's kind voice. There had to be more people in the world like Katherine.

"I'll be there as soon as I can."

"Theresa?"

"Call me Tess, hon."

"Tess, I can't thank you enough."

Tess hung up, and her front door opened so quickly that the screen door hit the wall. "Tess, call the police." Marty moved toward Tess as he spoke. "The man in the hat—I'm pretty sure it was him even though he didn't have his hat—and another man were in the backyard of Esther's house." Tess had contacted Marty the day after he called with the license plate number and had asked him to ride his bike in the area as an honorary angel and let her know if he saw anything suspicious.

"Slow down, Marty."

"Pick up the phone and call now. There are police sitting on Hillside Drive that could be here in… Please hurry."

Tess was able to contact the officer who wanted her to call with any suspicious activity by the house. He immediately contacted the two plainclothes officers who were parked only two houses down from the Duvall home. They were able to get to the back of the house while Jacob and Dylan were struggling to put something in the window well outside the kitchen. As Tess was leaving to pick up London, Marty asked if he could use her phone to call Esther. She asked him to just shut the door behind him when he left.

He heard someone pick up the receiver on the other end of the call.

"Esther?"

"Where are you?"

"The question should be: where have I been? And the answer: all over. You'll never believe what just happened."

Marty told Esther about turning in the "bad guys" and being an honorary angel for the day. After updating her, he left to finish delivering newspapers on Parker Street. Esther was growing impatient with Frankie's outbursts, running around the hotel room and singing loudly. After he knocked over a small side table, Esther came up with a game to calm him down and entertain Olivia. What none of them realized is that Frankie had also tripped on the phone cord and unplugged the telephone in the hotel room during his energetic episode.

The explosion was so loud that Marty almost fell off his ten-speed. He was heading away from the beige house and the Duvall house to deliver his last few papers when the loudest sound he'd ever heard came from behind him. The ground shook as he stopped and looked back at the Duvall home or what was left of it. The police had already handcuffed Dylan and Jacob to be taken in for trespassing and were walking them toward their car parked in front of the house when the explosive device went off.

Officer Craig Abbott directed Dylan and Jacob into the back seat of the police car as his partner, Yolanda Baker, called dispatch from the car radio. "There's been an explosion and now a fire at 8216 Parker Street. Please advise."

Marty couldn't look away, and his first thought was, of course, about Esther. He'd only shut the door to Tess Folten's house, so he dropped his bike in the yard, ran back through the door, and called the number he had memorized. The busy signal meant that either Esther was on the line with someone else, probably telling her about the explosion, or that the phone was off the hook in room number seven at the hotel down by the airport.

Across town in the police station, Ramona and Kemper, who had already been notified of the explosion of the Duvall home, were "noodling" on the next step in this strange chess game against Charles Armstrong, the evil man from the beautiful winery in California.

"An explosion? Seriously?" Ramona paced back and forth, relieved that they had taken the children from the house.

"The guy means business," Kemper said as he put his cigarette out in the ashtray on his desk. Kemper could really use a drink.

"From what Tess Folten told us of what he's done to people, I think he's dangerous." Ramona sat down in the chair across from Kemper's desk. "Charles Armstrong is a sociopath, that's for sure. Who knows what he'll do next? We need to stay one step ahead of this crazy man."

"Exactly," Kemper said. "I say we call him and tell him that we're on his side, so he'll back off for the minute until we find that key. For now, we do exactly what Charles is so good at doing in his game."

"What's that?" Ramona asked.

"We lie. We tell him that we have Tara in custody. That we just haven't told the news stations. We tell him that once we find the children, we'll have FBI agents on their way to his winery with the three Duvall children. And we do have agents on their way, but they're waiting to make an arrest outside of the grounds."

"I like it," Ramona said. "You could say that the authorities want to apologize for the pain he may have endured."

"Agree." Kemper had never seen eye to eye with the sassy oldest Duvall child, but she and her siblings were innocent victims in this travesty. Kemper had gotten off on the wrong foot with Esther. She was feisty and different than most kids her age. Still, he felt terrible that these kids were in hiding, without knowing what was going on or if they'd ever see their parents again. Now that their home was gone, he would do what he could to make things better for Esther and her brother and sister. "That should keep him in California for the time being. This way, he won't be sending any more of his men to blow things up…while we revise our plan." Kemper reached for the phone.

Back at Alice's apartment, Alice held Tara's hand as they watched the Breaking News on Channel Seven. "They blew up our house, Alice."

"I'm so sorry, hon. I really am."

"I'm not sad. I'm mad. I need to make several calls."

"Where?"

"The gas station on Dodge Street. I'll wear my wig and sunglasses. We wait until later, way later. They might be able to trace the call to the gas station, but they won't know I'm here."

"Who is 'they,' and who are you calling?"

Tara sat up straight and decided there would be no more tears. She was angry. "I'm calling Tess first to tell her of the changed plan. I want Esther, Frankie, and Olivia protected by the police from Charles. I'll call the authorities and tell them that we have important information. I'm just going to tell them, plain and simple, that we lost the key. To buy time, while we're looking for the key, the children should be with them. I want the world to know the kids are safe, so I'm calling all three TV channels to come to the station... I want Charles Armstrong to know that they are being protected. We need to get the audio tape and the pictures, Alice. The world needs to know that he's evil and that we didn't kidnap a baby. We saved her. More than ever, I need Clark."

In the office of Celestial Way's Mother House, Charles, Rocco, and Tex watched the grainy black and white television, the only one at the winery. NBC's David Brinkley was reporting on the nightly news. "A tiny house exploded this afternoon in Omaha, Nebraska."

Tex moved to the TV and turned up the volume.

"The home is that of a man in custody for the kidnapping of a baby." Behind Brinkley appeared a large picture of Clark Duvall or "Little Levi," the name Rocco used when talking about the son of the Irish truck driver. "Professionals are still attempting to see just what caused that explosion. While authorities are still on the lookout for the wife, who is also accused of kidnapping, the three children of Clark and Tara Duvall have been missing as well."

"Son of a bitch. That's good news. Right, Charles?"

Charles smiled and said nothing. It was the first smile in days. Dylan's news of the failure to get the children and the fact that his Direction Team had still not located any Doreen Whitfield meant that nobody could relax until Charles was happy.

Rocco answered Tex. "We still need to make sure that whatever London took was destroyed. She may not even be in Omaha."

"But the fire shows we mean business. Puts a little fear into Levi and Maureen. Don't you think, Charles?" Tex wanted confirmation. "Do you..." The ringing of the office phone interrupted Tex.

"Hello," Charles said, still looking at the screen which now showed footage of two fire trucks and several police cars in front of the blazing little house.

"We're trying to contact Charles Armstrong. This is Officer Kemper from the police department in Omaha, Nebraska."

"What can I do for you?" Charles said in a voice laced with a legacy of lies.

"It's more like what we can do for you," Kemper said.

Alice stood outside of the phone booth at the Sinclair gas station a block from her apartment. Tara made several calls as Alice kept her eyes peeled open for anyone who might recognize Tara.

"You're just going to have to trust me on this one," Tara said to the agent, who was fervently writing down notes about the information she was sharing with him. Alice looked up at the brightest full moon she'd ever seen.

That same beautiful moon, at that same moment, was shining into the back seat of a white Rambler driving up Interstate 29 from Red Oak, Iowa. The Junior Mints leaned into Esther, exhausted from a late night at a county fair, their tummies full and content, as Stav drove past the big screen of a drive-in theater on the way back to the Shamrock Hotel.

August 24th, 1976

"Do I have to wear socks?" Frankie whined.

Esther's patience was wearing thin, and Frankie pushing her buttons was a draining way to start another day. Stav had just discovered the reason why Tess had not called with an update on the plan. The cord to the phone had been disconnected all through the night.

"Nope."

"'Cause I don't want to wear them."

As Frankie pushed Esther's buttons, Stav pushed the button on the hotel TV. Frankie continued, "I hate socks."

The morning news weatherman had just finished the weather report when the face of the young, pretty reporter filled the screen. Sherry O'Hara stood out against the darkness of the burnt house like a shiny pink jewel in the dirt. "The explosion, which took place late yesterday afternoon at the home of the Duvall family, started a fire that destroyed most of the house until firefighters were able to put it out. Chief Thorfinsen of the Omaha Fire Department said that it was a good thing that no one was in the house. Presently, Clark Duvall is being held at the Douglas County Jail. Tara Duvall and her three children are still at large." The jewel may have been sparkly, but Esther couldn't tell if she was for real.

"Our house blew up?" Frankie asked.

Esther comforted her brother and sister as they cried about the news. She wanted to cry but didn't as she realized: no mother, no father, no house. Would the adults around her ever tell her what was going on? The phone rang, and Esther guessed the person on the other end of the line was Tess, the ringleader, the bossy lady of the angels, the no-longer-nosy neighbor. Esther longed to be playing in her living room, Esther's mom and Tess talking in the kitchen. Those days seemed so long ago.

"There's a new plan, kid."

The ominous sky hinted at a big summer storm, and Esther thought the rain might just make things better, cooler, calmer. Stav was silent as he drove the Duvall children past the airport into Omaha, again to a place that he hadn't divulged to Esther. Stav drove to the back side of the building. Esther had already seen the words on the front of the building. Omaha Police Department.

"This really doesn't make sense," she said as Stav parked his car behind a big, old building. The car leaving the parking lot as they had entered had been a blue Pontiac, Marty's dad driving, Marty shotgun. Marty had just identified both Dylan and Jacob as the men he had seen behind Betsy's bakery and in the back of the Duvall home right before the explosion.

"Life? Or this parking spot?"

"The police station? I can read. You've been hiding us for days, and now you're bringing us right to the people you were hiding us from? It doesn't make any sense at all!"

Tess and Ramona temporarily calmed Esther down, explaining that her identification of the man who had taken them from Dr. Vaughn's office would be a big help to everyone.

While still not happy with the never-ending challenges, Esther identified Jacob in a line-up as the man in the hat. The kids were then led to the back parking lot by Tess, Stav, and Ramona. Once the door opened, Esther knew at once what the adults had done.

"You lied."

The next two hours included Esther's meltdown and the calm down.

Tess explained how the plan had changed after the explosion of the house on Parker Street. Tara directed the plan from there, and Tess complied. Esther learned the real quid pro quo was the kids. Tara wanted the kids brought to the station for safety so that the media would come and expose them on a national level. Charles would know where they were and that he could not abduct or hurt them. The trade was that the police would not put Tara in jail, and they would let Clark out if they delivered important information that would lead to the undoing of the cult Celestial Way. The feds had been after Celestial Way for a long time, and the trade was worth it. They were willing to wait and see, hoping for that windfall. For now, they all needed to play the waiting game.

As Esther and the Junior Mints looked through the big MGM book, waiting with everyone else, Olivia shared her own secret. She pulled out the small envelope from behind the material of the ragged music box, the envelope she had seen her mom carefully place there the week before she had disappeared.

August 25th, 1976

"Did you know that if you put a frog in boiling water, it will jump right out? But live frogs will stay in the water as the water starts to boil, slowly, ever so slowly. They just stay, unable to perceive danger or the threat; they will stay until they die."

Dr. Vaughn's voice was soft and comforting as she talked about, of all things, frogs. Esther's brain was still foggy from the night before, sleeping in an office in the downtown Police Department of Omaha, Nebraska. Her brother and sister were on an adventure with Stav. She wondered what fun things could be discovered in the dark, depressing building. Esther focused on Dr. Vaughn's words, and she knew what the point of the frog story was. People stay in bad situations sometimes because they get into the bad situation slowly rather than suddenly.

Dr. Vaughn had asked Esther days earlier to name three true things in her life. The line between truth and lies had never been so blurry, and at that moment, as everyone waited to find out what the key from the music box would unlock, she knew she was about to find out more truth about her life. She wasn't quite sure she was ready for it. Esther's mind went back to a memory that seemed to come out of nowhere. Show and Tell in second grade had actually made her shiver at the time. Lisa Fertelli, possibly the only person odder than Esther in her class, brought a photo of a drawing for her Show and Tell item. Most kids brought Barbie Dolls or trucks; sometimes, the teacher even allowed pets if kids asked ahead of time. Strands of Lisa's long, unkempt hair hovered over her face as she talked about the picture of what Esther saw to be a beautiful woman looking away from the person who had made the picture, actually a drawing. Lisa explained, in what sounded like a forced, odd British accent, that the picture played tricks on your brain. You might see a beautiful young woman, or you might see an ugly old woman, depending on what your brain chooses to see. The quiet grins and laughter disappeared as students moved to get a better glance at the picture. Lisa showed the class where the features were for the beautiful woman, which Esther had seen right away, and then of the ugly old woman, and Esther suddenly saw what appeared to be a haggard old witch. Had the beautiful woman just disappeared? Her brain hurt.

How could a person's brain choose what to see? How could someone not see the truth when it was right in front of him? People saw lies several times a day- through advertising, from people, in pictures. Their brains choose which lies to accept.

During the frog talk, Ramona and Agents Curtis Michaels and Lori Fenway were listening to a tape recorder as they looked at several pornographic images of young girls. Sexual abuse, drug trafficking, murder. So many bad things. From the post office, lockbox 708 poured so much evil, and just like Pandora's Box, there was no putting those bad things back in the box. The tape and the pictures constituted enough evidence to make the arrest of Charles and his Direction Team at Celestial Way. Agent Curtis Michaels made the call to his contact, Agent Randy Gentry, in California, who was waiting a half mile down Cattle Ranch Road more than forty members of the FBI and the SWAT team, including several cadaver dogs, waiting to give the signal.

Officer Gentry gave the signal.

The federal team quickly yet quietly swarmed over the vineyard like a blanket of agitated bees. It was a perfect time to raid Celestial Way as it was noon, and the majority of the members of the community were in the Mother House for the noon meal, only a few people still scattered out on the hills with the vines. From Tara's description of the plantation, the FBI agents knew that Charles Armstrong and members of his team would, more than likely, be in the Main Office of the Mother House. The raid took approximately eighteen minutes, and the expression on the face of the Doctor, Charles Armstrong, the man who had always gotten what he wanted at whatever cost, was worth all the wine in California.

Once Charles and the Direction Team were handcuffed and taken to the trucks parked on the bottom of the winding dirt road, Agent Gentry spoke through a megaphone to the remaining Celestial Way community in the Gathering Room.

"Five busses are driving up Cattle Ranch Road as I speak," Gentry said in a cool, serious voice. "We are taking you all to safety as Celestial Way is now a crime scene." Confused and fearful faces in the crowd listened to Gentry's direction. "After the investigation, you will all be able to come back and gather your things, but for now, we need you all to take the busses to a place where there will be food and lodging. Thank you for your cooperation."

Other than Agent Gentry's announcement to the group, few words were spoken that afternoon. The SWAT team and investigators motioned directions to the bus. The Celestial Way community moved like a cloud, so overwhelmed with shock, that they barely moved at all. The faces of the men, women, and children gazing out of the bus windows before they took off for San Jose spoke the loudest. Despondence, disbelief, distress. The beautiful landscape of Celestial Way, laced with vines, all a beautiful proof of life, had been a lie. They had come here to escape the world and its bad things. They'd been duped.

Celestial Way was officially a crime scene, the scene of countless crimes. Once loaded, the busses left Celestial Way and drove down to an empty hotel in San Jose, where the passengers would stay until they could be processed. Before the last bus drove onto Cattle Ranch Road onto San Jose, agents and investigators scattered across the property to scour a place that had been home to countless people over the past two decades. Under the heat of an August day, only a slight and occasional breeze hovered over the team, moving from cottage to cottage, walking the grounds, and going over every inch of the Mother House, apartment, offices, cottages, and the winery.

The five men with cadaver dogs moved slowly, especially on the edges of the grounds. Agent Jeffrey Bryson, the youngest but biggest agent, followed behind Dakota, a seasoned, sassy, sniffing German Shepard, who pulled and made whiny sounds as she moved quickly through the Celestial Way Cemetery.

"What's up, girl?" Bryson called to his canine colleague, growing more anxious by the moment. "I'm right here with you, Dakota." Dakota yanked hard enough that she pulled free from the leash and raced beyond the Paradise Fields, beyond the big barn at the far end of the grounds, beyond the Beyond. Bryson followed but yelled back to nearby agents. "We've got something back here!"

17

Esther

FRIDAY, AUGUST 28TH 1976

The second time my mother died, we had chocolate chip pancakes for dinner.

It was my birthday.

I was ten, and I was a different person than I had been weeks earlier, not because I was ten, but because I had discovered the truth of me.

Dad—on a furlough from jail until the paperwork was finalized—had decided that breakfast for dinner would be fun for the Friday night birthday dinner, and even Olivia helped with making our unconventional meal. My parents flitted and flirted around Tess's small kitchen, flooded with rooster and chicken décor, the smells of pancake mix and bacon taking over the house. Frankie and I set the table as Olivia did not take her eyes off our parents, not for a minute.

"We've got company," Tess yelled from the front room.

Alice and Vincent were at the front door as Stav's white Rambler pulled up to the curb in front of the beige house, a woman sitting in the passenger seat, the Styrofoam smiley face back on the antennae. Frankie and Olivia ran up to Alice, and

Frankie hugged our new sparkly friend while Olivia stood back, waiting to be acknowledged.

"Don't you two look amazing! And there's the birthday girl." Alice handed me a box covered with purple and orange polka dot paper, a big purple bow on top. "For the one and only Ringleader."

"Thank you, Alice." I put the gift on the coffee table as Tess held the door open for Stav and the woman. I thought that maybe Stav had a girlfriend. That made me giggle a little. Before any introduction of the new woman could be made, Momma ran up to the woman and hugged her. Soon, the two were crying.

"Esther, Frankie, Olivia—I want you to meet London."

I remember thinking at the time, what a cool name. I wished I could have a name that was actually a place, like Nevada or Asia. London fidgeted but stared at us, and her eyes finally landed on Olivia. London looked at my mother; my mother nodded. "Dawn? Lovely, little Dawn." I could see that London wanted to hug Olivia, pick her up, and crush her with a strong embrace. She must have been advised, so she just stood and stared.

"London was a good friend of mine," my mother said as she bent down and rubbed Olivia's arm.

"Here it is," my dad said as he moved quickly to turn up the volume on Tess's big console television. "Sorry, we've been waiting to see…" Dad stepped back as everyone gathered near the TV.

The camera's view of the Celestial Way grounds on the national evening news was from the sky. The aerial perspective captured the men scattered across the landscape, countless restless ants on a big anthill. "The search continues for any other evidence of the crimes of the Celestial Way compound. So far, charged crimes of the cult leader Charles Armstrong and several of his followers include pornography, drug trafficking, sexual abuse, and now, after the unearthing of several bodies in a remote burial ground, murder." The adults in the room exchanged looks, and from what I could surmise, their shared reaction was not one of surprise. "FBI cadaver dogs were drawn to a recently deceased body, alongside six other skeletal remains in unmarked shallow graves."

The scene then changed from the aerial view of Celestial Way to the footage from the back of the Omaha police station. "There we are again!" Frankie announced, and his exuberance created comic relief to the shady days. The ever-precocious Nadia Comaneci wasn't the only face of national television that summer. The Duvall children and the uncovering of a cult, along with the amazing Olympic gymnast, would both be bookmarks for the unusual summer. I can't remember what the reporter said after that because so many things had been said about us that summer, and the reports all blurred together after a while. I do remember Ramona and Kemper stopped by around the end of the television report, just as Tess decided I could open my presents before dinner and the birthday cake.

"We can't stay long," Ramona said, Kemper, looking sweaty and uncomfortable as always beside her. "We both wanted to drop off some gifts for Esther and then we have to head back to work."

The gifts were all piled on Tess's coffee table, and I can say without a doubt that my tenth birthday was the most memorable birthday I have ever had. Both of my parents were with us. Momma promised a clothes shopping day before school for my birthday present. Tess gave me a cool red diary with a key attached to it with a ribbon. Kemper gave me a pencil case, and Ramona gave me a Nancy Drew book I'd never read before—*The Clue in the Jewel Box*. Stav gave me a souvenir spoon with the engraving: *San Jose, California Hotel Vendome* written on it. It looked like a baby spoon, but I suspected that the insinuation was a coffee spoon. I never did wear the beaded belt that Alice had made me, with the name Esther engraved in the leather by Vince, but I still cherish it to this day.

As Ramona and Kemper were leaving, Marty stood in the doorway. "I heard there was a party."

"Come on in, Marty," Tess yelled. "I hope it was alright that I invited Marty, Esther." I blushed and nodded my head. My mother smiled at me from across the crowded living room.

My dad moved toward Marty with an extended hand. "I believe we owe you a thank you." Dad shook Marty's hand. "We heard that you were a big help in the past few days."

"My pleasure, sir. I have a little something for you, Esther." Marty pulled something from his pocket and held it out to the room. "It's a rabbit's foot." The rabbit's foot was dyed sky blue, and Olivia and Frankie moved close to look at it. Marty explained to them, "It's for good luck. Plus, it matches Esther's blue eyes. Happy Birthday, Esther."

"It sure does," Tess said. "What a lovely gift, Marty."

"One more." The words came from London. "This one is for both Esther and Tara." London moved to pick up a book from the floor. It had a year on it that stood up from the green leather cover: *1953*. She opened the book and pulled out a Polaroid picture. Mom came and stood with me as London held the picture out to us.

"I could sure use the Junior Mints helping me put the right amount of chocolate chips in the pancake batter," Dad said as he walked toward the kitchen, Frankie and Olivia trailing behind him. "I could also use another man in the kitchen, Marty." Marty moved with the kitchen group. Mom took the picture and took my hand with her other hand, and we sat together on the couch. We both looked at the picture of a man and a beautiful woman. The words beneath it in messy writing read:

Charles and Katherine

January 30th, 1966

My mom's hand moved to her mouth as she said, "My mother, Esther."

"She's very pretty," I said, staring at the young, beautiful woman in the picture.

"And your mother, too," my mother said.

"What?" I thought of the ridiculous book we read at bedtime with the Junior Mints. *Are You My Mother?* Stav sat in an armchair looking out the front window, Tess sat next to me, and Alice and Vincent sat on the floor. I really wanted to be alone.

"I'm your mother too, Esther. Always will be."

"Katherine was an amazing woman." This time, London spoke as I saw tears cascading down my mother's cheeks. "She died last week after making sure you all were safe forever." The woman who was my mother, a woman I have no clear memory of aside from the smell of cinnamon rolls and a hug against an apron, had died days ago. I pretended to be moved by the picture as all the adults in the room zoned in on me. Truth be told, I wanted to throw up.

"And is that the bad man? The one they were talking about on the news?" I asked.

"Yes. He's also my father." My mom looked down as she answered.

"What? That's my dad?"

"No."

The room was quiet as all eyes looked down. I didn't ask. I wasn't sure I could take any more truths.

"Your father is a good-looking Irish man." Stav still looked out the window as he spoke. "Probably the nicest man I've ever known."

So many new truths in my life. I was overwhelmed.

The evening, despite the overload of truth, was, as I said, memorable. The pancakes and company were brighter after the moment in the living room. The evening was a calm island in the midst of the days of lies and the storm of later days, laced with even more reality.

So much more truth would be unveiled in the months to come. By December of 1976, twenty-two years almost to the day that Katherine first had gone to Celestial Way, the names of the seven identified bodies found on the compound, not in the cemetery, but beyond the Beyond - were announced to the world. Sally Evergreen was the first name on the list. That was because she was the most recent body buried, only weeks before the raid on the Celestial Way compound. She was identified as a runaway, only nineteen years old, a young woman from Medicine Bow, Wyoming. Names like Dorian Gray and Carl Minden, along with a few other names, meant something to those who had survived Celestial Way. They were names of people who had made waves and had suddenly disappeared, allegedly leaving since they were *unfamilied.* They had never left Celestial Way.

It was the names of two others that meant the most to London, my parents, Stav and Alice: Stacie Gates and Mick Sullivan, my father. Though London grieved the death of her sister, she had peace in her heart that Stacie/Stormy had not abandoned her baby girl. If anything, London could just speculate that Stormy had tried to leave with her baby, only to be stopped forever. The discovery of Mick's body was hard on everyone. He had, after all, helped so many leave the bad place seven years earlier. Expendable and disposable. More than anything, these bodies, once alive, had been in the way. If you were in the way of the Way, Charles Armstrong, you needed to be taken out of the way. They were a problem, so they were wiped away from the Celestial Way mission, campus, and Earth.

It was the last two names of the bodies found beyond the Beyond that would, in time, bring out the story of the vineyard and the lies that went along with it. Betty and William Gordan, of Cherokee, Iowa. The family members of the two contacted with notification of the deaths were shocked. Betty and William had gone to California after purchasing an old monastery, one that had sat for decades, to turn it into a vineyard. Friends and family had assumed they had just decided to live out their lives without maintaining connection. The estimated years of death by the forensic team was over twenty-five years. The couple had been on the land with the hills and a big monastery that needed some loving care for two years when they got in the way of two swindlers who had come to work for them in 1949.

One of the two men was Charlie, a young con man who had stolen most of his parents' life savings in Lawrence, Kansas, when he was seventeen and made his way west, conning and swindling people for more money as he traveled. In the process of conning a woman, a man named Walter had observed Charlie and pulled him aside after his scam. "You have much to learn." Charlie had found a mentor in his new friend Walter, a German drifter who had once worked with the circus. The two "grifters" were soon seeking out new marks as they both headed to the coast, swindling innocent people in every town along the way. Charlie was good at bringing in the ropers for the con; Walt was the man to close the deal. When they landed at Celestial Way, the name given to the vineyard by Betty and William Gordan, they found their final marks.

The two became the powerhouse behind the growth of Celestial Way as they were pretty good at manipulating people to do what they wanted, and so the community grew and thrived. They were good at finding the right people. They were good at getting rid of the wrong people. They were good at twisting a knife in your back so slowly that you didn't even know when you had died.

In the spring of 1977, we held a memorial service for Katherine, Mick, and Stormy. I hated how sad everyone was. I looked at my parents, Tara and Clark, with sadness. They had each lost a parent. I still had them.

People will make all sorts of profound statements about death. They might write a poem or a song about death. They might even personify death and address it: *Death, be not proud!* What people won't tell you about death is that it is the only truth about life. We can be sure of only one thing in this life: death. Also a lie. *It's a natural part of life, of human existence.* Nothing natural at all about it. Like almost everything else in life, death is a lie. A blurry, excusable deception that we accept and excuse, as we do most lies.

The truth of me.

It was complicated: a twisted family tree like no other. My mother was my sister, and my father was my brother. A woman in California who smelled like cinnamon rolls was my mother, and an Irish truck driver was my father. My brother was my nephew, and my sister was my sister from another mother. I was loved beyond measure, so the relation of the branches to one another was insignificant.

The truth of me.

The five of us stood on the edge of the lawn of our burnt house. Olivia had not left our mother's side since we had reconnected with her, and Frankie followed our dad like a puppy.

Almost a week after my birthday, a phone call to Tess gave us permission to go look at our house. Five days had passed, and the investigative team and the fire department had finally finished their work and had approved the visit, albeit with an escort from the team. A clean, smoky smell overtook us as we stared at the sooty scene. A very serious and stern man shook my father's hand. Roger was our chaperone. Roger's messy red hair capped his tall, thin body like an eraser on the top of a pencil. I wondered if Roger ever smiled. "Any salvageable items have been put in storage. We can drive to the storage unit after you're done here if you want. There wasn't much saved. A lot of the damaged items were thrown out. Some were ruined by the fire. Most were ruined by the water putting out the fire."

We all stood still as though stuck in mud. A loud bird chirped repeatedly, scolding us for disturbing the grimy scene.

"The insurance people were here earlier," Roger said.

The bird continued to reprimand us. We stood still, facing the mess that had once been our home.

"The firemen had to axe through the walls to help stop the fire. Sorry about that." Roger was uncomfortable with the silence from the notorious family that stood before him. He had probably read about the kidnapping, the disappearing kids, and the cult in California (oh, my) over the past several weeks. And here we were, silent and stuck, standing in front of him.

"The kitchen got the worst of it. That's where the explosive was. We think the gas oven might have been what made this worse than it should have been."

"Can we look around?" my dad asked. The smell was stronger as we moved toward the crispy ghost of the only home I had ever known.

"Sure." Roger looked relieved that someone had finally spoken.

Frankie ran ahead and shouted, "Look, Daddy. My truck."

The front end of a small yellow truck was barely visible, but Frankie spotted it. He ran up and stopped. Frankie looked at Roger. "Can I touch it?"

Roger walked up to the rubbish where Frankie found the truck. "It should be fine."

Frankie pulled the truck out and smiled at the rediscovered treasure. Olivia and Momma walked near where the living room had been. I walked a few steps behind. I didn't care about the loss of our house one bit. My family was back together, and we could go live at Memorial Park, sleeping outside every night for all I cared. We were a family again. Momma's hands moved to her face as she knelt down, her body shaking. Olivia leaned in on her, and I ran to see if she was alright. Frankie and my dad moved toward us.

"Babe, you OK?" Daddy tenderly touched Momma's hair.

We looked down in front of her. Displayed in front of us was a melted album with the singed yellow label in the center: *ABBA's Greatest Hits.* The melted black album had taken on the shape of the rubble below it. That melted mess, changed forever, never to be played again, no looking back. Note to self for the Seventh Grade Science Fair: How Different Things Melt in a Fire. How Different People React to Tragedy.

"We'll get a new one, Tara. Today." I hadn't realized how much I missed the voices of my parents, once my everyday directives, gone for so long, now here and treasured. "We'll head to the mall right after we leave."

Our dad hated the mall. Just another different thing in our world

My mom took her hands from her face. "What are we going to do, Clark?"

"We're going to start over. A do-over."

"A do-over?" Frankie asked.

"So many bad things, sad things..." My mom started crying again. My dad hated it when my mom cried.

"So many good things. You know that's true, Tara. We've done this before. We start over."

My mom sniffled and looked at my dad. The bird started chirping again.

"Maureen," my dad said and smiled.

"Levi," my mom said.

"Levi?" Frankie said. "What's a Levi?"

Momma and Daddy laughed.

Roger cleared his throat.

"Sorry, Roger." Daddy stood up. "We're almost done here."

"No hurry. I just wondered if you need anything else from me. Any questions or…"

"No questions." My dad spoke as my mom stood up. "We don't need to go to the storage unit today. We're staying with the woman across the street during the final tear-down and the building of the new house. I think we're set."

"Hope you don't think I'm out of line." Roger looked down as he spoke. "But I've just got to say that what you people have been through, well, I'm in shock. People are calling you heroes."

"Heroes," Olivia mimicked without looking at Roger.

"I'm not sure of all the details," Roger continued. "And I'm sure there's so much more to the story than we heard in the news, but ending that cult in California, well, that was big."

Momma and Daddy smiled at Roger.

"Kind of makes you wonder how it lasted so long, right under the nose of the authorities. In plain sight. Makes you wonder how many other places… there I go, rambling and… sorry."

"No need to apologize," my mom replied.

"Thank you," Roger smiled.

"Look!" Frankie shouted. He had found another treasure. "Esther, your charm!"

We all looked down at where Frankie was pointing. I had to get on my knees and look closer. There in the rubble was a charm from my bracelet: the little red slippers charm. Frankie picked it up as I looked at the faded bracelet on my arm. I had worn it the entire journey through the city that we had taken with Tess, Stav, and Alice. I hadn't even noticed that the charm was missing.

"The God Shoes," Frankie said as he handed me the charm. "You're going to need your God Shoes."

I looked at the ruby slippers charm. Though color no longer covered the charm, the charm had not melted. The fire had ravaged our home, and most things had perished, but a truck and a charm survived. Our life had been ravaged with death, separation, and so much loss, and yet my family stood together as we assessed the damage.

We had survived.

THE AFTER

There is no place like home.

Dorothy

18

Esther

JULY 4TH, 1996

Almost ten months pregnant in the lawn chair, with my children nearby, I sat with the other mothers from homes in our little cul de sac, watching the fathers of our children light firecracker displays in the middle of the street.

The children *ooohed* and *ahhhhed* as the discounted displays performed their light show for the simple audience. Not one of the people around me knew of the lies of my life or the story behind my mother's great disappearing act in 1976. No one—aside from one of the fathers lighting fireworks—knew that I was one of the children on the infamous cover of *Newsweek* magazine in the fall of 1976 with the headline, *The Cult Crisis in California.*

The photo was everywhere during the months following the raid at Celestial Way. At the time, I found it annoying. Today, I see the faces of the small children on the magazine cover, knowing what they went through, and I feel disconnected. *Had the seven days of lies really happened?* The in-depth expose had gotten it right, though, for the most part. And while the article held the cult epidemic umbrella over several notorious cults in California at the time, the editors had chosen to use the innocence of our faces for the cover as the victims who never signed up for the cults but who suffered, nonetheless. I could argue that we were exploited, but I won't. If the faces of the Duvall children lured readers into the fascinating story of our remote connection to an evil cult and that somehow helped in educating people on the problem, I was fine with that.

I was also fine with the fact that Marty's had been the first phone call to the police, among the dozen others, out of concern for the Duvall family the week my mother disappeared. He had lied to me when I told him not to tell his father. He had already told him. He says now that he had a crush on me and had always looked forward to collecting money for the newspaper. He had been genuinely concerned that Mrs. Duvall wasn't home and had expressed his concern to his father.

I was also fine with the birthday and Christmas cards I now received from a true uncle I never knew I had. Howard Wayman, brother to my biological mother, connected with us after the raid in 1976. We don't force a bond that isn't there, but we don't deny our relationship as we connect through simple Hallmark gestures a few times a year. In his initial contact with Tara, "Uncle" Howard told her that Katherine's father had died of a massive heart attack only three years after Katherine never made it home for Christmas. Katherine's mother had never been the same after Katherine's disappearance and her husband's death. Howard and Katherine's mother had lived fifteen years with sadness and anger, dying from cancer during the summer of The Great Escape.

Turns out Frankie was pretty smart, too, and he graduated last year with a master's in mechanical engineering and landed a job at Bechtel Corporation, where he will be on the design and construction team for the 1998 Winter Olympic Games in Japan. He and his wife moved last fall. Olivia lives with my family and walks to the library every day, where she helps Louise, a kind librarian who says that Olivia reminds her of her sister. We did alright for a bunch of carnival urchins, a ring leader, a wise guy, and a baby doll.

My two-year-old daughter Greta wiggled to get comfortable in my very pregnant lap. Rhett, my four-year-old and oldest son, pointed to the sky away from the display. "Momma, look! The moon's watching us." The beautiful moon above us is the only link I have to my biological mother, Katherine. We share the moon. The moon we were looking at was the same moon she must have seen every night in the California winery where I was born. I felt the death of a mother twice. Tara, the mother I had always known, "died" for two weeks in August of 1976. The mother I had never known died that same month. But a mother's love, biological or true heart, will always be a soft net catching you, even after she is no longer living.

"That's right. I think the moon likes the fireworks."

Rhett giggled.

If I were to measure out my life in coffee spoons, I would say that most of the little coffee spoons have been amazing, filled with goodness and filled with kindness. But I will not deny that coffee spoons are full of bad things. Life is just a big game board of chutes and ladders. And I will add that the spoons filled with little lies and big lies sometimes led down, down, down, but to bountiful spoons full of growth and maturity. No doubt, the lies, all the lovely lies, in my life had also brought beautiful gifts into my life, up, up, up: my husband, a former paperboy who is now the main accountant at the *Omaha World-Herald*, and my children, who had secured my honor to be a mother.

Once upon a time, a beautiful doctor asked me to name three things that I knew were true in my life. I struggled, but I did it. Today, I would not struggle to name three things about my life that are true:

1- I'm almost thirty.

2- I have a wonderful husband and three beautiful children.

3- Most of my life was a lie.

I guess you could say that I consider myself an expert on lies, by default, of course. I know a thing or two about the spectrum of deception. We lie for two reasons. Firstly, the truth isn't interesting enough. Believe me, there is nothing better than the exaggeration attached to a dull day. The second reason we lie is if the truth is too painful.

A lie is a lie.

That's a lie.

There are several kinds of lies on the spectrum of deception.

A little lie—or a white lie—is often made in kindness with no malice whatsoever. When Tess made me the ugliest sweater on the face of the earth for Christmas when I was seven, I lied.

"Thank you. It's really pretty." Momma smiled at my lie. Tess beamed in reaction to my deceit, and we all had a merry Christmas.

A medium lie is not good. No, a medium lie is about hiding the truth for your own gain. "I did clean my room."

I hadn't. I didn't want to be in trouble.

The worst lie is an evil lie. An evil lie hurts others at great cost.

Most people tell lies every day, sometimes even if they don't think they're telling lies. And most people, even though they don't change their names, hide behind titles or the pretense of juicy justifications. Some people lie so much and so often that they don't even think they're lying. When the lies are deliberate with a mission to manipulate, the lies are beyond the Beyond.

The one thing I have always found fascinating is that the word cult actually stems from the word cultivate: just as the winemaker manipulates and cultivates the soil with an agenda of growing grapes and good wine in mind, the cult leader—typically a sociopath or mentally ill person—manipulates the minds of those he must control.

The concept of Celestial Way, from what I've heard, was actually quite alluring.

The Releasing.

Letting go of the things in life that are holding us back or bringing us down. For some, it takes years of therapy to tackle that one.

The Revealing.

Showing the darkest corner of your life to another. Now, that is the deepest honesty.

The Rapture.

The Rapture is the ultimate joy. The purest state. As far as the Rapture goes, I made it. I'm there.

If you were to strip us all down to our purest purpose, the lowest common denominator would be always to keep safe and to trust those around us. And that just may be why parents tell children about a magical man who brings toys to them one day a year and a fairy who will give money for the baby tooth that came out. They tell them that there are no monsters in the world. And ultimately, most parents, on a daily basis, will lie to their children as they kiss them good night and tell them that they will always be there, and that they will always protect them.

So, what do you do in The After?

In The After, I hold no resentment toward the deception in my past. After the summer of 1976, after the seven days of lies, you might ask me: Would I lie to my little angels?

Absolutely.

Acknowledgements

Stories take a long time to move from the heart to the page to the shelf. Many people supported me on this writing journey, and for that, I am grateful.

Special thanks to the 'readers' of *All the Lovely Lies*: Robin Boeck, Mike Leatherman, Patti Grimes, Deb Ward, Amy Morris, Ande Leatherman, Bridgette Watson, Shelia Gleason, Diane O'Malley, Susan and Gary Boeck, Amy Jacobsen, Dave Ulferts, Beth Rivera, Katie Alitz, Lynn Weist, and Shawn Williams.

I am grateful to Shawn Williams and her expertise and advice on wineries and vineyards from her years of owning and running Williams Ranch Vineyard in Lubbock, Texas.

Special thanks to Emily and Rafe and the team of experts at KDP. Their guidance and wisdom through this process was priceless.

I especially want to thank my sister Robin, who was an amazing editor, marketing rep, cheerleader, and tear catcher, often all on the same day.

As always, I thank my husband and children for their patience on the days that I was lost in the story. A special thanks to my husband for his uncompromising encouragement for a project that was so important to me.

Made in the USA
Coppell, TX
10 November 2025

62831396R00203